The Cossack Hero in Russian Literature

Studies of the Harriman Institute

The Cossack Hero in Russian Literature

A Study in Cultural Mythology

Judith Deutsch Kornblatt

THE UNIVERSITY OF WISCONSIN PRESS

The University of Wisconsin Press
114 North Murray Street
Madison, Wisconsin 53715

3 Henrietta Street
London, WC2E 8LU, England

Library of Congress Cataloging-in-Publication Data

Kornblatt, Judith Deutsch.
    The Cossack hero in Russian literature: a study in cultural
mythology / Judith Deutsch Kornblatt.
    244 pp.   cm.
    Includes bibliographical references and index.
    ISBN 0-299-13520-9.   ISBN 0-299-13524-1 (pbk.)
    1. Russian literature—19th century—History and criticism.
2. Heroes in literature. 3. Cossacks in literature. 4. Russian
literature—20th century—History and criticism. I. Title.
PG2989.H4K67   1992
891.709'352—dc20   92-50254

To the Memory of my Grandmother
Franya Marshak Sobotka

Contents

Preface   ix

Acknowledgments   xiii

PART ONE: The Nineteenth Century

1. Introduction: From History to Myth   3
2. Folk Poetry, Pushkin, and the Romantic Cossack Hero   21
3. Gogol's Cossacks and the "Russian Soul"   39
4. Death Transcended and the Female Threat   61
5. Space and Time Unbounded   71
6. Conclusion: The Ambivalent Tolstoi   91

PART TWO: The Twentieth Century

7. Introduction: From Myth to History   99
8. Isaak Babel and His Red Cavalry Cossacks   107
9. Modern Poets and Their Cossack Rebels   126
10. Mikhail Sholokhov and Transfer of the Staff of Power   149
11. Socialist Realism and Death to the Cossack Myth   164
12. Conclusion: Nabokov's Postmortem   174

Notes   179

Selected Bibliography   211

Index   223

Preface

I AM OFTEN asked how a nice Jewish girl could become so preoccupied with the Cossacks. It would be ironically fitting to reveal that my blond hair comes not "from the milkman," as my family joked, but, according to the more macabre humor of East European Jewry, from the Cossacks who invaded my great-grandparents' shtetl. But my ancestors lived comfortably on the Kreshchatik in Kiev, and the closest my grandmother came to Cossacks was a handshake, when, as a young "menshevichka," she attained release from prison in the Caucusus through the aid of a group of "gallant horsemen," shortly before her precipitous emigration from Russia. "I have only the best of memories," she told me once, more than seventy years later.

My own interest began, instead, when after struggling through the florid and sometimes lurid prose of Isaak Babel, I heeded a suggestion that I might look back to Nikolai Gogol to find the origins of the later writer's strangely attractive Cossack heroes. On first reading, no story could seem more distant from Babel's *Red Cavalry* than the jingoistic, dully romantic *Taras Bul'ba* of Gogol, the heroes of which, I felt, had been forever etched in my mind's eye by Yul Brynner and Tony Curtis. But I was wrong. Not only did one movie director miss the point of *Taras Bul'ba,* but Babel's subtly ironic Cossacks indeed step right out of Gogol's Ukrainian stories of the 1830s, regardless of the fact that Babel himself met not Ukrainian but Russian Cossacks in the Polish campaign of 1920. What did that Jew, trying to define his place in the changing reality of postrevolutionary Russia, see in the anti-Semitic Cossacks of yesteryear? How did the Jew-who-would-be-Russian find the core of his Russianness in Gogol's exotic Cossacks of the steppe?

My interest in the Cossack as a national myth deepened when an anonymous reader, having read a blind journal submission, responded vituperatively that my article was obviously written by a male-chauvinist anti-Semite. To analyze the Cossack hero meant to step, apparently, on sacred and very sensitive ground.

The present study has several goals, and thus addresses several audiences. In the largest sense, I would hope to have written a *useful* book, one that would provide if not answers, then provocative new questions for the study and teaching of some of the most important texts in the history of Russian literature. The Cossack is an ambiguous hero, both Russian and not-Russian at once, oppressive and free, buffoonlike and cunning, and to be able to draw on his ambiguous literary image is to enrich the reading of the texts through which he marauds.

Equally important, this book should cause specialists on single authors to ask hitherto unasked questions about the Cossack heroes in otherwise familiar texts, about how they differ from the Russian characters, and likewise from the other "exotic" characters of the stories, and how they might participate in a larger Cossack myth.

Theoretically, the Cossacks are a case study in the transformation of historical phenomena into a literary image, and, perhaps practically, one which might tell us much about the amorphous Russian "soul." Particularly now, when the Soviet Union has disintegrated and Russian society opens up more and more to the Western world, and as our American students choose to study Russian instead of the more familiar French or Spanish, we need to recognize ways in which Russians may be like as well as essentially unlike ourselves.

This book does not fit easily into any traditional critical genre. Although it adopts a roughly chronological structure, it is not merely a survey. Nor is it a purely conceptual study, although it grapples with the definition of cultural mythology and studies the development of national self-consciousness. Similarly, the study is more than a series of close readings, although the reader will, I hope, find some of the readings provocative. Instead, it attempts a thematic analysis of a rich and pervasive image in the Russian cultural imagination. The chronological format is conceptually necessary, for despite the reliance I show on the early Barthes and his definition of cultural myth, I am attempting more than a structural analysis that isolates the topoi of the myth and then lays them bare in text after text. Instead, I analyze the *development* of the Cossack myth, and the dynamic relationship of that myth to changing reality in nineteenth- and twentieth-century Russia. Cultural myths exhibit tremendous elasticity, but stretched too far they may no longer represent that which they once did. As I hope to have shown, Gogol's Taras Bul'ba, ossified by Stalinist dogma, stopped reverberating in the Russian imagination sometime in the 1940s or 1950s.

The reader of this study will find that some authors receive more attention than others. The depth of study is dictated by the relative richness of the author's involvement in the Cossack myth. Pushkin is seminal, but not as influential as Gogol, who establishes the myth for the next hundred years. Tolstoi is only peripherally related. Babel, again, is central to the now even more complex myth, as are the Futurist poets Khlebnikov and Kamenskii, all of whom feed the Cossacks of Sholokhov. It is Sholokhov who begins the rewriting of the Cossack myth, and ironically moves it toward its death. Perhaps out of respect for the once vibrant mythic hero, I have chosen not to parade his corpse through more Stalinist novels than necessary to confirm the autopsy. Here I rely on the reader's ability to extrapolate.

Thus, this study aims at both analysis and description, speculation and explanation. It is my hope that specialists will discover new corners in old rooms, and the generalist, whether in literature or cultural history, new doors into the unknown.

On a technical note, in an effort to balance readability and consistency, I have chosen a modified Library of Congress transliteration system, with the sole exception of the elimination of the final apostrophe from both Gogol's and Babel's names.

And finally: I began research on this book in the final years of stagnation, and wrote and revised the manuscript during the Gorbachev era. The copy-editing process coincided with the collapse of the Soviet Union in the closing months and days of 1991. As I reread my analysis of the Cossack hero for one last time, I have tried to keep in mind any changes in the world order that might affect the book's final form. In most places I have done my best to respect the wishes of Ukrainians to refer to their homeland without a direct article before "Ukraine," and all references to Soviet literature now reflect a historical period and not contemporary fiction of the 1990s.

In these days of cataclysmic reversals, one must be wary of predictions concerning the future of post-Soviet culture. Yet one might wonder whether the renaming of the Belorussian republic to Belarus' might augur a similar reversion in Russia to holy Rus'. If so, it would be fair to ask whether or not the Cossack hero of Russian literature will find a place in this new/old cultural mythology.

Acknowledgments

IN THE TEN YEARS that I have lived with these mythic Cossacks I have incurred a great deal of debt, and I would like now to repay with my gratitude all those who have helped me grow as a scholar, and who have forced me to ask harder questions about my work than I sometimes felt prepared to do. All errors and misconceptions that remain in the text, however, are solely my own. First of all, I am thankful to the W. Averell Harriman Institute for a yearlong postdoctoral fellowship, during the tenure of which I was able to begin to see the book potential of a "loose, baggy" dissertation. I also appreciate the vote of confidence of the members of the Harriman Institute Publications Committee, who saw fit to include this book in the Series of the Harriman Institute. Heartfelt thanks to my readers at Columbia University, especially Robert Maguire, Richard Gustafson, and Robert Belknap (who first suggested to me the Babel/Gogol connection), Mark van Hagen, and Carl Hovde. And to Lynn Solotaroff for her editing advice. Robert Maguire has been a steadfast support through the long years of revisions and submission, and I must single him out for special thanks. May he continue to be a good reader and friend. Thanks also to Caryl Emerson, who discovered pearls in my manuscript that I didn't even know were mine to drop, and to Hugh McLean, whose careful reading saved me from more than one infelicitous error. And thank you, in these final stages, to the thoughtful director and editors at the University of Wisconsin Press.

Colleagues, friends, and family offered invaluable encouragement, especially Judith Weil, Richard Borden, and more recently, Clare Cavanagh. Special mention goes to J. Thomas Shaw who read and reread my Pushkin chapter, and to David Bethea, who believed in me even in moments when I did not. Most of all, I would like to express my loving debt to my husband, Marc Kornblatt, who crossed out superfluous verbiage from countless drafts of this study, and who has always stood with me one hundred percent. A final thank you to my late grandmother, Franya Marshak Sobotka, who first nurtured my love of Russian, and to whose long life I hope I brought joy by my decision to follow in her footsteps.

Part One

The Nineteenth Century

Ilya Repin, "The Cossacks of Zaporozje." Courtesy of Scala Fine Arts/Art Resource, New York.

ONE

Introduction:
From History to Myth

Hᴇ ᴊᴜᴍᴘꜱ on his horse and gallops off on a tour of pillage and rape, with billowing trousers and forelock blowing in the wind. He sleeps in the saddle and makes his home on the open steppe, burning Turkish villages in the morning and Polish churches at noon. He can drink his weight in *gorelka*, dance the *kazachok* until he drops, and all the while swear allegiance to the Mother Russian Church. Rattling sabre and gun, he abandons his family to ride off with the host, ignoring all obligations that tie him to the past and to the land. The Cossack is free and expansive, wild and energetic, uncompromised and unbounded.

Or so we believe. We feel we know his type so well that Lev Tolstoi could call Natasha in *War and Peace* a "little Cossack" without further commentary. The epithet had been naturalized. It is enough to know that Natasha is spontaneous and carefree, so unlike both her elders in the novel and the readers of her story, in Tolstoi's day and in our own.

How do readers form such an idealized image of men with whom they have had no actual contact and about whom they know only the sketchiest of historical details? And why do these mythic men play such frequent and consistent roles in Russian literature, a literature more often touted as home for superfluous men, petty clerks, and an occasional holy peasant? The answers to these questions lead us toward a cultural mythology of Russia, and hold within them further questions: why do we form myths in general and, more important for us here, why such a myth in particular? Why these attributes and not others? Why glorify the Cossacks at all?

Russians, like all peoples, define themselves by the myths that grow out of and evolve in response to their cultural and historical context. The Cossacks are part of the Russian context much like the cowboys or the gold rush are part of America's. Often contrary to historical evidence, Americans believe the land and the life it supports provide limitless opportunities; this is one

3

way in which to understand themselves. That the ever-expanding western frontier no longer exists has little to do with its ability to continue to generate mythic signs. And that those signs sometimes change evinces the fact that a culture constantly reshapes its own myth of self.

Americans have a special relationship to the Cossack myth, born no doubt from the power wielded by deceivingly similar myths of pioneers made wild in the process of civilizing the West. But the works under consideration in the present study were written for a Russian audience, in Russian, and by authors who principally identify themselves as Russian. It is true that Cossacks captured the imaginations of writers of other nationalities as well, and the historical characters played significant roles in Poland's as well as Russia's past, and in the formation of Ukraine as a political entity separate from the Polish-Lithuanian or Russian empires that successively ruled over it. I am nonetheless concerned here only with how Russians formed their own imaginative relationship to the Cossacks.[1] How, I want to ask, does the Cossack hero participate in a Russian's understanding of self?

By isolating the Cossack's role in Russia's cultural mythology, we can better understand the governing assumptions that unconsciously make up the nation's self-definition.[2] Part of my endeavor here will be to wrest power from myths by "denaturalizing" them, by showing the myth of the Cossack in particular to be a system like any other, composed of analyzable elements or *topoi* that relate in a specific way to each other and to the context that produced them. Only then can we begin to understand why the romantic *vol'nyi kazak,* the ontologically "free Cossack," became codified as part of Russia's self-image.

Furthermore, we can then extend our research into a secondary system, into the conscious use made of the Cossack myth in Russian literature. Myths are passively incorporated into a people's self-definition. But individual writers, aware of the power of the mythic image, can actively manipulate and sometimes dismantle the structures of myth. This process of adaptation is particularly interesting when the image is an ambivalent one, as with the Cossack. Much of the Cossack ethos must be morally unacceptable to modern readers, and yet writers in this study could nevertheless embrace Cossack characters. How Russian writers could transform the Cossacks into heroes, often without irony, will be addressed in the following chapters.

The appeal of the heroes has several related explanations. The Cossack myth, as do all cultural myths, mediates oppositions in Russian culture. It allows Russians to represent themselves as a comprehensible whole by organizing a definition of the Russian self and its relationship to reality. Myth reduces or purifies the multifarious and often contradictory elements of that reality.[3] To associate with the Cossack hero as myth need not mean to condone missions of rape and pillage. Rather, it is to accept the material of the

4

myth as a structuring mechanism of inherently chaotic reality. Thus, a uniform mythic image of the Cossack began to emerge in Russian literature in the early nineteenth century. That myth "transform[ed] history into nature";[4] it leveled reality by erasing contradictions, purifying, freezing, and eternalizing the hero. The Cossacks became THE COSSACK.

The Cossacks in fact were men like any others, with differing backgrounds and ideologies. The word *Cossack* itself is ill defined, and has been applied to groups as varied as fifteenth-century Tatar soldiers, nineteenth-century tsarist cavalrymen, and, most recently, Soviet collective farm workers living near the Don River. Historically, however, these men are linked by their home on the physical and cultural edge of Russian society, and their ambiguous role as defenders of and rebels against the order they brought to the frontier.

As border people, the Cossacks themselves incorporated opposites, reconciling elements on the frontier of wilderness and civilization. In the myth, as we shall see later with Gogol, geography became identity. Wanderers with no fixed spatial coordinates, the Cossacks could begin to represent unbounded or liminal experience in general. And their liminality, imagined or real, transformed the historical Cossacks into ideal mediators.

Before proceeding with an analysis of this idealized image, we must paint a clearer picture of the various historical Cossacks whose stories were transformed in the texts under consideration.[5] The discussion is purposefully brief, designed only to introduce the nonspecialist to important figures and events, and to begin the process of demythologization for those readers already under the influence of the ideal Cossack image. The names of Cossacks like Razin and Pugachev are familiar to many readers, Russian and Western alike, but the relationship of their stories to the societal and historical factors that shaped them is often ignored. Heroes are born ex nihilo only in myth, where their heroism is unquestioned. The vagaries of history, on the other hand, force upon us questions about the Cossacks, and emphasize the paradoxes that in fact form their portraits.

The History

If the mythic image eventually emerges as a perfectly reconciled whole, the historical Cossack was nothing of the sort, and the myth's surface homogeneity only barely covers the contradictions that truly give it depth. Cossack originally meant "independence" but came to mean "oppression"; warriors who proclaimed the equality of their society actually adhered rigidly to a military hierarchy; rhetoric proclaiming pride in purely Slavic heritage contradicted an ethnic composition that was in fact quite diverse.

As early as the fourteenth century, the name "Cossack" was already in use in the steppe, the southern and eastern plains of Eurasia, deriving from the Turkic word for vagrant or wanderer, and referring to Turkish or Tatar brigands, or by extension, to any horseman of the steppe. A number of Tatar mercenaries were employed by Moscow for border defense beginning in the mid-fifteenth century, and referred to as "Service Cossacks." Although the later Russian and Ukrainian Cossacks may not have descended directly from these ethnically non-Slavic guards, they did inherit a great deal of vocabulary, patterns of dress and ritual, as well as a tradition of military valor and horsemanship.[6] Many Tatars in fact joined the newly forming hosts, lending the Slavic people and their customs a markedly Eastern caste.[7]

The "Slavic" Cossacks originally were not an ethnic group at all, but a self-formed community of the homeless and disenfranchised. The hosts principally comprised Ukrainians, Great Russians, and Poles, but accepted into their midst Western Europeans, Turks, Tatars, even occasionally Jews, and often intermarried with the non-Slavic women of the steppe and frontier lands. Newcomers were required to abandon their former names and titles, a practice that led to faster assimilation and the formation of customs peculiar to the Cossacks themselves.

The Cossacks in Ukraine, then a part of the Polish-Lithuanian empire, originated around 1450 when a large number of families migrated from the old principalities of Kiev, Podolia, and Volhynia toward the fertile area at the edge of the steppe. These migrants were mostly farmers who sought freedom from debt or peasant service, which would soon translate into serfdom further west and north. The settlers were forced to develop military prowess, defending themselves against Tatar raids. Although the Mongol Tatars had largely retreated from the European section of the continent by the mid-fifteenth century, the steppe lands as well as the Caucasus continued to provide a home for nomadic and warring tribes for centuries to come. The new Slavic inhabitants of the borderland adopted the name Cossack from the surrounding tribes as an indication of their own free and newly militarized way of life. It was bands of these Cossacks, mostly in close-knit male communities, who continued still farther south beyond Polish-Lithuanian control to found the Zaporozhian Sech toward the end of the fifteenth century.

The Zaporozhians were the Cossacks most influential for the Cossack hero of nineteenth-century literature. The Sech, the term for their military association as well as the physical camp, began to gather in the late fifteenth century, "beyond the rapids" (*za porogami,* thus the name *Zaporozh'e*) of the Dnepr River. For security, the camp moved frequently from island to island, as the Cossacks found it necessary to protect themselves and their booty from attack by Tatar, Turk, Pole, Muscovite, and Russian Imperial Army alike.

Cossack Territories in the Seventeenth Century

An odd assortment of people made up the Zaporozhian Cossacks. Most had run away from the political, military, economic, and penal systems of Polish Ukraine or Muscovy to live on what they hoped would be the freer frontier. Outside of the Sech, they settled on the left (southeastern) bank of the Dnepr and spread progressively eastward as the land closer to the administrative centers became populated. They retained their military center on the Sech, with only a short interruption, until the end of the eighteenth century.

Zaporozhian Cossacks eschewed agriculture and family life, unlike the more settled Ukrainian Cossacks who did not migrate as far as Zaporozh'e. Many of them were single men who lived year-round in barracks on the Sech itself, in a constant state of military preparedness. Even the married men, leaving the camp to live with their wives during part of the year, would abandon their homes when the call came to ride off on raids with the host. The primary means of livelihood on the Sech itself were fishing, hunting, some herding, but mostly pillage.

The Zaporozhians continued to draw extensively from the Ukrainian Cossack ranks, but the latter remained closer to the Polish authorities, and thus less independent, often accepting pay or land in exchange for their

7

border defense. The Polish king eventually organized the Ukrainian Cossacks and placed them under direct control of a crown-appointed *hetman,* or leader. Although these Hetmanate Cossacks often showed dissatisfaction with Poland by banding with the Zaporozhians against the Poles, such allegiances were fluid and periodic.

Similar migrations began to take place on Russian territory in the beginning of the sixteenth century, several decades after the formation of the Sech. Peasants, criminals, and adventurers fled Muscovy and headed toward the fertile, basically uninhabited wedge of land between the Don and Volga rivers. These new frontiersmen also took for themselves the name "Cossack," and soon formed the second most powerful group after the Zaporozhians, the Don Cossack Host. Like the Zaporozhians, many Don Cossacks rejected farming, for it represented slavery to the rich landowners and an oppressive government, not to mention to the land itself. The host continued to attract young discontents as serfdom took hold in Muscovy and the later, renamed Russian empire. New hosts—the Kuban Cossacks, the Black Sea Cossacks, the Grebensk and Iaik Cossacks, to name only a few—were formed as the frontiers of the empire expanded, creating ever more difficult to defend but freedom-promising territory. Like their Ukrainian counterparts, these Russian Cossacks drew extensively from Tatar bands in the wild steppe, learning from them while fighting against them, intermarrying with them, and living their life of self-proclaimed independence.

The unfettered society sought by new Cossack members may have been more apparent than practiced, however, for a strongly hierarchical political system formed among the runaway individuals almost from the start. The Ukrainian and Zaporozhian Cossacks had a hetman, the Russian Cossacks an *ataman,* from the Tatar word for chief, and all were organized in strict military fashion into increasingly smaller units, with a lesser-ranked chief at the head of each.

Nonetheless, the Cossack society did differ substantially from that of the empires to the north and west, for it constantly was forced to confront the excitement as well as hardships inherent in life on the frontier.[8] Just as anyone could freely join the host, all could leave. But to separate yourself from the Cossacks meant to face the unpredictable steppe alone, not to mention the law, that might be in pursuit and from which Cossack protection offered some immunity.

As time passed, the Cossacks ironically became tied to the land and to the official military, both of which they had originally fled. The Polish government waged a moderately successful campaign to register the Cossack males into the official military, handing out land rewards in return. Though inhabiting land claimed by the empire, the Cossacks were a constant source of embarrassment to the central authorities, for they continued to see them-

8

selves as a separate political entity and thus to implement their own ad hoc foreign policies. During periods of war or treaty between Poland and Turkey, or with other neighboring lands, the Cossacks would recognize neither party's claims over their own sovereignty. By registering the Cossacks, the Polish government hoped both to control the number of warriors and thus the threat of internal attack or rebellion (unregistered Cossacks were to convert to the status of peasants or town dwellers), and to enlist the Cossacks into its own service. The register proved of only limited use, for while the Cossacks were permitted special tax status, they apparently did not feel obligated to return special allegiance.

The Russian government tried to subordinate the Don and other Cossack hosts in its own territory, especially toward the end of the seventeenth century. At this time much of the Ukrainian lands had fallen to Russian control, greatly increasing the number of Cossacks in the realm. Peter the Great fostered gradual russification and imperialization of the Cossacks by organizing a number of hosts by fiat, with Cossacks forcibly relocated to new territories demanding experienced border guards. A second practice "created" Cossacks from the indigenous population of the borderlands, labeling them as Cossack and requiring them to defend their land from incursion by nomadic tribes. This naturally precipitated the gradual loss of military prowess as well as the prestige attached to the Cossacks. A study of the Cossacks from the seventeenth century until as late as the Second World War proves especially complicated because of this frequent renaming and relocation of Cossack hosts. Don Cossacks were found on the Kuban River and Zaporozhians in the Caucasus.

Some Cossacks became landed gentry and grew rich in the course of rapprochement with the central authorities. Animosity developed between the more settled Cossacks (called *domovitye* or "house-owning") and the newcomers (*golutvennye* or "destitute") who still sought the dangerous life promised by the Sech and the frontier land. The so-called Cossack freedom fighters, the defenders of the oppressed of the seventeenth and eighteenth centuries, began to spend as much time fighting among themselves as rebelling against the central Polish or Russian authorities. By the time Catherine the Great finally disbanded the Sech in 1775, and dispersed the remaining Zaporozhian Cossacks to other localities—for Poland had by then been partitioned, and Catherine had full control over all Cossack lands—many Cossack families had long since settled onto the land and into the life and value system of the rest of the agricultural community. The nineteenth-century Cossack was almost fully domesticated. We find him settled along the Don and Volga rivers in central Russia, the Terek in the Caucasus, or the Iaik River in the Urals, renamed the Ural River by Catherine the Great to dissociate it from the former Cossacks of Pugachev's rebellion.

9

Although the nature of the Cossacks shifted radically over the course of four centuries from the fifteenth to the nineteenth, Cossack hosts are usually identified in space, not time, and referred to by the river around which they lived. Furthermore, Russian Cossacks are distinguished from Ukrainian Cossacks, the latter title designating the Zaporozhian warriors on the Sech as well as the Hetmanate Cossacks under Polish dominion on the right (northwest) bank of the Dnepr. Communication between the various groups was extensive, however, and fostered a certain similarity among all the Cossacks.[9]

The two most famous Cossack leaders, Razin and Pugachev, drew support from hosts other than their own and relied on the prestige of the earlier heroes, especially the Cossacks Ermak Timofeevich[10] and Bogdan Khmel'nitskii,[11] in their rhetorical addresses to the peasants and their own Cossack followers.

Stepan (or Sten'ka) Razin (1630?–1671), the most popular Cossack in Russian folk poetry, lived in the Don and Volga regions on Russian territory. He was born into an established and influential Cossack family among the rich, downstream *domovitye* Cossacks, but apparently felt drawn to the *golutvennye* Cossacks of the upper regions, whom he eventually organized, along with the poor peasants and townsfolk who joined them, to rebel against the rich boyars and aristocrats. Few Cossack-led revolts were directed specifically against the tsar or the institution of tsardom per se. The victims were usually the nobles, although the throne was expected to take ultimate responsibility.

The mid-seventeenth century in Russia was a period of extreme social upheaval, and Razin's rebellion must be understood in this context. The tax burden on the poor increased substantially, as did military obligations, necessitated by an ever-present war with Poland.[12] The chasm between haves and have-nots in Russia grew ever wider. Furthermore, religious fanaticism was on the rise. Based on their reading of the Book of Revelation, a number of sects were anticipating the end of the world in the year 1666. When the apocalypse did not take place, immense psychological adjustments were necessary among the illiterate poor who had rallied around the prophets of doom. To add to economic, social, and spiritual pressures, the very nature of piety itself—usually a highly conservative and binding force—was shaken when Patriarch Nikon introduced reforms, albeit minor, in the holy books and ritual practice.[13] Nikon's reforms, decreed as orthodox, led to the *Raskol,* or Great Schism, and the formation of a large group of "Old Believers," who clung to the established ways as the true Orthodox religion. These Old Believers were severely persecuted by the Church, and many fled for protection to Cossack territory. To this day, some farm workers of Cossack ancestry on the Don follow the ways of the Old Believers.

Razin's leadership during these troubled times began no doubt as brigandage, but turned into social rebellion, with support from the poor and socially or religiously disenfranchised elements within the empire.[14] Many of the Cossack rebels from the 1600s to 1800 followed the same path. As the richer Cossacks of the lower regions often sided with the empire in order to protect their own rights, the Cossack uprisings must be understood as the truly complex phenomena they were: apolitical brigandage, social jacquerie, conservative monarchist impulse (many rallied under the banner of a pretender to the throne, a "true" heir thought to be dead but somehow resurrected), and, finally, civil war among the Cossacks themselves.

Moscow, or St. Petersburg after Peter the Great moved the capital to the newly founded northern city, was faced with no small dilemma regarding the Cossack rebellions. The government could not afford to lose the important military service that the Cossacks provided, particularly on the borders. Yet the authorities found they could not control that force successfully, and even more could not afford to let the Cossacks run free. The situation remained volatile for a hundred years after the capture of Razin in 1671, at least through the career of perhaps the second most infamous Russian Cossack, Pugachev.

Emel'ian Pugachev (1742?–1775) lived during the reign of Catherine the Great. His area of influence began around the Don River, but spread as his Cossacks rallied peasant support in their rebellion against the government. The Iaik Cossacks of the Ural Mountains eventually formed his strongest allies. In the uprising of 1773–75, called the "Pugachevshchina" after its leader, the peasants believed Pugachev to be Tsar Peter III, the husband whom Catherine had murdered. They joined him in such numbers that the Cossack and his followers proved a significant military and social threat to the regime.

Soviet historians considered Pugachev one of the first genuine revolutionaries in Russia, for he seemed to take up the cause of the poor and downtrodden against the landowners and the court. In much of the popular literature as well, he and Sten'ka Razin are seen as Robin Hood figures, taking from the rich and giving to the poor.[15] As Razin had been quartered and beheaded, Pugachev too was caught and hanged just outside the Kremlin walls. The great independent age of Cossackdom passed as the rebels were overcome and their followers submitted again to central authority.[16]

Thus the early nineteenth century saw the Cossack as largely assimilated into the agricultural community and thus in a position diametrically opposed to his earlier profile as willful freedom fighter. These are the Cossacks whom most Russian writers and readers of the romantic period might possibly have encountered. The Sech had been disbanded after Pugachev's rebellion, and the Cossack hosts dispersed and reorganized in carefully controlled areas. The practice of forming new hosts from relocated and/or renamed Cossacks continued throughout the late eighteenth and nineteenth centuries.

The Russian throne virtually always named the atamans, many of whom had no previous Cossack connection.

Within the Imperial Army, the Cossacks formed special cavalry units and proved influential in a number of campaigns. They were largely responsible for confounding Napoleon's army in the War of 1812, and marched behind the retreating French all the way to Paris, creating a sensation among the Europeans. But discipline among the Cossacks deteriorated, and even their military role diminished. Well into the twentieth century, units with appropriated Cossack names were formed and disbanded as soon as the pomp had served its purpose.[17]

By a twist of historical fate, the flesh-and-blood Cossack met by late-nineteenth- and early-twentieth-century Russians had regained some of his martial, violent aura, but, seemingly, at the expense of his freedom. The Cossack of the tsarist army, of the anti-Jewish pogroms, and of the White Army in the Civil War no longer fought for his right to a carefree life of community, dance, and drink. Rather, he appeared to fight on the side of the oppressors. As a military force, he became little more than a weapon in the imperial arsenal.

The first two decades of the twentieth century did witness renewed cohesion among the Cossacks as a group, probably as a result of the chaos of revolutionary times and the desire of the Cossacks to defend their land. (The role of the Cossacks in the Russian Revolution and Civil War will be taken up further in the second part of this study.) Some joined the White Army, some the Red, and others rallied with Cossack or Ukrainian nationalist units in an effort to guarantee Cossack independence from whichever regime would finally gain control. In general, however, the Cossacks as a viable group virtually disappeared in the first decades of Soviet rule.[18]

Ardent Cossack nationalists in emigration have tried to renew a sense of community in the hope that the Cossacks can regain their land after the fall of the Soviet Union. Some have gone so far as to claim that the Cossacks predated the Russian people in the land of Rus' (called Cossackia by one author) and that Cossacks should be granted separate nation status distinct from the Russian people.[19] Nonetheless, the Cossack presence remains a more or less moribund issue in Russia today, its expression limited to the publication of histories about the Cossacks' past and their patriotic devotion to the tsar, or about their revolutionary fervor, depending upon the rhetoric prompted by the situation. Some Cossacks may remain who identify themselves as such, particularly in the Don basin, but the hosts have passed from history to myth.

Curiously, the Cossack people themselves virtually disappeared—were assimilated, exterminated during Stalin's collectivization policy, or emigrated to the West—at about the same time as the literature that elevated them into heroes. New manifestations of the myth of the Cossack today are all but absent from the Russian literary imagination.

The Historico-Mythic Appeal

In 1870, Tolstoi claimed that "Cossacks have made the entire history of Russia. Not for nothing do the Europeans call us Cossacks. The Russian people all desire to be Cossacks."[20] Tolstoi asserts here that both Europeans and his own countrymen somehow equate the inner essence of the Russians with Cossacks. The Russian man wants to define himself as sharing vital qualities with the Cossacks. No doubt Tolstoi was not referring, or not referring *only,* to Cossack murder and drunken debauchery. If his comment is any indication, there must be other aspects of the Cossacks that attract the reader, and allow us to overlook or transform the Cossacks' violence while embracing their essence. These aspects not only enter into an individual Russian's self-definition, but become in some way coterminous with the history of all of Russia.

Cossacks did not "make the entire history of Russia" any more and probably even less than a figure like Daniel Boone "made" America. Despite any concrete role the Cossacks may have played in Russia's past, their mythic service has been greater. In retrospect, the Russians had no Trojan War upon which to base a positive image of themselves as victors. There were no militant Crusaders who valiantly fought a holy war. No brave pioneers battled savage Indians to make way for civilization, having successfully rebelled against their mother government. Instead, *The Lay of Igor's Campaign,* considered by many a national epic, is the tale of a defeat.[21] And the first two national saints, Boris and Gleb, preferred to lay down their lives passively rather than fight for their rights. The Cossacks, however, provide the Russians with an aggressive and colorful portrait of part of their past and of themselves.

This picture first grew to prominence during the romantic period in the 1820s and 1830s. At that time Russian writers were looking inward to determine their own psychological core, and backward to remember, recover, and sometimes invent their unique national personality.[22] Through the romantic obsession with the soul—individual and cultural—the Cossacks were reclaimed as an exotic yet essential Russian phenomenon. That they were not necessarily exotic, nor always Russian, did not prevent their transformation into myth.

As a national symbol, then, the Cossack enjoyed tremendous popularity beginning in the first third of the last century. We still find him proclaiming his heroic stature in Russian literature through the first half of this century.

Despite his drunken and savage reputation—widespread in the Jewish literature about Cossack-instigated pogroms that has largely influenced the Cossacks' image in the West—he appears repeatedly in Russian texts as a hero of superhuman proportions. His violence is not ignored in these tales, but elevated along with the Cossacks' other characteristics to mythic stature. Conventional morality gives way to standards of a higher or at least utterly unordinary domain.

We can now return to the original questions of this introduction: Why the Cossacks? Why were these less than patriotic, often morally reprehensible historical figures seized upon and transformed by the popular imagination? And how could members of the literary intelligentsia who were not Cossacks, or at best were Cossacks by birth but not way of life, come to associate themselves with the Cossacks? Why did the Cossack hero have such a strong appeal that he could remain throughout more than a century of changing Russian and Soviet reality? And why, of course, did the myth then die out?

As already suggested, the Cossacks in Russian history often served as seminomadic border people, and, in the Russian imagination located in the established centers of society, became representative of the margin of more than just geography. Descriptions of rituals of initiation found frequently in literary texts elaborate on the popular association of Cossacks with the limen of experience itself.[23] In these rites, strict hierarchy is reversed and traditional barriers separating ruler and ruled are effaced. As described by Gogol in *Taras Bul'ba* (1842), the election of host leaders involves twice-repeated refusal of the honor by the candidate, who has been dragged to the Cossack gathering place. When the newly elected official finally accepts leadership, represented by a ceremonial mace, four of the oldest Cossacks step forward and anoint the head of the new chief with mud.[24]

Daniel Mordovtsev (1830–1905) elaborates another aspect of the ritual in his novel *Sagaidachnyi: A Tale from the Times of Free Cossackdom* (1882). After election, the new chief is placed upon a huge mound of earth. This "throne" is referred to as "the grave," associating the receipt of power with death. Garbage from huge baskets is next dumped on his head, a practice parallel to the anointment of mud described in *Taras Bul'ba*. "To happiness, to health, to the new father," the Cossacks cry out triumphantly, and proceed to climb up the grave mound and "do with 'the new father' whatever comes into their heads. One smears his face with dirt, another tugs at his forelock. . . ."[25]

In this ceremony, the powerless berate the powerful, the untouchable is soiled, and the living are treated as dead. On a practical level, the electoral process reminds the chosen one that pride must not carry him away, that he owes his position to the people's decision. Its elaborate nature, however, suggests a deeper meaning as well. By performing reversals of the normal order, the Cossacks here participate in a liminal experience; they exist on the threshold of our world, removed from the restrictions of ordinary behavior. As in carnival when beggars dress as kings and men as women, these Cossack rituals suspend the traditional laws of government, propriety, causality, and morality. This is true of all liminal rituals, as Bakhtin suggests in his discussion of medieval carnival, which "expressed this universal renewal and was vividly felt as an escape from the usual official way of life."[26] Participants exist for those moments outside the restrictions of mundane time and space.

Once associated with barrierlessness, the Cossack hero could easily absorb negative traits connected with him. He could be, for example, violent, since ordinary societal restrictions did not apply. Writers who, as native speakers of Russian culture, absorb the liminal mythic image could thus incorporate and even glorify the ambivalent aspects of the Cossack. Violence, reconciled with its opposite, could be transformed into a mark of Cossack energy.

By combining opposites, the Cossack becomes an ideal and vital whole. A Russian who reread the Cossack past as his own could then himself reconcile the contradictory phenomena of his world. For nineteenth-century readers, the Cossack myth helped reconcile at least two major sets of related oppositions that plagued their society: Asia and Europe, and repression and freedom. The first set, sometimes referred to as the dichotomy of self versus other, is the larger category of any number of nineteenth-century Russian preoccupations all superimposed on the question "Who are we?" The nineteenth-century intelligentsia endlessly debated whether Russia was East or West, Asiatic or European, natural man or civilized man, and so on with related oppositions. The Cossacks strike a curious chord in this debate.

By most criteria, the Cossack is an exotic character, living a life separated from civilized Russia by more than geographic distance. His clothes, his hairstyle (the traditional forelock), his way of life, even his colloquial language depart drastically from that known to nineteenth- or twentieth-century Russians. In this regard, our picture of the Cossack does not differ substantially from that of Pushkin's gypsies, the mountain dwellers of writers like Marlinskii or Lermontov, or even the original "noble savages," the cannibals of Montaigne. Certainly European poems by Byron and Victor Hugo about the Cossack Mazepa, as well as many writings about Cossacks by Russians themselves, fit securely into the literary tradition of the romantic and pre-romantic noble savage.

Yet the Cossacks ultimately are not interchangeable with other exotic characters. Those noble savages exist somewhere totally removed from our civilization, so that the city-dwelling hero can travel to their habitat, glorify them, perhaps learn from them, but ultimately cannot remain among them.

15

The savage, no matter how noble, lives across an unbridgeable abyss from the hero, as well as from the author and audience. The gypsies, such as those in Pushkin's poem by that title, are of this type. They are depicted as alien or "other," definitely, categorically *not* Russian. The Cossacks, on the other hand, *are* Russian. In fact, they are both "other" and quintessentially "self." Geographically, they live distant from the main centers of Russia, and their overexuberant revelry and pillaging challenge all civilized decorum. Yet, and here we find the essence of the myth, the popular image would have the Cossacks as the principal upholders of the Russian Orthodox faith and preservers of the purity of Rus'. Rus' was the Kievan kingdom known as the origin of Russian civilization, a culture destroyed by the Mongol invasion, but whose soul, the intangible *russkaia dusha,* remained somewhere alive. The Cossack heroes of literature repeatedly evoke this soul, the Russian origins in old Rus', and thus represent continuity through the disruptive period of Eastern domination.

Furthermore, the Cossack heyday in pre-Petrine, pre-Nikonian Russia represented a period in history that the Russian people would hope to reclaim for themselves. By the early eighteenth century, Peter the Great had reorganized the empire into a European-style bureaucracy, even subordinating the Church to a government ministry, and brought in advisors from Europe to reshape his society. The Cossacks signify an era that allegedly existed before dilution of the Russian people by the corrupt and corrupting West.

A Russian writer of the nineteenth century might then choose a Cossack hero and a Cossack setting to express some truth about the so-to-speak essential Russian core of himself and his world.[27] A romantic writer particularly was engrossed in this search for self-definition, but later supposedly realist writers also replayed and refocused the mythic Cossack hero. The self/other paradox makes the Cossacks much more than another item in the list of gypsies, Indians, and other exotica. It allows the author to identify a part of himself and his culture that might not be apparent. He can assert that he and the aggressive Cossacks are one, that the Russians too are whole, united, integrated, and spontaneous.

The second, related set of oppositions that explains the appeal of the Cossack myth—freedom and repression—allows the author to proclaim not only that he is like the Cossack in a general sense, but that he shares the particular Cossack pursuit of freedom within a restricted world.

Why the Cossacks proved popular for so long as signs of freedom relates perhaps to the Russian's close familiarity with its opposite. Other countries may have rival claims to a history marked by tyranny and oppression, but it is possible that none has been as obsessed by it. Although the Cossacks organized into hosts only after the end of Tatar domination of the Russian

16

land (the so-called Mongol Yoke), and their flight was from Russian and Polish, not Tatar, oppression, they became the sworn enemies of all non-Slavic nomads in the steppe. As such, they anachronistically represented a strong, militant response to the Mongol oppression. Many Tatars of the Golden Horde had converted to Islam, and thus became associated in the Russian mind with the Turks, also sworn enemies of the Cossacks, as well as of the Russian Empire. If the Cossacks were part of the American myth, we would say they helped make the world safe for democracy. In the Russian context, they regained and preserved territory on the frontiers to make it safe for the Slavs. From the Great Russian point of view, of course, Slav could be quite narrowly defined, for it excluded the "infidel" Polish Catholics, whom the Cossack also opposed.

Ironically, the Russian civilization that the Cossacks supposedly guaranteed in the steppe was not democratic but feudal at best, despotic at worst. And the Cossacks themselves were fugitives from just that repressive system. Official serfdom began in Russia in 1550, with increased restrictions in 1581 and again in 1649, when "fixed years" were abolished for runaway serfs, and landowners received unlimited rights over them. Serfdom was not abolished until 1861. Thus, as the Cossacks fought the infidel and represented freedom from foreign oppression, they could signify the negation of repression within Russia as well. The Zaporozhians and some of the Don and other Russian Cossacks rejected agriculture completely, lest they have any contact whatsoever with the ideology of serfdom. Again, many Cossacks of history did indeed till the soil, and some eventually owned their own serfs. But the Cossacks of myth remain unbounded.

The relationship of Cossacks to the issue of freedom and repression in a politico-historical sense is thus multitiered. The Russians are Cossacks and the Cossacks are free. The Russians too, then, are free, or retain their essential freedom in the midst of temporary bonds. Myth reinforces reality, for it allows opposites to coexist in time, reconciling the traditional binary pairs upon which Russian society models itself.[28] The Cossack hero guarantees that historical oppression and metaphysical liberation need not be contradictory.

On another level, the Cossack myth provided a way for nineteenth-century Russians to understand themselves in a native context, and not simply as slower stepbrothers of the West, enslaved to European custom. For in the latter relationship, Russia always came up short. The Westernizers, in their decades-long debate with the Slavophiles, repeatedly emphasized Russia's backwardness, and the need to learn from the West.[29] As Petr Chaadaev wrote in his first philosophical letter:

> One of the worst features of our peculiar civilization is that we have not yet discovered truths that have elsewhere become truisms, even among nations that

17

in many respects are far less advanced than we are. It is the result of our never having walked hand in hand with other nations; we belong to none of the great families of mankind; we are neither of the West nor of the East, and we possess the traditions of neither. Somehow divorced from time and space, the universal education of mankind has not touched upon us.[30]

According to Chaadaev, Russia must now join with its European neighbors, whose histories had developed "hand in hand," and "go through the education of mankind from the beginning."[31]

Others, however, claimed that Russia's woes were caused by too much contact with the West, not too little. From Peter the Great on, they claimed, Russia had became a slave to European bureaucracy and the moral corruption it fostered. The petty (or, as Russians would say, *poshlyi*), disillusioned, or ineffectual citizen was seen as a direct result of sociocultural repression from France, Germany, and England.

The Cossack myth, then, provided an antidote to Pushkin's or Turgenev's superfluous man in nineteenth-century literature. It allowed authors to create, and readers to identify with, characters who expressed positive aspects of their definition of self. Russian writers could demonstrate that Russia was not like the West; it was no worse, and in terms of energy and vitality, in fact much better. The mythic Cossack hero turned the clock back before Peter and could subvert the paradox of freedom and repression on a social as well as political plane.

If Russia felt it had shouldered more than its fair share of cultural tyranny from the West and of political tyranny from the East, in terms of the Mongols and the inherited autocratic government, it also could point to the severity of its censorship as a mark of artistic tyranny from within. The Cossacks, as we will see in Part 2, were conveniently, if ingeniously, appropriated from the historical realm by writers in the early twentieth century to represent artistic freedom, freedom from aesthetic norms as well as from censorship. On political, social, and artistic planes, the Cossack myth helped Russians cope, as it were "aesthetically," with their own repressive reality; it provided a definition of self that could neutralize the repressive pole of the opposition.

Although cultural or historical reality and the Cossack myth are interrelated, there is not necessarily a one-to-one correspondence between periods of increased repression in Russian life and the popularity of the Cossack hero in literature. Occasionally our desires for a neat relationship are satisfied, as in the case of the Cossacks used as symbols of freedom by the Decembrists, who opposed the reactionary policies of Alexander I in the 1820s. The Cossacks of the Decembrists, however, are less interesting by far than those of writers we might feel lived in somewhat freer periods. In fact, we are dealing with the complex phenomenon of the development and adaptation of a cultural myth through literature. A given manifestation of the Cossack hero can never simply respond to a particular political or social situation, for the influences on any given writer include the history of the myth itself, the interplay of other myths of the society, generic and other intertextual considerations, and personal idiosyncrasies, among others in a perhaps endless list of interactive systems. This study will continue to refer to historical influences on the various texts it examines, but it will repeatedly suggest the whole range of factors involved in the propagation and perpetuation of the myth.

To this point the discussion of Cossacks as a representation of freedom has avoided psychological implications of the Cossack hero. By deemphasizing the appeal of the Cossack myth as rebellious wish fulfillment, I do not mean to ignore its importance. Warrior heroes from the Three Musketeers to the American cowboys have seized the hearts of readers from country to country and generation to generation. Their sexual potency is most surely attractive to many writers as well as readers. For a woman reader and critic, perhaps this psychological explanation for the Cossack's continued appeal is less compelling than cultural and aesthetic ones. More to the point, however, are the aims of the present study on the one hand to examine those aspects that differentiate the Cossacks as a uniquely Russian phenomenon, *unlike* other heroes, and on the other to go beyond local readings of the intentions of individual writers, in order to theorize about a larger cultural mythology. No doubt a writer like Gogol was attracted to the image of the Cossack on a sexual level. And the same may well be true of Pushkin and Tolstoi, or Isaak Babel and Marina Tsvetaeva who inherited the myth in the twentieth century. The assumption behind this study, however, is that the myth involves many more variables than machismo, and that much more is at stake than the revelation of violent and rebellious emotional desires. The appeal of the Cossacks in the Russian cultural tradition is both deeper and more nationally specific.

As a child, the poet Marina Tsvetaeva fell in love with one particular hero of the Cossack myth, Pushkin's Pugachev in *The Captain's Daughter*. As an adult she wrote about him: "We do not want to, but we see, we do not want to, but we love."[32] Tsvetaeva enunciates here a basic truth about the myth, if not necessarily about Pushkin's text. The Cossack demands our attention, so that even his murderous force is compelling. Russian authors were attracted to this Cossack hero for more than a century. They transformed the historical figures, who lived from the fifteenth century to the twentieth, in Ukraine, the Don basin, the Caucasus, and the Urals, into a single appealing, in fact invigorating and self-defining, myth.

Many of the important texts for the Cossack myth seem to fall short of

19

greatness. Especially to a contemporary audience unaccustomed to the more acceptable melodrama of nineteenth-century literature, the plots may seem trite, the language hackneyed, the bravura of the heroes unconvincing. To ignore the complexity of the myth in nineteenth-century texts, however, because we find distasteful the genre chosen by individual authors in which to shape it, or to read those texts ignoring the impact of the myth within them, is to continue to be in the myth's power. Readers within the culture will find that the assumptions of the text are natural and self-evident, and foreign readers will continue to understand them according to their own implicit national myths.

We must decode the image of the Cossack as a segment of Russian cultural mythology in part to discern the underlying assumptions that make Russians *Russian*. They may resemble Americans, as their steppe might resemble midwestern prairies, and their frontier, the frontier of the American West. But Russians are also unlike Americans, and this study may turn us in the direction of understanding why.

The remainder of Part 1 of this study will suggest the specifically Russian elements in the Cossack heroes, and unwrap the major topoi that echo throughout the myth in the nineteenth century. Chapter 2 examines the various strains that merge to form the Cossack hero, especially in the works of Aleksandr Pushkin. The remaining chapters of the first part, however, analyze the elements of the Cossack in his fully mythic form, represented most clearly in the stories of Nikolai Gogol. Although Pushkin, and later Tolstoi, play on the underlying contradictions and complexities of received assumptions about the hero, it is Gogol's Cossacks who are largely responsible for the image of the Cossack adopted and adapted in twentieth-century Russian literature. Part 2 examines those adaptations in light of the oeuvres of several major poets and writers, and of the changing cultural climate. The final chapters chronicle the death of the once-vibrant Cossack myth, and the last pages take an ironic look back upon it.

All whose ancestors came under the Cossack sabre celebrate the extinction of the Cossack hosts. The death of a cultural myth, however, is a more ambivalent issue; rebirth of the COSSACK may still lie ahead.

TWO

Folk Poetry, Pushkin, and the Romantic Cossack Hero

IN RUSSIAN belles lettres, the historical Cossack begins his transformation into a mythic hero within the romantic works of Aleksandr Pushkin (1799–1837) and his contemporaries. Although the treatment of the hero by Pushkin is varied and characteristically contradictory, it nonetheless, and perhaps by virtue of its ambiguity, reveals the Cossack's influence on the Russian literary consciousness.[1]

Russian readers' exposure to Cossack characters in the early part of the nineteenth century came in one of three related forms: romanticized accounts of the history of the Ukraine; newly published collections of folk poetry; and European romantic accounts of Cossacks or, by analogy, historical fiction in general. All of these fed the Russian public's newly found interest in the past, and in its own national history in particular. Following the success of Nikolai Karamzin's *History of the Russian State* (1818–26), historical figures of all sorts became material for generic transpositions,[2] and the Cossacks were no exception.

Folk Poetry and Folk Imitations

Since the sixteenth century, Russian folk poetry had made extensive use of Cossack heroes. Historical songs with roots in the Russian *byliny* (heroic epic tales) and in lyrical folk ballads glorified the Cossack brigands, minimizing the horror of their destructiveness and glamorizing their unconventional adventures.[3]

Line length and rhyme scheme are variable, but motifs in the folk songs are stylized and repetitive. Certain settings and plot elements immediately identify the Cossack songs: the heroes sail on the Mother Volga River, the Quiet Don, or the great blue sea; they plunder merchant ships; miraculously escape Turkish prisons; and outwit the tsar himself. Over and over the Cossack leaders speak in the parallelisms typical of folk poetry, "like a trumpeter trumpeting" *(kak v trubu trubit);* "they went reveling-carousing" *(khodili-guliali).* And the clever Cossacks of folk imagination are virtually immortal. As the heroic Razin claims: "You needn't waste your gunpowder and burst your shells— / The little bullet won't touch me, the shot won't take me."[4]

The earliest poems and tales repeatedly evoke the figure of Ermak, conquerer of Siberia. Others tell the story of a siege of the Turkish-controlled town of Azov by a group of Don Cossacks,[5] and later ones relate episodes, real or invented, from the lives of Razin and Pugachev. Many of the Cossack topoi found in romantic literature were first popularized in the historical songs. Personification of the vast land and rivers over which the warriors roam, especially of the Don River as father, the Volga as mother, and the steppe as fiancée, is particularly typical. The intimacy with nature that the folk poetry champions reflects a desire on the part of the people to see their lives in harmony with the rich land that provides their sustenance.

Only when the folk songs were published at the end of the eighteenth and first half of the nineteenth centuries did they become a significant factor in the history of the literary character.[6] At that time poets, Pushkin included, began to create folk imitations, incorporating imagery and diction of the older songs and tales. Despite stylistic similarities, these new poems differed from their prototypes in their self-conscious formulation, and by the very fact that they were published under the names of individual poets. As such, readers were forced to confront a clash in values between the Cossack ethos and that of "civilized" literary society. The Russian poets, unlike the people among whom the folk songs originated, could not present the heroes as representatives of themselves. The voice they used was "other," and the folk imitations remained nonmythic.

Pushkin was an avid collector of folktales and poetry, and his imitations are generally recognized as closer to a folk tone than those of his contemporaries. He successfully incorporates Cossack motifs in his narrative poem *The Brigand Brothers (Brat'ia razboiniki,* 1822) and exploits the rhythm, vocabulary, and typical repetitions of folk poetry in three poems based on Razin songs, *Songs of Sten'ka Razin (Pesni o Sten'ke Razine,* written 1824–26).[7] Thus he imitates: "So began Sten'ka Razin / To think some thoughts" (Stal Sten'ka Razin / Dumati dumu); and "No trumpet trumpeting is heard from the field" (Ne truba trubacha s polia slyshitsia); Razin is called "To carouse upon the sea, upon the blue one" (Poguliat' po moriu, po sinemu) and to "Escape upon the sea, upon the blue one" (Pobegi po moriu po sinemu); "And he stares at the mother at the Volga" (A gliadit na matushku na Volgu).

Pushkin called Razin "the only poetic figure in Russian history,"[8] and the brave "Stepanushka" was indeed particularly popular in folk poetry. Because of his notoriety, Razin's name was grafted onto songs and historical ballads composed long after his lifetime, glorifying exploits of an entirely different Cossack and another era altogether. But despite the fact that more "Razin" songs have thus been collected than ones devoted to any other Cossack hero, Razin as a character never fully developed in nineteenth-century literary texts.[9]

Actual documentation on the life of Razin was scarce in Pushkin's time, and his story may possibly have had less appeal to those prose writers increasingly enamored of the many historical references typical of the historical novel. More likely, his tales of brigandage on the Volga River seemed too anarchic to censors and authors alike. Razin was less a border guard, with at least quasi bonds to society, and more an uncontrollable brigand, as he appears briefly in Pushkin's own songs. Even Pushkin's cycle was not published in his lifetime, having been refused by no less rigorous a censor than Nicholas I, and appeared only in 1881. Politics played a large role in early romanticism, from the Decembrists' calls for constitutional liberties to monarchists' support of autocratic rule, but anarchy was not considered a political option by any part of the intelligentsia until much later in the century.

Even more important is the Ukrainophilia of early Russian romanticism. A number of writers of the teens and twenties turned their attention to Ukraine and thus to specifically Ukrainian Cossacks. The relatively unknown land to the south inspired works of all genres including ethnographic studies and romanticized histories, imitations of folk forms (which nonetheless often found themselves accepted as genuine folk songs), "native" Ukrainian comedies, and historical novels. Ukraine was far enough away, and different enough in custom and costume, to fulfill the romantic fascination with the exotic. Yet by the nineteenth century it was also a fully established part of the Russian empire, and its writers could move to Petersburg and easily assimilate into Great Russian society. It also happened to be the home of the Zaporozhian Cossacks and of the perceived mother of Russian cities, Kiev. All three concepts, then—Ukraine, Cossack, and Kiev, or in fact all of Kievan Rus'—could become associated with each other, and in turn with the origins of Russia and with a way of life closer to the essence of Russian nature and to the folk, or *narod,* than that of the Europeanized Russians of the capital.[10]

This fascination with Ukraine was not without its political dimension. The official term for this territory throughout the nineteenth century was "Malorossiia" or "Malaia Rossiia," literally "Little Russia." The term "Ukraina" meant "borderland" and referred to the southeastern "Russian" land under the Polish Empire. It had a largely historical-geographic, not ethnic significance.[11] When Ukraine was united with Russia in 1654, it officially became known as Little Russia. Yet "Ukraina" often recurred in folk poetry, and was claimed by Ukrainian nationalists in the growing movement of the nineteenth century. For them it took on a definite national rather than merely regional feeling.[12]

The label "little" is technically a reference to the land's lesser distance to Constantinople (for the purposes of trade and pilgrimage), rather than to its smaller size or political significance. Other connotations of the epithet were not lost on Ukrainians, however, many of whom objected to "Great" Russian condescension. Disagreement continued throughout the nineteenth century as to whether Ukrainian was a dialect of Russian or an independent Slavic language, and whether the contemporary inhabitants of the Ukraine were emigrant Russians (many Russian historians believed that Ukraine had been totally depopulated when the Kievan principalities fled before the Tatars) or, in fact, the direct and legitimate descendents of old Rus'.[13]

Justifiably, Ukrainian nationalists of the later nineteenth century objected to the russifying tendency of the early Romantic writers. Ukrainian historians to this day insist on the purely Ukrainian origins of the Cossack. The issue is extremely complex, since the historical status of the Ukraine as a separate nation distinct from either Poland or the Russian empire is in question. For the purposes of the present study, however, the historical distinction between Ukrainian and Russian Cossacks recedes. As in folklore, Cossack texts often arbitrarily substitute one Cossack's name or characteristics for another.[14] If this study betrays a Great Russian bias, it is because nineteenth-century Russian literature dictates it.

Ukrainian folk literature, even more than its Russian counterpart, personifies the steppe, emphasizes the limitlessness of the territory, and, most of all, glorifies the Cossacks. Originally called "Cossack songs," these traditional Ukrainian folk forms, or *dumy,* were popularized among Russian readers through politicized imitations by the poet Kondratii Ryleev (1795–1826).[15] Collectors of Ukrainian folk material praised the native *dumy* for their supposed aesthetic purity, and for the intensity that they believed reflected a more passionate relationship with nature than that of Russians.[16]

The original Ukrainian folk songs were sung and often composed by wandering bards, called bandurists, who accompanied their tales on a stringed *bandura.*[17] When reference is made in Russian literary texts to these musical performers, they are frequently described as blind, associating them with the proverbial blind Homer, and their songs with the *Iliad,* the archetype of national epics. This elevation of the *dumy,* and thus their heroes, to epic stature reflects a perception about the Ukrainian experience, and particularly the Cossack experience, as intimately in touch with national origins and the elemental power of nature.

Romantic Historiography and the Cossacks

The popularity of Cossack themes in Pushkin's day was more than a sentimental attraction to rural life kept at an aesthetic or scholarly distance. Little, after all, was sentimental about the Cossack that a historian might discover. Russian fascination with the Cossacks was also more than a vague yearning for exotic and fantastic subjects. It was fostered, instead, by romanticism's interest in national history.[18] In their understanding of the historical discipline, however, Russian romantics drew little distinction between ethnographic material and other documentary data; romantic historiography sought to recapture and refashion the entire spirit of an age, in all its organic vitality.[19]

In Russia as well as the West, historians were turning more and more toward studies of the people and their folk customs to explain the vicissitudes of history. The Russian people, the *narod,* was understood as the repository of native values, preserved in their historically original forms. Under the influence of Schelling, with whom, as one twentieth-century historiographer points out, "philosophy changed into mysticism, and history into art,"[20] the historians used data drawn from popular legends and songs to create a picture of life as they imagined it to be.

The most important historical work in this context first appeared in manuscript in the 1820s and was probably read at that time by Pushkin.[21] *Istoriia Rusov,* or *The History of the Russes or Little Russia,* erroneously ascribed to Bishop Georgii Koniskii,[22] paints a highly romanticized portrait of the Cossacks.[23] Later historians, sifting through the fragmentary data on the Cossacks, have repeatedly complained of the inaccuracies of *The History,* many of which made their way into popular renditions of the myth.[24]

The account renders an idealized history of the Cossacks, and in so doing implies that they represent all Ukrainians.[25] As a further step, the introduction to the published version claims that the history of the Ukraine (and thus of the Cossacks) in fact forms the core of *all Russian* history: "The history of Little Russia before the time of the invasion of the Tatars with their Khan Batyi is united with the history of all of Russia, or rather it *is* the one, single Russian history."[26]

The text of *The History* itself begins with a chronicle of the origins of the Slavs, tracing them back to a son of Noah, and leads quickly into a description of Kievan Rus' and then to the first Cossack hetmans. This attempt to portray the Cossacks retrospectively as pure Slavs, and the Slavs as descendents of biblical personalities, filtered into many of the later Cossack texts. It is a technique common to ancient chronicles and imperial genealogies, designed to legitimize figures in power by associating them with the primeval origin of mankind.

Since the remainder of *The History* organizes itself around the succession of Cossack leaders, it creates the impression that the Cossack warriors dominated or were, in fact, coterminous with the history of the entire area. Its author stresses the heroism and cunning of the Cossacks vis-à-vis Poland, and their efforts toward freedom, efforts that eventually, under the Cossack Bogdan Khmel'nitskii, brought Ukraine into the Russian empire.

Although *The History* supports the claims of Ukrainian national independence, it does so by asserting the legitimate descent of the Cossack leaders from Kievan Rus', that same Rus' that Great Russians claim as their own origin. Ukrainian nationalists have understood this text as evidence of the Ukraine's historical right to cultural and political independence. It could equally well be and was embraced by Russians as proof of their own uninterrupted connection to Rus' through the Cossack presence in so-called Little Russia, and the assistance of Cossacks in returning the territory of Rus' to its Russian heirs. For a Russian audience, *The History* presents the Cossacks as freedom fighters, organically and historically united to Russia. The Cossacks, as mythic heroes, are here related in some way to the origins of the Russian people.

The attraction of these heroes was no doubt increased by an association with medieval texts that also evoke Russian origins in old Rus', texts newly discovered and read avidly by early-nineteenth-century intellectuals. Similarly, the translation of Homer's *Iliad* by N. I. Gnedich, begun in 1807 and completed in 1829, influenced Russian writers to search for Russia's own epic heroes. Romantic writers found what they were looking for in the Cossacks appropriated from historical works, which themselves had begun the process of mythologizing the Cossack hero.

The newly popularized Cossacks proved fashionable among writers in the 1820s and 1830s from widely differing political camps, including the reactionary Faddei Bulgarin on the one hand, and many of Pushkin's friends, the reform-minded Decembrists, on the other. The prolific poets among the Decembrists of the late teens and early twenties (so-called retrospectively after their attempted coup on December 14, 1825) had a connection with Ukraine and by extension with the Ukrainian Cossacks through their Southern Brotherhood and the Ukrainian-based Society of United Slavs that merged with it. They tended to draw themes from the south, rarely advocating Ukrainian independence, but more often using the Ukrainian struggle for its national, cultural, or political independence as an allegory for their own situation in Great Russia. The Decembrists concentrated on the political reorganization of Russia, and to this end called for an assimilation of non-Russian nationalities and the "several varieties of the native Russian people" into a single culture, under a unified republic.[27] For them, the Ukrainian struggle was a general Slavic one. Reaching maturity on the heels of the

Napoleonic War in 1812, these young educated nobles dreamt of forging a country free of autocratic caprice, based on the Enlightenment ideals of individualism, but fully infused with romantic nationalism and pan-Slavism. The Ukrainian Cossack defiance of Polish autocratic domination provided a model.

The Decembrist Fedor Glinka (1786–1880), for example, began a novel about Khmel'nitskii in 1817, ostensibly chronicling the attempts of that Cossack to liberate the Ukraine.[28] Yet the manuscript repeatedly confuses the Zaporozhians with the Don Cossacks, associating the Ukrainian heroes with rebellions on Russian territory and with Russian attempts at liberation from Russia's own autocratic rule. Kondratii Ryleev's (1795–1826) fragments collected under the title *Nalivaiko* (1825) imply that the Ukraine is the Rus' of old, and her defense is in fact a defense of an uncorrupted Russia, freed from the foreign influences of "the Pole, the Jew, and the Uniate."[29]

Glinka's poem "The Foray of the Zaporozhian Cossacks from the Sech to the Volyn'" (1826), subtitled "From the history of the seventeenth century," takes another mythologizing step. It suggests a relationship between the Zaporozhians and the medieval heroes *(bogatyri)* of Russian folklore, thus transporting the Cossacks out of their own historical context, despite exact historical and geographic references within the text. By so doing, Glinka obliquely associates the Cossacks with contemporary *"bogatyri,"* his fellow Decembrists tried in 1825, who supposedly shared with the medieval heroes a noble tradition and dedication to the pursuit of justice. The Zaporozhians, of course, were noble in neither social class nor sentiment. Under Glinka's pen they lose their local specificity, becoming not so much myth as an abstract emblem for freedom from oppression.

Embrace of the Cossack by Decembrist writers was therefore less a glorification of the liminal hero than yet another argument for replacement of the tsarist government with a republic. Ryleev drew themes from Russian history (*Oleg the Wise, Sviatoslav, Sviatopolk,* and *Dmitrii Donskoi*) and published the poems as *dumy* in 1825 alongside *Bogdan Khmel'nitskii* and a long narrative poem about the Cossack Voinarovskii (1823–25). His heroes are virtually interchangeable, representing not the Russian essence as a whole—as would be the case in the established myth—but only those like-minded republicans who saw themselves outside or alien to the central ruling power and who martyred themselves to their cause.

Another writer of the 1820s, Vasilii Narezhnyi (1780–1825), took a less political stance when he wrote about Ukrainian Cossacks, turning to history in order to indulge in popular romantic exotica.[30] His novel *The Zaporozhian* (1824) is more interested in the Cossacks' daily escapades than in their rebellion, as is also true of his novel *The Seminarian: A Little Russian Tale* (1824). Over the next few decades, Narezhnyi was joined by a long series of writers interested in the seemingly exotic nature of everyday Cossack life, many of whom fabricated stories of their own Cossack roots. Such an assertion of Cossack blood ostensibly lays claim to historical veracity, but actually further mythologizes the Cossacks. The passionate heroes of the past are thus transformed into close relatives and embraced as self as well as other.

Foreign Sources

Some Cossack works of the romantic period borrowed their subject from foreign sources rather than native histories. This is the route through which the Cossack Mazepa came into Russian romantic literature.

Ivan Mazepa (1639?–1709) spent his childhood in the Polish court in the middle of the seventeenth century. His story, popularized by Voltaire through Byron, has come down to us in variations of the following: Accused of courting his master's wife, the young Ukrainian was tied to the back of a wild horse and sent off into the steppe to die. He was found starving by a Ukrainian girl, nursed back to life, and went on to become a great hetman of the Zaporozhian Cossacks.

Facts, however, suggest that Mazepa rose to the hetmancy by more political, less romantic means. Mazepa apparently arranged for his election with strong support from Moscow after decades of fighting in Ukraine among Russians, Turks, Poles, Zaporozhians, and Hetmanate Cossacks, the friction aggravated by Khmel'nitskii's treaty with Moscow and constant war with Poland. The new hetman suppressed further uprisings and brought Ukraine more securely under the jurisdiction of the Russian empire.

Mazepa was advisor and friend to Peter the Great until the first decade of the eighteenth century. For still somewhat unclear reasons, however, the Cossack leader chose to side with Charles XII of Sweden against the Russian tsar at the battle of Poltava (1709), thus betraying the Russian empire, now guardian of his own Ukraine.

Mazepa's image remains contradictory in the Polish, Ukrainian, and Russian literature about him, depending, to a large extent, on the political stance of the writer. Those who believe he legitimately opposed Peter in order to secure a free and independent Ukraine tend to glorify his behavior. His earlier friendship with the Russian throne in this case is understood as a cunning plan to gain influence that could ultimately profit the unjustly colonized Ukraine. Russian nationalists, however, label Mazepa a traitor and intriguer for his own personal gain. The latter writers refuse to elevate Mazepa to the level of mythic hero, although they do often mythologize the Ukrainian Cossacks whom Mazepa abandons. Since readers also bring to

28

critiques of Mazepa stories their own political prejudices, analyses of the literature on this Cossack tend to be particularly biased.

European visitors to Russia occasionally reported back to their countrymen on the exotic land to the east in the form of travelogues and histories. Voltaire had access to such materials for his *Histoire de Charles XII* and *Histoire de la Russie sous le règne de Pierre le Grand*. Two short comments in these histories about Mazepa's role in the late seventeenth and early eighteenth centuries then provided the background for Lord Byron's poem *Mazeppa* (1818).[31] The poem is presented as a tale told by the Cossack himself to Charles XII, who is having trouble sleeping after the battle: "'But I request,' / Said Sweden's monarch, 'thou wilt tell / This tale of thine, and I may reap, / Perchance, from this the boon of sleep, / For at this moment from my eyes / The hope of present slumber flies."[32] Byron concentrates on Mazepa's apocryphal ride upon a wild horse that takes him home from captivity in Poland: "'They bound me on, that menial throng, / Upon his back with many a thong; / Then loosed him with a sudden lash— / Away!— away!—and on we dash!— / Torrents less rapid and less rash" (ll. 370–74), so that: "'Away, away, my steed and I, / Upon the pinions of the wind, / All human dwellings left behind; / We sped like meteors through the sky, / When with its crackling sound the night / Is chequer'd with the northern light'" (ll. 423–29). The poem as a whole therefore exudes irony: a romantic journey, impelled by images of freedom and bondage, does no more than lull the listener to sleep. Although the poem does not necessarily have a national character, readers who seek to glorify the Ukrainian Cossack can essentially ignore the frame, and interpret the internal story about the wild ride as a symbol of the Cossack's relentless drive for freedom.[33] Byron's Mazepa becomes a Cossack hero living an exotic life so intense as to be utterly alien to our own, and to the Swedish king's.

Drawing extensively on Byron in his own poem titled "Mazeppa" (1828), Victor Hugo further stresses the distance of the Cossack's essence from the reader's. In the first half of the poem, the poet recapitulates the flight of the wild horse with Mazepa tied to its back; in the second, he transforms Mazepa into an artist who is misunderstood and unappreciated by prosaic society. As the inspired romantic poet is alienated from the general public, so is the Cossack removed from everyday experience:

Ainsi, lorsqu'un mortel, sur qui son dieu s'étale,
S'est vu lier vivant sur ta croupe fatale,
  Génie, ardent coursier,
En vain il lutte, hélas! tu bondis, tu l'emportes
Hors du monde réel, dont tu brises les portes
  Avec tes pieds d'acier![34]

Byron's and Hugo's poems, which emphasize the exoticism and ahistoricism of Mazepa, stimulated native reassessments of the Cossack. Aleksandr Pushkin began to exploit the paradoxical nature of the Cossack in his own version of the Mazepa story, the narrative poem *Poltava* (1828), in response to a narrative poem by the Polish poet Adam Mickiewicz, *Konrad Wallenrod* (1825–27).[35] The latter had been an answer to an earlier depiction of Mazepa in Ryleev's *Voinarovskii*.[36] In Ryleev's poem the eponymous hero, Mazepa's nephew, has been exiled to Siberia, and tells the story of his life and that of his uncle to a sympathetic ethnographer. The latter comes to appreciate Voinarovskii's love of the Ukraine and the desire to free it from foreign domination that was Mazepa's nephew's if not necessarily the hetman's own cause.[37] As Voinarovskii confesses: "I must live; within me still / Burns love of my native land."[38] The ethnographer later returns to inform the Cossack of his pardon, only to find Voinarovskii frozen over the grave of his wife.[39]

Pushkin's *Poltava* in turn provoked a response from Faddei Bulgarin (1789–1859) in the form of a tendentious novel *Mazepa* (1833–34).[40] Bulgarin's prose was never known for its high literary quality, and as a man and litterateur he was detested by many members of the intellectual community, Pushkin among them.[41] A Pole by birth, he entered Russian literature and service after fighting *against* the Russians under Napoleon in 1812, and as a new imperial citizen he brought the ardor of a recent convert to his patriotism. Bulgarin calls his Mazepa a Judas bereft of God's blessing, for the hetman clearly allies himself with the enemy Poles among whom he grew up, and betrays Peter and both Russia and Ukraine for personal gain. By the end of the novel, this Mazepa causes his own death, a potentially incestuous relationship between his unsuspecting son and daughter, and the suicide of that son.

Pushkin

The protracted polemic, examining so-called patriotic or traitorous elements in the story of Mazepa and Peter the Great, suggests the breadth of the growing myth, for each work exposes a different side of the Cossack hetman.[42] Pushkin's *Poltava* displays the complexity of the historical narrative, and never itself chooses sides. While depicting Mazepa's anarchic selfishness in contrast to the attempts of Peter to preserve a civil and united Russia, it at the same time draws a compelling portrait of a traitor nevertheless capable of love and guilt, and with at least plausible personal reasons for his hatred of and desire for revenge against Peter.[43]

Pushkin's long poem begins with an epigraph from Byron: "The power and glory of the war, / Faithless as their vain votaries, men, / Had pass'd to the triumphant Czar."[44] These words are strangely more fitting for Pushkin's than for Byron's poem, for the former takes a decidedly politicized, less lyrical view of Mazepa than had the English version, and treats an entirely different and more military period in his life.

The first few stanzas tell of the Cossack hetman's shocking abduction of Mariia, the daughter of a rich nobleman, Kochubei. Mazepa is here no longer young: "He is old. He is dispirited with age, / By war, cares, and troubles; / But passions burn within him, and again / Mazepa knows love" (V:20, ll. 41–44). More important, he could not have legally married Mariia without special dispensation from the Orthodox Church, for the Cossack was her godfather and a union would have been considered incest under religious laws. Unlike her parents, the girl herself is not averse to this illicit match to a man much older than herself; she has refused all eligible suitors and fallen in love instead with the romantic image of Cossack life that Mazepa represents to her. Pushkin tells us that she "always sang / The songs, that he composed," and "loved the cavalry formations, / And the martial peal of kettledrums, and the cries / Before the mace and Cossack staff / Of the Little Russian leader" (V:22, ll. 119–20 and 124–27). In a note to the first of these lines, an "editor" who is one of Pushkin's narrative voices in the poem informs us that tradition ascribes several folk songs to Mazepa, and that Kochubei himself refers to a *duma* written by Mazepa. By reminding his audience that Mazepa himself wrote folk poetry, Pushkin ties his hero to the tradition out of which grew his own *Songs of Sten'ka Razin*. He furthermore suggests that Mariia at least, but no doubt his readers as well, would "read" this Cossack through the topoi of the COSSACK.

Thus, Pushkin presents a complex psychological portrait for which he recognizes that passion may not be so much blind as blinded by myths and tradition. Mariia rashly abandons the safe, noble house of her parents in order to become part of the exciting Cossack life she knows only from folk literature and the ceremonial trappings of the Cossacks paraded before her. Like Pushkin's sentimental heroines from *The Tales of Belkin,* but in her case not at all comically, Mariia misunderstands her situation because of an equation of literary image and reality, making her the first fictional character to fall under the influence of the Cossack myth. She takes Mazepa to be the Cossack she nurtures in her imagination, and recognizes that he is not that hero only later, after the death of her father, and ironically in a mad delirium:

I took you for another,
Old man. Leave me.
Your gaze is mocking and horrible.
You are ugly. He is beautiful:

In his eyes shines love,
Langour in his speech!
His moustache is whiter than snow,
But yours is dried with blood! . . .
(V:62, ll. 399–406)

Mariia's misreading is our own, and the power that myths hold over her is as strong as over all "readers" of national culture. The potency of her confusion of mythic image and life is perceptively, and tragically, captured by Pushkin in the rhymes of *krov'* and *liubov'* (blood and love), *uzhasen* and *prekrasen* (horrible and beautiful).

But Pushkin leaves the romantic story of Mariia's elopement and turns to a historical account of the political situation faced by Peter the Great, and the role of Mazepa as hetman. Kochubei waits in the background to take revenge on his daughter's unlawful husband. The remainder of the first part presents possible motivations for Mazepa's treason. Ukraine under his rule is seething with discontent at Moscow and Great Russian domination, and in desperation her patriots are ready to join with Charles in Sweden's fight against the Russian tsar. Mazepa at first holds back, ostensibly out of loyalty to Peter. But it soon becomes clear that the hetman is contemplating treachery.

Part 2 begins with a dialogue between Mazepa and Mariia, including a declaration by Mazepa that he has the independence of Ukraine at heart. Yet at the same time he refers elliptically to the imprisonment and imminent execution of Kochubei that he has arranged. "Tell me," Mazepa demands, "Who is dearer to you / Your father or your spouse?" (V:37, ll. 95–96). Mariia does not understand Mazepa's words; she resists making a choice of loyalty between her lover and her father, and cannot understand the implications of the betrayal of her father eventually forced from her. Mariia's mother makes a secret visit on the eve of the execution. With difficulty she convinces her daughter of the truth and probable consequences of Mazepa's actions against Kochubei and persuades Mariia to go with her to plead for her father's life: "Come to your senses, my daughter! Mariia, / Run, fall at his feet, / Save your father, be an angel for us: / Your glance will bind the hands of the villains, / You can remove the ax from them" (V:46, ll. 352–56). But the women arrive too late. In this very dramatic section, first Mazepa's, then Mariia's inner confusion and guilt are highlighted, as Pushkin juxtaposes the political and personal dilemmas.

The third part of the *poema* suggests new motivations for Mazepa's eventual betrayal of Russia: grief over Mariia's absence; shamed pride from a previous affront by Peter;[45] again his love of Ukraine; or, finally, mercenary interests. Pushkin's Great Russian patriotism becomes clear in this section when his narrator calls Mazepa "a Judas"; this Mazepa ultimately betrays

Russia in the hope of personal gain. Yet, the story ends on a private rather than political note: Mariia, driven mad and wandering alone at night in the vast steppe, calls out to her traitorous husband, while he tosses in his sleep: "Mazepa's dreams were troubled" (V:61, l. 6). After a delirious exchange with her anguished husband, partially reproduced above, Mariia disappears into the darkness, leaving the hetman, his heart heavy, to heed Charles's call. Mazepa follows the foreign king, "bidding farewell to his native land" (V:63, l. 424).

The final stanza, set apart from the main text, then removes the scene a hundred years hence, to Pushkin's age and present-tense narration, and remembers the former "strong, proud men, so full of the free power of passions" (V:63–64, ll. 426–27). This concluding section calls into question an unambiguous interpretation of certain facts presented by the "historical" voice of *Poltava*. We are, for example, told that Mazepa was buried together with the foreign king, as though eternally alienated, and forgotten by his own people. He is spoken of once a year only, when the Church reaffirms its anathema. But the poet actually contradicts these statements, and concludes his poem with the declaration that a blind Ukrainian singer—a traditional epic bard—will continue to sing Mazepa's songs.

Although he asserts at the beginning of the last stanza that the past has disappeared, the poet's reference to a bard emphasizes the immortality of the Cossack. The songs that Mazepa wrote, which Pushkin first mentioned very early in the poem as having so affected Mariia, and which he informed us in a note were connected to Ukrainian folk poems, guarantee his impact on later generations. Composed when he was still young, that is, during the romantic youth glorified in Byron's poem, and sung already in his own lifetime, the songs in fact provide a link through the legendary Razin of folk song fame to Pushkin himself. The *Songs of Sten'ka Razin,* written by Pushkin, like the ones sung here, written by but not necessarily about Mazepa, relate in both theme and poetics to the lyrical-narrative *dumy.*[46] Thus, despite Mazepa's questionable patriotism and/or morality as revealed in any historical rendering, on one level in this *poema* he nonetheless implies a Cossack ideal.[47] His lyrical and romantic songs, mentioned at the opening and closing of Pushkin's poem, bracket the historical and in some sense prosaic text (including the notes), and transform it into myth. We might say that Mazepa creates the Cossack ideal in *Poltava,* although he himself does not live up to its image.

If Mazepa's motivations in the poem are at best ambiguous, the attitudes of the youthful Cossacks, whom Mazepa leads but eventually abandons, are clearly not. As a group, they explicitly desire to defend "Rus'," "ancient Moscow," and Ukraine. But this group as well is not unambiguously ideal in *Poltava,* for a strong voice within the poem, perhaps closest to Pushkin's

Great Russian viewpoint, supports Peter's claim for a unified Russia and thus condemns "Young Ukraine." The Cossacks are at best naive for having been duped by Mazepa, and at worst simply wrong.

There is yet a third Cossack image presented, however, and one that complicates the picture even more. He is the nameless Cossack who is a rival for Mariia's affection, and who, though unsuccessful in love, is granted the Byronic wild horseback ride, carrying to Peter the Great Kochubei's denunciation of Mazepa. In this minor figure, Pushkin has coopted for the Great Russian cause the apolitical but romantic Cossack of Byron, and the very political yet still romantic Cossack hero of Ukrainian folk poetry.

On top of his reading of Western European literature and native folk poetry, Pushkin was extremely interested in historical genres, both as documentary and in their relationship to fiction. Like the other romantic writers who turned to historical themes, Pushkin read the novels of Sir Walter Scott, and at least one scholar suggests parallels to Walter Scott as well as Byron in *Poltava*. [48] Scott's *Waverley* (1814) was first reviewed in Russia in 1815, and issued along with others of his works in at least forty separate Russian translations between 1820 and 1830.[49] In addition, Russian journals and publishing houses printed huge numbers of translations of Scott's European imitators. In 1828, an Englishman in St. Petersburg wrote to Scott that "Your works are as much esteemed on the banks of the Neva and Wolga [*sic*] as on those of the Tweed or Thames."[50] And although some critics in the 1830s and 1840s—notably O. I. Senkovskii, the editor of the conservative journal *Library for Reading*—complained of Scott's perversion of literary taste,[51] influential critics including Belinskii, Pushkin, and Gogol repeatedly came to the Scotsman's defense.

Many of the Russian works influenced by Scott are first-person accounts of a fictional hero, an insignificant participant in the cataclysmic historical events being described in the background. The reader views these events through the naive eyes of the protagonist, a stranger to the men who make history. The hero's maturation, usually abetted by a romance, provides the narrative line through which weave his meetings with actual historical actors on both sides of the struggle.

Pushkin, like many of his contemporaries, attempted to adapt the Scottian genre for the Russian soil as a way of developing Russian prose. Unlike others, however, he undertook detailed historical research as background for his fiction. Along with research in the 1820s into Ukrainian and Don Cossacks, especially Razin,[52] Pushkin with great difficulty received permission to examine archival material on Emel'ian Pugachev. He traveled to Kazan' and Orenburg, centers of Pugachev's activity, examined the documents available to him, and interviewed aged eyewitnesses to the Pugachevshchina. A historical study of Pugachev and of his rebellion was published by Pushkin in

1834, originally titled *The History of Pugachev*. Nicholas I personally required the title changed to *The History of Pugachev's Rebellion*, claiming that a rebel does not have the right to his own history. Two years later, Pushkin reused the material in his novel *The Captain's Daughter*.[53]

The tsar apparently read *The History of Pugachev* as a single-minded confirmation of his own ideas about the control of rebellious chaos, and rushed the work into print without the usual delays of censorship.[54] But Pushkin portrays in it a number of contradictory aspects of the Cossack and of the rebellion itself. Although Pugachev's atrocities are well documented by Pushkin, we sense nonetheless a certain attraction to the clever, powerful Cossack as well.

Pushkin does not hesitate to confirm Pugachev's military skill, and reports on one occasion that it surprised even a Russian commander, "who had not expected of him such knowledge of military tactics."[55] Yet the Cossack's success did not stem only from his superior maneuvering. Nor did the droves who joined Pugachev solely decide the progress of the revolt, although so many disaffected enlisted men deserted the official ranks that commanders could never rest assured of their own men's loyalty. Delays and bad judgments on the part of Russian officers were equally to blame, and by faithfully reporting these Russian errors, Pushkin suggests Pugachev's ability to take advantage of his luck.

The author's portrait of the captured Pugachev's entrance into Moscow is largely sympathetic: "He was in fetters. The soldiers fed him from their hands, and told the children who clustered around his sledge, 'Remember children, that you saw Pugachev.' Old folks still tell of his bold answers to the questions of passersby. He was cheerful and calm the whole trip."[56]

Pushkin's guarded attraction to Pugachev grows even greater in his fictional account of the Cossack.[57] *The Captain's Daughter* presents a Russian, Petr Grinev, who is guided to safety from a blinding snowstorm by an unknown peasant. The next morning, out of gratitude and youthful exuberance, Grinev presents his savior with a hareskin coat. Only later does Grinev learn that the peasant is in fact the feared Cossack rebel, Pugachev. The latter, though challenging the tsarist Russian army to which Grinev has vowed allegiance, nonetheless pays back his benefactor multifold. Not only does he spare Grinev's life and that of his beloved after seizing the fort where they are stationed, but he also allows the young Russian officer to return to his company and continue the fight *against* the Cossacks. Pugachev's generosity sits side by side with his violence. As Grinev himself exclaims: "I could not help but marvel at the strange concatenation of circumstances: a child's coat given to a tramp has saved me from the noose, and a drunkard, reeling from inn to inn, lays seige to fortresses and shakes the very foundation of the state!"[58]

Grinev's first encounter with Pugachev's paradoxical nature comes in the form of a dream about his father's death. The peasant, whom Grinev's still does not know to be the Cossack ataman, acts as a proxy for the boy's father, from whom Grinev must receive a deathbed blessing. In the dream the peasant appears at once kind and threatening; he glances gaily *(veselo)* and calls out tenderly *(laskovo),* but he is terrible *(strashnyi)* and fills the room with bodies mutilated by his axe (VIII:289). We are later told that Pugachev's features do not betray a violent personality, although we know that he has just ordered the hanging of the father of Grinev's fiancée, and that he condoned the brutal rape and murder of her mother (VIII:330). His merriment, in fact, is infectious, and Grinev begins to laugh in the Cossack's presence without knowing why (VIII:331). The Pugachev whom Pushkin presents is by no means a simple embodiment of evil divorced from the good Russian soul, the latter characterized by the nobleman Grinev. Rather, exotic destruction and familiar sympathy coincide within the dreaded Cossack rebel.[59]

Pugachev is nonetheless not yet a fully mythic Cossack. The ataman, as representative of the *narod,* is contrasted to the westernized but nonetheless fully Russian gentry in the figure of Grinev. The two characters share a friendship and mutual respect, but ultimately Pushkin describes a conflict, not a unity. As much as the author may sympathize with the Cossack, his allegiance, and the reader's, remains with Grinev.

By gentle irony, we are led to understand that the legendary "signs of the tsar" upon Pugachev's chest are no more than scars from boils, and his epic ability to eat huge quantities and withstand unbearable heat in the bathhouse are the self-delusions of his followers (VIII:329). What is not a delusion, as Pugachev tells us by analogy with a folktale, is the Cossack's conscious choice to settle for a short life enjoying the food of an eagle, rather than live a raven's life of three hundred years, and eat off the flesh of carrion (VIII:353).[60] Pugachev chooses the heroic path, fully accepting its mortal and, yes, amoral consequences.

But Grinev, although in awe of Pugachev's power, remains skeptical of the Cossack's heroism. His interpretation of the tale immediately follows and differs from Pugachev's: the "eagle's" food—the Cossack spoils of war—differs in no way from the carrion it supposedly eschews, and the brutal murder of the parents of his fiancée cannot be a heroic act. For his part, the Russian's heroism is defined by blind devotion to his sense of honor. His sentiments, and Pushkin's concerns, remain decidedly noble. Self and other, violence and humanity may coincide in the figure of Pugachev, as they do in Mazepa, but ultimately they do not raise the Cossack and his milieu to the level of myth.

Excerpts from folk songs head five of *The Captain's Daughter's* fourteen chapters, and proverbs precede another two (often believed written by Pushkin himself), but the juxtaposition of the folk forms and the literary sections they introduce only distances the book further from a folk milieu. Perhaps only when the Cossacks themselves break into song are we close to an actual evocation of the Cossack ideal. Grinev reacts to the singing with appropriately contradictory attraction and repulsion:

> It would be impossible to relate the effect on me of this simple folk song about the gallows, sung by people themselves destined to the gallows. Their fierce faces, harmonious voices, and the mournful expression given to the words, expressive enough on their own, all this shook me with some kind of poetic horror. (VIII:331)

Only two pages after we are told that Pugachev "shook" *(potriasal)* the foundations of the state, the Cossack song and its singers all shake *(potriasalo)* the poetic sensibility of the noble Russian. As Mazepa's song in *Poltava* leaves its mark on the reader as well as Mariia, transforming into myth the real treachery of Cossack war, the song inserted here raises the specter of the Cossack ideal.

Nonetheless, *The Captain's Daughter* more closely echoes Scott's historical romances, in which fictional main characters interact on a broad tableau with historical personages.[61] The central focus of the novel never shifts from Grinev. Thus, Pushkin tells his story *via* a young Russian nobleman who travels into the country soon to be ruled by Pugachev; a non-Cossack intrudes into Cossack life. The story is about the lad and how he reacts to the Cossacks, and not about the Cossacks themselves. And the centrality of the love story between Grinev and the captain's daughter clearly distances the short novel from native Russian sources. Except for the initial meeting of Grinev and Pugachev in peasant attire, the Cossacks do not appear until chapter 6, almost halfway through the novel. By then, Grinev has already fallen in love with Mariia Ivanovna, and has twice attempted a duel in defense of her honor. The friendship between Grinev and Pugachev proves there is a close relationship—and the proxy dream suggests that Pugachev serves as a symbolic father for the young man[62]—but Grinev apparently has not assimilated vital traits from his unlikely friend. Cossacks of tradition make war, not love.

Thus, despite the kernel of myth within it in the form of the self/other or attraction/repulsion paradox, Pushkin's work differs from the more mythic stories of Gogol and those influenced by him. The choice of a single, historical Cossack, supported by strong historical verisimilitude, gives the tale less than epic proportions. As is the case with most great writers, Pushkin had a diverse agenda: attempts at a Walter Scottian narrative; refining of the Russian prose idiom; comments about imperialism in the figure of Catherine the

Great, who emerges as a second benefactor (and alternate parent figure) at the end of the story, and only finally, the reworking of a Cossack ethos.

Pushkin chose a national historical theme, filtered through its folk variations, but his interest lay elsewhere. If anything, the ambiguity surrounding the character of Pugachev produces irony, not mythic mediation. Humor, created by the juxtaposition of Grinev's tender romance and the bloody Cossack rebellion, seems more to the point. Ultimately, Pushkin had aesthetic concerns: to outdo the romantics in his own romantic parody. The Scottian convention of an "editor" who merely publishes another's manuscript, which Pushkin introduces at the end of *The Captain's Daughter*, in this case brings us back to *The Tales of Belkin* and *Poltava*, with their respective comic and tragic play on the reader's assumptions of psychological verisimilitude and consequent involvement in the romantic story. The "romance" he creates, of course, is as much between Grinev and Pugachev as it is between Grinev and Mariia.

Once established as a famous writer himself, Nikolai Gogol acknowledged a debt to Pushkin for the anecdotes that ostensibly motivate several of the former's great works, including *The Inspector General* and *Dead Souls*. Gogol's use of the Cossack hero, however, and his elevation of that hero to national myth, may have been influenced by those same factors that acted upon the man he proclaimed his literary father, but show little direct lineage. Pushkin's Cossack works suggest some of the topoi upon which Gogol expands, but they spend as much time ironically undermining as developing their mythic potential. Irony, as we will see, is not Gogol's principal mode when creating his Cossack heroes, and the stories about them therefore stand out sharply from his other works. The following chapter will suggest reasons for Gogol's glorification of the Cossack, and further clarify the Cossack topoi. The complete myth of the Cossack cannot be found in any single text, but Gogol's *Taras Bul'ba,* as we will see, perhaps comes closest.

THREE

Gogol's Cossacks and the "Russian Soul"

EXTERNAL CHARACTERISTICS of the Cossack hero derive from elements associated with specific historical hosts: the shaved head and forelock, Turkish trousers, and the *dzhigitovka* (trick horsemanship of the Kuban and Terek Cossacks). Regionalisms and technical Cossack military terms immediately identify the characters, so that reference to a *chub* or *oseledets* (forelock), a *kuren'* (Zaporozhian military unit) or an *ustrug* (boat used on the Volga in Razin's time) signals to the reader that the surrounding material must be understood as part of the Cossack world. Just as a ten-gallon hat in a story tells us to draw on our shared knowledge about cowboy stories, a character with a *chub* invites a Russian audience to compare the present text with earlier Cossack texts, and to use the code those texts have developed.

It is more significant elements, however, that raise the character to the level of myth. In this chapter we can begin an analysis of topoi that transform the Cossacks into a part of a Russian cultural definition. The first aspect of the Cossacks that must be examined is a progressive russification that began through association with another important national myth, so-called holy Rus', and gradually allowed the Cossacks to assume the role of embodiment of the "holy Russian soul."

Folk tradition first associated the Cossacks with holy Rus'. One of the variations of the seventeenth-century "Tale of the Taking of Azov," the so-called "Poetical Tale about the Azov Seige, 1642," reflects a popular image of the Cossacks by calling them "holy-Russian heroes."[1] The Cossacks are the defenders of Holy Russia, the purity of which is attacked by the "heathen" Turks, or in other works by the "infidel" Tatars, or the "heretical" Poles supported by the "unholy" Jews. We find the same vocabulary in Ukrainian Cossack tales; "Lament of the Captives of the Turks about Ransom" sings of heroes who long to be delivered back to their "holy Russian bank."[2]

The Cossack as defender of holy Russia became a staple in Cossack literature through the works of Nikolai Gogol, as this chapter will examine. Later writers constantly repeat this topos, so that Daniel Mordovtsev's *Sagaidachnyi* describes this Cossack hero's desire to move the entire Zaporozhian camp to the Crimea, to the place in which Saint Vladimir—the father of Christian Rus'—was supposedly baptised.[3] Sagaidachnyi's wish demonstrates the close association felt between Cossackdom and the origins of the Russian people. It is no doubt one of the aspects of the novel that caused the editor of Mordovtsev's collected works to call the author a "Russian Walter Scott," who harmoniously unites English traits (his facility using the Scottian genre) with the "noble Russian soul that knows how to love and to suffer, that knows how to be great. . . ."[4] Mordovtsev himself had Ukrainian Cossack ancestors, but this claim to *russkaia dusha,* or Russian soul, draws more from his Cossack characters than the nationality of his parents or his "native" poetic talent.

The association of the Cossack and the Russian soul became so strong after Gogol that otherwise sophisticated critics often read into Cossack characters traits that the texts themselves might not supply. Pushkin, it is often asserted, embodied in his Pugachev character only truly Russian qualities. The Cossack-rebel may have been a murderer, a treasonous pretender to the throne, and even, as Pushkin himself shows in his history of Pugachev's revolt, a coward and a blasphemer, but his image in the novel *The Captain's Daughter,* we are told, subordinates those traits to the overwhelming dominance of his "Russian soul." As one Soviet Pushkin critic claims:

> Pugachev is abundantly endowed in *The Captain's Daughter* with all these qualities. It is he who appears as the embodiment of an inexhaustible creative energy and the high moral and intellectual qualities of the Russian people: a clear mind, love of freedom, generosity, fairness, fearlessness, resourcefulness, boldness, and breadth of nature.[5]

Western critics also often see the Russian soul in Pushkin's Cossack hero:

> There is an element of admiration, however grudging, for Pugachev himself in Pushkin's [*The History of Pugachev*]. Pushkin waits, of course, until his novel *The Captain's Daughter* to suggest that Pugachev may also have been a warm, perceptive, and understanding, though certainly unpredictable, human being on a personal level, perhaps in some sense an amalgam of many traits, both laudable and reprehensible, of the Russian national character.[6]

Whether or not Pushkin actually intended his readers to view the Cossack as an embodiment of the Russian soul, the previous quotations indicate that readers are prepared to do so. And that that soul is holy, somehow representative of the ideal image of God still present, if hidden, in Russian man is supported by a long tradition in the national literature.

A holy Cossack would seem to be an oxymoron, if not altogether heresy; murder and pillage are far indeed from Christlike humility. Nonetheless, this is the first indication of the Cossacks' dual nature. Larger, stronger, less vulnerable than normal men, they transcend the boundaries imposed on mortals, be they spatial, temporal, moral, or metaphysical. Viewed from another angle, they absorb otherwise profane or taboo traits and, as liminal and ambivalent types, develop out of them a hagiography of their own.

Gogol and the Cossacks

Cossacks appear frequently in the early work of Nikolai Gogol (1809–52), culminating in the rewritten version of *Taras Bul'ba* (1842), analyzed in depth in the second part of this chapter. The stories of his first collection of fiction, *Evenings on a Farm near Dikan'ka,* feature Cossacks, as well as two important articles published in *Arabesques* ("A Glance at the Composition of Little Russia" and "About Little Russian Songs"). Four fragments now gathered under the title "The Hetman" portray Cossack heroes, as do two stories in the collection *Mirgorod* ("Vii" and the original 1835 version of *Taras Bul'ba*). Cossacks also find mention in scattered though significant passages of Gogol's correspondence.

Cossacks do not simply demonstrate Gogol's juvenile attraction to exotic, carefree characters, as has been suggested by a critic no less eloquent than Vladimir Nabokov.[7] Rather, it would seem that Gogol's fascination with the Cossacks was as important for his definition of the essence of the Russian man as were his masterpieces *The Inspector General* and *Dead Souls,* whose characters live in the heartland of Russia, in an era roughly contemporaneous with Gogol's own.

Though his personality has eluded biographers for more than a century, romanticized accounts of Gogol's precocious passion for the land of his birth, based on evidence from letters and contemporary reminiscences, surface repeatedly in Gogol scholarship. The assertions pale, of course, in the face of an equal number of reports regarding the writer's propensity to lie about both his emotional life and his literary or academic accomplishments. Nonetheless, Gogol undeniably crossed paths with Cossack material at a number of significant junctures.[8]

Not only was Gogol himself descended from, or led to believe he descended from, a long line of Cossacks,[9] but we learn from correspondence that the peasants who surrounded him in childhood still retained some ancient Cossack traditions. The Zaporozhian Sech had been destroyed in the not too distant past and the domesticated Cossacks still felt ties to it.

As a boy, Gogol exhibited a strong interest in history in general and in local Ukrainian history in particular, fed by the library of his distant relative D. P. Troshchinskii, and promoted by his teachers at school in Nezhin. After moving to Petersburg in 1828, he continued to find encouragement for his fascination with "Little Russian" customs and history through his acquaintance with historians and folklorists such as M. P. Pogodin and M. A. Maksimovich. His first meeting with Pushkin occurred at a time when the latter was at work on his own historical research, including an investigation into Ukraine. As we saw in the last chapter, *Poltava* and *The History of Pugachev* both benefited from that research.

Gogol began to gather ethnographic material in his school exercise book as early as 1826, and continued to request information from his family on Ukrainian traditions throughout the 1830s, much as he would ask for data on Russia and Russians when he wrote to friends from abroad in the later 1830s and 1840s. The requests suggest the value Gogol placed on ethnographic detail in his writing. He believed he could not write without the facts (or *statistika*) his research provided him. Yet we must remember that Gogol insisted on receiving his facts secondhand, from a distance, and thus filtered through others' interpretation, a type of "hearsay" reality.[10]

Unlike Pushkin, Gogol did not travel to the locus of activity or interview participants and eyewitnesses. Pushkin approached historical data with skepticism, and we can distinguish a definite generic shift when he moved from history to fiction in *The Captain's Daughter*. Gogol from the start, however, proved more interested in the myth than in the evidence, in THE COSSACK than in the Cossacks.

Gogol criticized historians for their dry treatment of the past and looked instead toward folk songs and *dumy* for authoritative historical accounts. He called songs "a living, talking, resounding chronicle of the past."[11] Contrasting traditional histories with folk song collections, he wrote to Maksimovich: "What are all those stale chronicles I'm digging around in when faced with these resounding, living chronicles?" (Nov. 9, 1833, X:284).[12]

In his article "About Little Russian Songs," Gogol repeats that songs resurrect the past: "They are a tombstone of the past, or even more than a tombstone; a stone done in elegant relief with a historic inscription is nothing compared to this living, talking, resounding chronicle of the past" (VIII: 90–91). A historian will search through them in vain for dates and accurate reports, says Gogol,

> but when he might want to discover the true way of life, elements of character, all bends and shades of emotions, anxieties, sufferings, and rejoicings of the

people depicted, when he might want to draw out the spirit of an age gone by, the general character of the whole nation and of each individual, then he will be completely satisfied. The history of the people will reveal itself before him in crystal clear grandeur. (VIII:91)[13]

The only history for which Gogol reserved consistent praise was "Koniskii's" *The History of the Russes.* Gogol's respect for it stemmed, no doubt, from the highly romanticized quality of its interpretation of the past. According to N. S. Tikhonravov, who did important early research on Gogol's sources, *The History* served for Gogol not only as a store of facts but as an inspiration, for he found in it "love of his homeland, which often lures him beyond the limits of strict accuracy."[14]

As for more literary sources of the Cossack character, Gogol was surely aware of the work recently produced in Ukrainian. His own father had written Ukrainian comedies, and Gogol apparently wrote and performed some of his own while still at school in Nezhin. Moreover, fragments of the most important Ukrainian work of the day, Ivan Kotliarevskii's mock epic *The Aeneid,* appear as epigraphs heading chapters in Gogol's "Fair at Sorochintsyi" from *Evenings on a Farm near Dikan'ka.*

Gogol, however, left no reading list for scholars to confirm his acquaintance with contemporary Russian or European literature, and there are critics who question whether there was any breadth to his literary knowledge at all.[15] Yet to live in Petersburg in the 1820s and 1830s and not to have read, or at least be aware of, the important actors in the new and growing drama of the Russian literary scene is improbable. We do know of Gogol's interest in Pushkin, and that he read *The Captain's Daughter* between the writing of his two versions of *Taras Bul'ba.* We can also easily detect parallels with Narezhnyi's work; *The Seminarian* probably provided material for Gogol's "Vii," and "Two Ivans or a Passion for Litigation" no doubt suggested to Gogol "The Tale of How Ivan Ivanovich Quarreled with Ivan Nikiforovich."[16]

The Russification of Gogol's Cossacks

In all of his work, Gogol deemphasizes the distinction between Russians and Ukrainians in a broad sense, and Russians and Cossacks more specifically, just as he refuses to draw a decisive distinction between his own Ukrainian heritage and Russian allegiance. As he wrote to his friend A. O. Smirnova: "Not even I know what kind of a soul I have, Uke or Russian [*khokhlatskaia ili russkaia*]" (Dec. 24, 1844, XII:418–19). He continues in this letter to deny any real difference between the two nations, for, though historically distinct, they have now fused together *(slivshis' voedino)*, reinforcing one another. Furthermore, Gogol claims that his early writings (that is, his Cossack stories) provide no conclusions as to his ethnic heritage. They are neither Russian nor Ukrainian, but both. Thus in this later nonfictional statement Gogol continues to assert what his fiction suggested ten years earlier; he recognizes no contradiction between "them" and "us," either in himself or in the Cossacks.

On the surface, Gogol develops those aspects of the Cossacks that would suggest their exoticism. Temporally, they live in a past era that has disappeared because of assimilation with the Poles and Europeanized Russians; spatially, they inhabit faraway rural Ukraine where the spoken language differs enough from the reader's to warrant a glossary (as in *Evenings*). Despite Belinskii's assertion (referring to *Taras Bul'ba*) that the story "is true to life down to the last degree, [and Gogol] presents an actual portrait of life in which everything is captured with amazing verisimilitude,"[17] its Cossacks differ significantly, as we will see, from those of both history and Gogol's own day.

In *Taras Bul'ba*, Gogol forces his Cossacks into roles larger than life. When preparing for battle, for instance, "the Cossack commander grew a whole yard," to become a "limitless leader" (II:80). As in all his fiction, Gogol obliterates the boundary between metaphor and fantasy. The souls of dead Cossacks ride up to heaven in the arms of angels, suggesting an extraordinary interaction of the heroes and divine agents, and a corpse in "A Terrible Vengeance" grows to mammoth proportions, struggling to burst from his confinement underground. The frequent comparisons of the Cossacks to birds further conjure up superhuman, epic associations: Ostap flies into battle "like a hawk soaring in the sky" (II:119), and all the warriors glance around the field "like eagles, seated upon the summits of tall, steep mountains" (II:131); "Having roused themselves [by shaking their wings] like young falcons, the young Cossacks repeated:—For the Sech!" (II:131).

Readers who concentrate only on the fantastic elements correctly perceive the stories' divergence from historical or contemporary reality. For them, the Cossacks act out a romantic fairy tale in an unattainable "other" world, a *trideviatoe tsarstvo* or never-never land, as the sociological critic V. F. Pereverzev claimed.[18]

Those readers, however, fail to recognize the familiar aspect of Gogol's Cossacks. On the most obvious level, the author repeatedly calls the Cossacks "Russian," thus identifying them with the audience for which he wrote. They have a "Russian soul," "Russian tenderness," "Russian bravery." And unlike Pushkin in *The Captain's Daughter*, Gogol does not begin by describing a Russian hero who leaves his homeland, journeys into the exotic Cossack territory, and then returns home to Russia, enriched by his exposure to the untamed warriors. He does not present the Cossacks in contrast to Russians, but as though they themselves *are* the Russians.

Gogol begins his distorted equation of the Zaporozhians with Russians by considering them not just as inhabitants of a part of Ukraine, but as representative of the entire Ukrainian nation. In his article "A Glance at the Composition of Little Russia," he calls the Cossacks a "diverse assemblage of the most desperate people of the bordering nations" (VIII:47), but then goes on to find proof in their language and faith for the claim that most were original inhabitants of Little Russia. He writes only of the Zaporozhians for the rest of the article (VIII:47–49), thus equating these Cossacks with all of the Ukrainian past. In "About Little Russian Songs," he again considers "Cossack" and "Ukrainian" synonymous terms. He claims that "the extensive freedom of Cossack life penetrates and breathes everywhere" in Little Russian songs (VIII:91), and examines no music other than the Cossacks'.

The next step in Gogol's identification of the Cossacks with Russians is his repeated use of the term "Little Russia" instead of "Ukraine," a common practice in his day. He eventually drops the qualifier "little" almost entirely, however, and speaks of the Cossacks not as a separate people, and not as Ukrainians, but as Russians.[19] In *Taras Bul'ba* he calls his heroes "an unusual demonstration of Russian strength" (II:46) and boasts that they are capable of "galavanting recklessly, drinking, and carousing as only a Russian knows how" (II:47).

Here Gogol capitalizes on the mythic richness of the adjective *russkii*, derived from *Rus'* and not *Rossiia*.[20] He claims that the Cossacks live in the Russian land *(russkaia zemlia)* and contain the "kernel of Russian feeling" *(krupitsa russkogo chuvstva,* II:134). His reference to "the Russian land," a term familiar from Old Russian epic and folk texts, associates his heroes with historical Rus' and implies a connection between the Cossacks and the supposed origins of Russian civilization.

Having established a metonymic relationship between the Cossacks and the Russians through the mediation of Rus', Gogol repeatedly emphasizes the ability of the former, and by extension the latter, to reconcile contradictions. He locates the Cossack Sech in *Taras Bul'ba* at a point midway between the Poles in the West and the Turks or Tatars in the East. The Cossack adventures involve movement, on land or water, between the two opposing geographic areas and cultural entities. In *Evenings,* the Cossacks' travel also unites two opposite areas, here the north (both Vakula in "Christmas Eve" and the grandfather in "The Lost Letter" travel to St. Petersburg) and the exotic south, in which devils and witches walk the streets beside the peasants. Furthermore, Gogol explicitly states in "A Glance at the Composition of Little Russia" that the Cossacks are a people belonging to Europe in terms of their faith and location, but at the same time totally Asiatic because of way of life, customs, and dress. They are a people in which two opposite parts of the world, two differing essences have so strangely come together: European carefulness and Asiatic abandon; simpleheartedness and cunning; a strong sense of activity and the grandest laziness and satisfaction; a drive toward development and perfection, and at the same time a desire to appear scornful of any perfection. (VIII:49)

Russians, too, traditionally see themselves as situated midway between West and East, neither one nor the other, but the reconciler of the two. According to its popular self-definition, Russia absorbed the shock of the Eastern Mongols, saving Europe from invasion. And from the nineteenth-century Western point of view, Russia itself was almost Asia. As Gogol writes in *Taras Bul'ba*, foreigners saw Poland as "that half-Asiatic corner of Europe," and considered Muscovy and the Ukraine to be located in Asia proper (II:160). Yet Russia also assimilated much of European culture, particularly after Peter and Great opened his famed "window to the West." Russians, Gogol included, could travel freely to Germany, France, and Italy and feel as at home there as in their more "Eastern" land. Russians, thus, felt able to combine, indeed reconcile, the two cultures. In Gogol's day, this synthetic quality of the Russian soul had particular currency among both the Westernizers and the Slavophiles. Although espousing different solutions to Russia's problems, the two groups fundamentally agreed on the unique superiority of their people and the historical mission thus entrusted to them. Russians allegedly retained the pure and elemental spirit associated with the East, and were therefore in a position to reinfuse a decaying West with life.

Gogol's metonym, then, has many tiers: Cossacks are Ukrainians are Russians are East *and* are West.[21] Just as the Cossacks are able to reconcile the paradox of self and other, they can combine the differing qualities of Asia and Europe, wilderness and civilization, unknown and known, and, as becomes increasingly clear, opposites of all kinds. They are old and young, good and bad, noble and drunken. "You would simply have to see this frontiersman in his half-Tatar, half-Polish dress on whom the borderland was so sharply imprinted," writes Gogol, and goes to describe how he could fight frightfully one minute, then throw away his plunder and carouse drunkenly the next (VIII:48).

The seamless combination of opposing traits is a hallmark of the Cossack myth; it raises the hero above the fragmented human level where the reader exists. And since the Cossacks are in some sense representative of Russians in a less corrupted and original form, the "Russians" of holy Rus', a Russian reader can claim that he, too, transcends the mundane.

The Cossacks' "Russkaia Dusha"

Gogol's article "A Glance at the Composition of Little Russia" begins with an analysis of life in Rus' during the thirteenth century, before, according to his estimation, the Cossack nation emerged. In the first few pages, Gogol stresses aspects of the era that diverge from what he will shortly describe as Cossacklike. The people all resembled one another—he uses terms such as "of a single faith," "of one tribe," "with a single language," "marked by a single general character" (*edinovernye, odnoplemennye, odnoiazychnye, oznachennye odnim obshchim kharakterom,* VIII:40). His Cossacks, however, are a diverse assemblage (*pestroe sborishche,* VIII:47). The idea of *pestrota,* or multicolored diversity, remains constant throughout the Cossack myth.

The pre-Cossack, single-faceted people gathered together into small appanage kingdoms that, despite their overwhelming uniformity, were "divided among themselves to an extent you rarely encounter even among peoples of widely differing characteristics" (VIII:40). Brother fought brother and father fought son (VIII:41). The picture that emerges of the thirteenth century is one of fragmentation within a forced union: "Relatives gathered together against their will." The Cossacks, however, are an organic unit able nonetheless to incorporate oppositions: "Despite the diversity [*pestrota*] of the population, internecine wars did not exist here" (VIII:43).

The pre-Cossack inhabitants did not enjoy the support of a religion which can, "more than anything else, bind and develop nations" (VIII:40). The vocabulary Gogol uses to describe the powerlessness of their religion that "did not evolve in close connection to laws or life" evokes failed military endeavors: the monks and priests did not know how "to seize power over the people with the aid of their powerful weapon—faith—and with that faith to ignite a flame and zeal to the point of enthusiasm . . ." (VIII:40).[22] Productive militance, on the other hand, marks the Cossacks, that "martial people, powerful because of their unity," who were "committed to the goal . . . of eternal war with the infidels" (VIII:46, 47).

Most condemning of all, Gogol emphasizes three times that the early people lacked passion: "Strong passions did not reach here" (VIII:40); "No hatred, no strong passion aroused them" (VIII:41); "Not one strong feeling, no fanaticism, no superstition, not even a prejudice inflamed it" (VIII:41). Thus, Gogol continues, "it seemed that almost all of mankind's strong, noble passions had died within them" (VIII:41). Passion is here positively associated with vitality. Not only were the pre-Tatar, pre-Cossack inhabitants of the Russian territory fragmented, but they were pale and stagnant as well; theirs was a "monotonous life, moving separate parts, but immobile as a whole" (VIII:41).

The unfavorable tone Gogol uses to describe early Kiev must strike the reader as unusual; the holiness of Rus' is generally untouchable in Russian letters. Yet examined in light of the growing Cossack myth, its purpose becomes clear. The Cossacks, who Gogol believed emerged during the re-population of southern Russia following the Mongol invasion, exhibited all the traits lacking in the earlier inhabitants, as well as in Russia's more northern citizens. First of all, the "new" Russians preserved the purity of their Slavic blood, "in its former wholeness, with all the pagan beliefs, childish prejudices, songs, tales, Slavonic mythology, mixed so simple-mindedly with Christianity" (VIII:43). Paradoxically, the people remained pure as they united with other nations: "A wild mountain dweller, a plundered Russian, a Polish servant escaping from the despotism of his masters, even, perhaps, a Tatar refugee from Islam all formed the core of this strange society" (VIII:47). Gogol is not clear as to where these Russians/Cossacks acquired their pure Slavic blood and culture, but he implies by this paradox that the blood they had was so thick that the absorption of foreign elements did not dilute it. Quite the opposite, in fact, is the case; non-Slavic elements were transformed, and thus further strengthened the Cossack whole.

Theirs was a true society of equality, claims Gogol. The Cossacks formed a tight brotherhood *(tesnoe bratstvo),* unlike the forced, volatile union of the early Kievans, but equally unlike the central papal control of the ascetic Catholic knights of the West. The Cossacks "were untamable like their Dnepr rapids and oblivious of the whole world during their frenzied feasts and revelry" (VIII:48). The unmediated force of nature itself was their model.

In "About Little Russian Songs," Gogol suggests an actual identity between the Cossacks and nature that surrounds them. The equation of geography and inner essence helps explain the soul of the people who live in the Russian land. He writes: "they run to [nature] for no other reason than to express the emotions found in their souls. . . . The same phenomenon presents itself simultaneously in the external and internal world" (VIII:94).

Gogol's belief in the intimate connection between nature and a man's, as well as a people's, soul leads him to see great significance in the association of geography and national identity. This identification becomes fully developed in *Taras Bul'ba,* where the freedom and expanse of the steppe are inwardly projected onto an essential element of the Cossack himself. In his nonfiction, Gogol states the association between geography and history (i.e., the formation of a people). He instructs teachers in "Thoughts on Geography":

When enumerating nations, the teacher is necessarily obliged to demonstrate the physiognomy of each, as well as those traits which its character acquired, so to say, through geographic influence. He must group all nations of the world into large families and present the general traits of each group before they branched out. He must then present their physical history, i.e., the history of alterations in their character, in order to clarify why, for instance, the Teutonic tribe, of all the peoples of Germany, are marked by the resoluteness of a phlegmatic character and why, on the contrary, the Germanic people take on all the playfulness of a light character once they cross the Alps. (VIII:105)

Thus Gogol develops his theory that the outer world explains and defines the inner, as though no barrier exists between the two. Internal and external are reconciled; the expansive Russian land and the all-encompassing Cossack/Russian soul are one.

By identifying the Cossack spirit with Russian geography, Gogol is able to draw on a well-established system that valorizes the land as free and most assuredly transhuman. In an effort to create heroes who could themselves transcend the limitations of contemporary life, Gogol finds confirmation within another cultural myth. And like Peter Pan who never grows up, or space creatures who travel through time, the Cossacks are able to transcend the bonds that tie mortal man to this ordinary world.

Taras Bul'ba and the Wholeness of the Cossack Soul

In *Taras Bul'ba,* the Cossacks take on a decidedly religious aura, although admittedly a religiosity mediated by Gogol's romanticized and unique interpretation of the Russian Orthodox image of God. Strangely, the influence of his story was so strong that Gogol's definition of the holiness of the Cossacks survived well into the Soviet era, and not always stripped of specific religious terminology. Gogol's Cossacks defend the "Holy Russian Church," and in *Taras Bul'ba* pause to pray before riding off on a "holy" mission to destroy the Poles. But his Cossacks also manifest a unity regardless of diversity and a propensity to sing and dance that represent for Gogol divine vitality. Gogol's later nonfictional statements on Orthodoxy indeed stress humility and obedience, but his earlier fiction glorifies passion instead. Gogol's Cossacks, despite their violence,[23] are ideal because they are whole, spontaneous, and alive.

Gogol suggests the organic unity of his Cossacks by showing the loss that results from asserting one's individual ego as separate from the group and by personifying the Cossack environment as the collective female counterpart of the Cossack male host.

Taras Bul'ba begins with a scene in which the two sons of Bul'ba, Ostap and Andrii, have just returned home from their study at the Kievan Academy, sometime in the sixteenth or seventeenth century. Taras makes fun of their academic pursuits—although he sent them and had himself gone to the Academy as a youth—and insists on taking them to the Zaparozhian Sech where they can learn something useful. When the three Cossacks arrive in the Cossack camp, Taras discovers that many of his former cohorts are long since dead or in slavery in Turkey, and that the rest sit idly, unoccupied by the "holy" Cossack deeds of war, pillage, and plunder. Taras stirs dissent among the warriors, who finally decide to travel to the western Ukraine to fight the infidel Poles, a decision supported by scouts who coincidentally return at that moment to tell of atrocities committed there against the Mother Russian Church. At last, the Bul'ba sons will have a chance to grow into full-fledged Cossacks.

The situation is complicated, however, by ever more perceptible differences between Ostap and Andrii. When the narrator first introduces Andrii, he does not distinguish him from his older brother. As he begins to describe their school days, however, the narrator tells us that Ostap "was always considered one of the best comrades" (II:55). He rarely leads, but always joins in the antics of the group. He would never, even under the worst threat of punishment, betray one of his comrades, and he is always straightforward with his equals. In short, Ostap is an ideal member of his school community.

Andrii, however, stands out from the rest of the schoolboys. He is brighter and more enterprising, and often instigates the activities that the others follow. Tragically, Andrii discovers an obsession during his school years that the rest of the group does not share. He longs for women, a dishonorable feeling for a Cossack until he has seen battle, and this urge isolates Andrii from the other Cossacks. He has to hide it from his comrades and begins to spend more and more time alone, wandering the streets of Kiev. On a solitary walk he meets a Polish girl, out of love for whom he will eventually betray his fellow Cossacks.

When the two boys arrive at the Sech, the narrator again does not differentiate between them: "Ostap and Andrii threw themselves into that revelrous sea with all the ardor of youth" (II:67). Within the same paragraph, however, the narrator singles out Andrii, commenting on his strong reaction to the typical Cossack punishment for murder. We are told that Andrii has intense emotions (II:56), in contrast to all the rest of the Cossacks, including his brother, who are repeatedly referred to as cool and composed (*khladnokrovnye*—the typical Cossack epithet). A Cossack must be outwardly calm, despite the vital energy bursting within his soul.

Once again, the narrator speaks of the two sons together when describing their characters in battle. He calls them "our young Cossacks" and tells us that "Taras was pleased to see that both his sons were among the first" (II:84). The narrator then indicates the difference in their characters. Ostap acts "with composure" (*s khladnokroviem*—again the typical epithet for all the Cossacks) and "could measure the entire danger and situation in an instant" (II:84). Andrii, however, acts like a drunk. He is not composed, but mad, and rushes into situations where "no calm [*khladnokrovnyi*] and rational man would dare." While Ostap could measure the entire situation (*mog vymeriat'*), Andrii "did not know what it means to consider or calculate or measure out beforehand his or the enemy's strengths" (On ne znal, chto takoe znachit . . . izmeriat' . . ., II:85).

Before the battle of Dubno the Cossacks surround the city, hoping to starve out the Poles. On the evening of Andrii's defection, all the Cossacks sleep under the stars, including Ostap, who had "long since gone off to be with the Cossack units" (davno otoshel k kureniam, II:87). Andrii, however, "did not go off to the units" (ne otkhodil k kureniam), the exact opposite of Ostap's community-oriented action. While all the other Cossacks sleep, Andrii lies awake staring at the sky. "It was all open before him," says the narrator of the expansive view above. "The air was clean and clear. The thick starry mass of the Milky Way crossed the sky like a belt, and all was flooded with light" (II:88–89). The description of the universe infused with light strongly contrasts with Andrii's loneliness and separation from the group. It is at this moment, when Andrii is most isolated from the cosmic whole, that a Tatar servant woman appears, like a phantom, to lead him to the Polish girl.

When Andrii yields to the temptation of his love for the girl, he cuts all ties with the group and abandons his integral place within the ancestral line: "And what is a father to me, or a comrade or a fatherland?—said Andrii, tossing his head sharply and straightening his stance, as erect as a black poplar.—If that's how things are, then this is what I have to say: I have absolutely nothing. Nothing, nothing" (II:106).

Andrii spends the remaining few days of his life among foreigners, for once he has forsaken the unity of his community, his Cossack nature and all that is essential within him dies: "And a Cossack perished! He was lost for all of Cossack knighthood!" (II:107). This symbolic death is soon followed by his actual death at the hands of his own grieving but steadfast father. Ostap, on the other hand, distinguishes himself in battle, and is elected ataman, although he is eventually captured and executed by the Poles. To the last moment he remains a hero, never crying out from pain or fear. He dies with a call for his father on his lips, forever cementing his union with the Cossack brotherhood.

The revised and expanded version of *Taras Bul'ba,* published in Gogol's collected works in 1842, takes a more sophisticated view of wholeness than had the original version from *Mirgorod.* Gogol does not merely associate his Cossacks with monolithic oneness, but suggests vitality by describing their union as formed of multiple, symbiotic parts.[24]

In the 1835 edition, Gogol speaks of the Cossacks as a unit, a horse column *(konnaia kolonna)*, that is not formed by the aggregate of separate bodies but is rather a single, integrated, organic force. Their power and skill come from their union, "as though arising from the fact that their hearts and passions pulsed in unison to the single tempo of a universal thought" (II:329).

Gogol altered this passage when he rearranged and lengthened the battle scenes and added more historically accurate description. One striking addition is his introduction of names and short biographies of many of the Cossacks, ascribing to them differentiated characters. Yet the individual warriors—Kukubenko, Mosii Shilo, Balaban, Borodatyi, and the rest—unite organically, as though in a single body. Gogol implies the symbiotic nature of their union in the choreographed movement of the troops: "The Zaporozhians all fired, without pausing for breath: the ones in back simply loaded and passed the weapons to the front, causing consternation among the enemy, who could not understand how the Cossacks shot without reloading their guns" (II:135). Again as though choreographed, one Cossack springs up immediately behind another who has fallen, or senses an enemy approaching a comrade and calls out to warn him. The Cossacks respond chorally to Taras's rallying cries so that variations on the following verses punctuate the battle descriptions:

> "What's the story, men?" said Taras, calling out to the units. "Is there still powder in your powder flasks? The Cossack strength has not weakened? The Cossacks do not waver?"
> "Yes father, there is still powder in our powder flasks. The Cossack strength has not yet weakened. The Cossacks do not yet waver!" (II:138)

Gogol also added a crucial complexity in the 1842 version when he set up a comparison of the Cossack troops with the Poles. The Poles also form a single unit—a force or *voisko*—but they are regimented and mechanical, not organic. They are organized by a foreign engineer *(inozemnyi inzhener*—the adjective means "of a foreign land" and the noun is borrowed from the French, a double condemnation) who tears his hair at the "artlessness" *(neiskusstvo)* of the Cossack warriors.

Gogol describes in detail how the Poles arrange themselves in rigid rows: first the embroidered hussars in even mounted formation; then the soldiers in chain mail; then the cuirassiers with spears; then warriors in copper helmets; and finally the best gentlemen, each dressed in his own fashion (II:117). The Polish unity, however, is artificial and easily deteriorates. After a single battle, "many were not counted among their ranks. But among a hundred Cossacks perhaps only two or three were killed" (II:135).

The careful attention to articles of clothing and weapons in this passage parallels a similar description of the Poles still safe inside their town. The narrator heaps detail upon detail to describe what he calls a "living picture":

> The copper helmets shone like the sun, feathered with plumes white as swans. Others wore light caps of pink or sky blue with peaks inclined to the side. Their caftans had rolled-up sleeves, sewn with gold or simply laced with cords. Some had sabres and rifles in expensive settings for which the gentlemen had paid dearly. How many were the types of adornment! In front the Budzhakov colonel stood arrogantly in a red cap decorated with gold. The colonel was heavyset, taller and fuller than the others, and his broad expensive caftan barely reached around his belly. The other colonel stood opposite, almost at the side gates. He was a small, shriveled man, but his tiny, keen eyes looked out sharply from under thickly grown brows and he turned about quickly to all sides, pointing briskly with his thin dry arm, passing out orders. . . . (II:115)

In comparison, the narrator tells us about the Cossacks only that "There was no gold on anyone, save perhaps here or there where it glittered on the sabre hilts and rifle casings. Cossacks did not like to deck themselves out richly in battle" (II:115).

Contrast is obvious in the length and detail of the two descriptions, as well as in the content. Gogol, in fact, rarely bothers to describe the outer appearance of the Cossacks at all, with the exception of a few fixed epithets, such as references to Taras's moustache, the Cossack forelock, and, as mentioned before, the composed *(khladnokrovnyi)* expression of the warriors. Gogol's restraint in describing the Cossacks not only serves to impress us with their disregard for material possessions in contrast to the Poles' wealth. It also impedes the reader from forming a mental picture of the heroes. While the Poles appear as an ornamented, purely two-dimensional picture, the Cossacks defy specific description.

Gogol creates a similar contrast between the Cossack environment and the Polish environment. Just as the Poles are composed of inorganic fragments, their town, too, is composed of discrete, lifeless parts. The narrator describes the Polish monastery and town through Andrii's eyes as the enamored Cossack makes his way to the Polish girl trapped inside. He enters through a dark, narrow, underground passage past coffins and loose human bones, as though he is descending into the region of death itself. As Andrii emerges into the street, the narrator tells us that the square is completely empty, but then proceeds to describe meticulously the benches, buildings, and walls which occupy or surround it. Obviously, the town is empty not of objects but of life itself. "The square seemed dead" (II:97), the narrator tells us, and was strewn with dead or dying bodies, again described for us in horrid detail. The narrator then devotes a paragraph to a description of the various parts of one home, including the guards who "resembled statues more than living beings" (II:99). There is a pseudo-unity between things and people in the starving Polish town; all are lifeless, inorganic objects.

Gogol scarcely describes the Cossack Sech at all. Instead, the narrator explains the form of life found in it: "It was some kind of an endless revelry, a ball which had begun noisily and lost track of its conclusion. . . . That communal revelry contained something captivating within it. This was not a collection of carousers who had become drunk out of grief, but simply a mad spree of gaiety" (II:64). In this passage, Gogol differentiates between a group which is a mere assemblage of individuals *(sborishche brazhnikov)* and an indivisibly whole unit, signified by the abstract noun "revelry" *(razgul'e)*. He thus implies that the Cossack environment cannot be defined by the walls which surround it (of which there are none, in any case) but only by the wholeness and activity of life within.

Gogol similarly describes and personifies the other natural environment of the Cossacks, the steppe: "Her whole multicolored expanse was embraced by the last bright gleam of the sun . . ." (II:59); "Nowhere did they chance upon any trees. There was nothing but the same limitless, free, beautiful steppe" (II:60).

The structure of the Russian language allows Gogol to refer to both the Sech and the steppe (sometimes called steppes in English) using singular, feminine pronouns and endings. He can thus establish them as the partner of the singular, masculine Cossack group. As we shall see in the next chapter, actual women play no part in the Cossack life; Gogol refers instead to the Cossack homeland as both mother and fiancée. When the Bul'bas ride into the steppe, "she" is called a "green, maidenly expanse" (II:58). Perhaps the best example of Gogol's personification of the steppe as the female counterpart of the Cossacks occurs immediately after the narrator relates Andrii's memories of his enchantment in the arms of the Polish girl. He switches back to the narrative present and tells us: "But meanwhile the steppe had long since taken them all into her green embraces . . ." (II:58). The contrast between the single Polish girl who entraps the alienated Andrii, ensuring his total isolation, and the life-nurturing steppe which embraces but does not contain the group emphasizes the aspect of organic wholeness that unites Gogol's Cossacks and their environment.

The Cossack Soul through Music and Dance

Gogol's Cossacks are not only whole, but vital. In the first chapter, both sons have just returned from the Kiev Academy and are home only long enough to prepare to go to the Sech. The next two chapters of the story develop a contrast between the type of learning the boys received in school and the learning through activity which they will experience during their mature Cossack lives. Taras tells them:

> Everything they cram into your heads—the academy, and all those books, grammars, and philosophy—all that's rubbish. It doesn't mean beans, and I couldn't care a damn about it all! . . . Here's a better plan. This very week I'll send you to the Zaporozhian Sech. That's where learning is really learning! [Vot gde nauka tak nauka!] There's your school. That's where you'll get your smarts. (II:43).

The contrast between scholastic, logical learning (on the Western Latin model used in Kiev) and actual life experience is a common device in romantic literature. "Book learning" is static, fragmented, and dead. As the narrator in *Taras Bul'ba* explains about the academy education of the Cossacks:

> Teaching in those days was sharply divorced from reality: all those scholastic, grammatical, rhetorical, and logical subtleties had no relationship to the times; they never adapted themselves to nor did they repeat themselves in life. Those who learned them could in no way apply even the least scholastic parts of their knowledge. The very scholars of the day were the most ignorant of all, for they were totally distanced from experience [*opyt*]. (II:53–54)

In the Sech, however, one learns through experience, or the *opyt* of the above passage: "The Sech did not like to waste time troubling itself with military exercises; the young were brought and educated in the Sech through experience [*opyt*] alone, in the thick of the battles that, for that very reason, went on continuously" (II:64).

The juxtaposition of static book learning and active life seems to condemn the former as useless. Gogol, however, does not simply choose the latter form of learning over the former. In this area as well as others, the Cossacks are able to encompass contradictions. At the very beginning of the story, the narrator tells us that every worthy Cossack sends his sons to Kiev to be educated. Taras himself surprises Ostap by mentioning the Latin poet Horace and later demonstrates his belief in the importance of rhetoric: "Taras knew that no matter how strong a good, old wine may be on its own, and how able it may be to fortify man's spirit, if you also add to it the proper word [*prilichnoe slovo*], then the power of both the wine and the spirit will be doubly strong" (II:130). Taras has apparently not forgotten his Western-style education. Clearly, Gogol's Cossacks do not totally reject rational learning. True knowledge *(nauka tak nauka)* can come only by means of the dialectical union of learning and active experience.

Gogol once wrote to his friend M. A. Maksimovich: "I swear, we have all become terribly distanced from our primitive elements. We, and especially you, just can't get accustomed to looking at life with a who-gives-a-darn attitude in the way the Cossack always looked at it. Have you ever tried, having just gotten up from bed in the morning, to dance a *trepak* all over the room in nothing but your shirt?" (X:357).

"Our primitive elements" *(pervozdannye èlementy)*, also translatable as essential or original elements, apply to the Cossacks because of their simple ability to act. They are primitive because they exhibit the true being of the first man, the image of God, and not only because they lived in an earlier historical time.

In *Taras Bul'ba*, Gogol often uses dance and song as metaphors for the Cossacks' activity. A passage from the 1835 edition of the story does not veil his suggestion that their music and dance represent man's essential state:

> Man has freedom in music alone. He is in fetters everywhere. Wherever he comes into contact with life he forges for himself fetters even more oppressive than those which society and authority lay upon him. He is a slave. He is willful only when he loses himself in wild dance, when his soul does not fear his body. (II:300)

Ostap and Andrii are first introduced to the Sech and Cossack life by the sight of a wild dancer who, although perspiration is pouring down his face, asks the musicians to "play livelier" (II:63). Because his drinking is as wild as his dancing, he will not remove his heavy winter jacket since he knows that whatever he removes he will sell for vodka. The narrator tells us that this dance, which is "the freest and wildest that the world has ever seen" (samyi vol'nyi, samyi beshenyi), is called a *kozachok,* a word which derives from the Ukrainian spelling of *kozak,* or Cossack. In this way Gogol unites the freedom and wildness of the Cossacks' dance, music, and drinking with the Cossacks themselves.

Gogol also compares the Cossack battle to music: "Andrii immersed himself in the enchanting music of the bullets and swords" (II:85). And like the Cossack dance, the battle is wild and free. In another passage from the original edition of the story, Gogol has his Cossacks march together into battle to the whistle of bullets, which he compares to wedding music (II:328). In the comparable battle section in the 1842 edition, Gogol takes the music image one step further and realizes the metaphor. The Cossacks not only march to a musical rhythm, but their fighting actions actually become the music. They punctuate their choreographed movements with the musical refrain cited earlier; thus the musicality of the Cossack battle suggests that Taras and his comrades embody activity defined as music and dance.

Like the Cossack dance in the Sech and the battle on the field outside Dubno, the open steppe is also immersed in music. One paragraph that describes the steppe begins with the words "all the music which rang out during the day became quiet and was replaced with another music," and continues with such characteristic phrases as "the steppe was deafened with whistles," "the chirping of the grasshoppers become louder," "a cry was heard," "they heard with their own ears the entire, infinite world," "a crackle, a whistle, a chirring," "it resounded sonorously," "the slumbering ear," and other aural descriptions. The Cossacks not only listen to these sounds, but become intimately united with them, so that "the night stars gazed directly upon them" (II:59–60). Surrounded by the music of nature, the Cossacks commune with the heavens. The music unites their true essence with that of the universe.

Gogol's article on Ukrainian songs in *Arabesques* praises Cossack music for the fact that it was born in moments of freedom, never composed pen in hand. It exudes strength, joy, and might—qualities connected with the active experience of life (VIII:90–97). In his article on the history of Ukraine, Gogol calls the period he describes in *Taras Bul'ba* a "poetic era" *(poeticheskoe vremia),* a time when everyone took up the sword and wanted to be an actor instead of a spectator (VIII:48). This definition of poetry in terms of action is coincident with Gogol's ideas about his own work. His letters and nonfiction writing betray his conviction that he was called by God to a life of service. He evidently first considered this service to be in the government. As he matured, however, it became increasingly clear to him that his mission lay not in the realm of bureaucratic service but in literature. He began to see his poetry as the ultimate union of word and deed; as his active part in the cooperative effort toward the realization of his own true essence. By writing "poetry," he would become an actor in life and a participant in the divine movement of the world.

In contrast to music and dance, the artforms most closely connected with movement, Gogol uses static, visual imagery to characterize the enemy troops, the Poles. He describes their clothes and armor in great detail, but does not show them in motion. Instead, he calls them a tableau vivant (*zhivaia kartina,* II:114); they are no more than sculpture in flesh and bones. Toward the end of the story, when Gogol describes the scene in Warsaw at the execution of Ostap, he again pays close attention to the pictorial aspects of the Polish crowd. He carefully describes their clothing and jewelry, and particularly concentrates on a young girl and her beau who are standing in the "foreground" (*na perednem plane,* II:162), as though within the immobile frame of a picture. By contrasting the Poles' stasis with the Cossacks' movement,

Gogol emphasizes the important traits which he bestows upon his heroes: the ability to act, to experience life, to demonstrate the active soul within them.

The Soul of Russia Inverted

The appeal of *Taras Bul'ba* as an adolescent adventure story is obvious. But few critics have recognized that it fits firmly within Gogol's oeuvre, all of which is concerned with the mission and role of Russia. Unfortunately, Russian and Soviet schoolchildren were force-fed the story as proof of Russian nationalist strength, and Western readers tend to prefer Gogol's less epic and more ironic tales of Petersburg and the famous "laughter through tears" of *Dead Souls* and *The Inspector General*. Knowledge of the Cossack myth is vital to appreciate *Taras Bul'ba* fully and to fit it into the context of Gogol's interest in the Russian soul and into all of Russian literature.

An understanding of the mythic nature of Gogol's Cossack can perhaps best be enriched with an examination of its opposite: the author's brilliant descriptions of the dull triviality (*poshlost'*, or, as he preferred, *zemnost'*)[25] of this world. In turn, an appreciation of the Cossack hero can reveal new meanings in Gogol's non-Cossack masterpieces where the mythic ethos is inverted. Two examples, both from *Mirgorod* where *Taras Bul'ba* was first published, suggest comparison, although most of Gogol's stories could be brought forth, including *Dead Souls*.

"Old-World Landowners" ("Starosvetskie pomeshchiki"), the first story in the *Mirgorod* collection, begins with a detailed description of the estate, with a repeated emphasis on the fences, walls, and trees that enclose the area.[26] Unlike the marauding Cossacks, the landowners do not leave their isolated enclosure. There is a strong parallel between this "old-world" estate and the fortified Polish town in *Taras Bul'ba,* which is also described in terms of the surrounding ramparts and walls.[27] The Poles prefer to stay enclosed and starve in their lifeless fort rather than venture out into the world and face the power of the Cossacks head on. The landowners also choose to die passively (and even their isolated life resembles death) rather than experience the real-life terrors of the surrounding woods and world. The final pages of "Old-World Landowners" abound in terms suggesting absence *(pusto, otsutstvie, tishina, pustynia, nichego ne ostalos', opushchenie),* confirming that the carefully guarded enclosure really contains nothing at all. The vital presence of the divine found in the Cossacks and their land is here totally absent.

Andrei Belyi and G. A. Gukovskii, two perspicacious students of Gogol's work, have both pointed out the inverse relationship between *Taras Bul'ba* and "The Tale of How Ivan Ivanovich Quarreled with Ivan Nikiforovich" ("Povest' o tom kak possorilsia Ivan Ivanovich s Ivanom Nikiforovichem"), the final story in *Mirgorod* and often considered a transition to Gogol's non-Ukrainian works.[28] The two Ivans share some superficial similarities with their Cossack ancestors, but their quarrel unfolds in the law courts, not on the battlefield or even the metaphoric field of life, and their weapons are words, ineptly handled, rather than skillfully wielded sabres and rifles. In fact, their ridiculous battle arises in the first place over possession of a gun that is never even fired. The story explicitly portrays men who do not exhibit the essential vitality, whether metaphorically erotic or militaristic, of the ideal Cossacks.

Before their quarrel, Ivan Ivanovich lies under his awning and wonders, "What is it that I don't have" (II:228), as though his worth is established by his possessions. The heroes of *Taras Bul'ba,* on the other hand, are far from acquisitive. They squander their booty on drink and have no desire to exhibit their wealth (II:115).

The narrator of "The Tale of How Ivan Ivanovich Quarreled with Ivan Nikiforovich" begins the story highly sympathetic to Ivan Ivanovich, but does not move beyond a description of his belongings in praising his good qualities, as though he defines Ivan's character only in terms of the objects with which he manages to fill his world. That his world is never wholly full, however, is demonstrated by the fact that he desires yet one more object, the rifle of his neighbor, Ivan Nikiforovich. The latter, who seems less needy of fine clothing and objects than the first Ivan, is greedy in another way. He constantly feels compelled to stuff his belly (as does Afanasii of "Old-World Landowners") in order to fill the shell surrounding his empty internal world. He eats so much that the Cossack jacket he wears is bursting at the seams. Gogol reduces this inwardly empty ex-Cossack to the level of an inanimate object by apparently listing him along with his other possessions that the maid is hanging out to air: "'What a stupid woman!' thought Ivan Ivanovich, 'next she'll drag out Ivan Nikiforovich himself to air!' And so it was . . ." (II:229). Gogol's suggestion that the two Ivans are no different from their inanimate possessions contrasts with his assertation that the Cossacks exhibit some sort of true being.

Although the lack of humor and the jingoism of *Taras Bul'ba* often turn readers away, its centrality within Gogol's oeuvre can scarcely be ignored. Its Cossacks represent man at his most vital. They exhibit "essential elements," as Gogol claimed in his letter to Maksimovich, for they violate all barriers that tie men to this trivial world. Taras Bul'ba explicitly rejects the sweets (*pampushka, medovik, makovnik, pundik*—all listed in diminutive forms of endearment, II:43) that the landowner Afanasii Ivanovich, the overfed Ivan Nikiforovich, and many of Gogol's other *poshlye* or *zemnye* characters repeatedly stuff into their mouths in order to fill the voids that constitute their bodies and their lives. Taras and his fellow Cossacks have no need for these external means of fulfillment. Infused with Gogol's passionate ideal, they represent the whole, active Russian soul.

Implied but not stated to this point is the fact that, for Gogol at least, the soul is decidedly male. Simon Karlinsky perhaps overemphasizes but nonetheless provocatively points out the importance in Gogol's work of what has become popular to call male bonding. According to Karlinsky, the intrusion of female heterosexuality into the story of the two Ivans (in the figure of Agafiia Fedoseevna) destabilizes the relationship between Ivan Ivanovich and Ivan Nikiforovich and motivates the breakdown in their friendship and their world, culminating in the notes of pathos at the end: "It is boring in this world, gentlemen" (II:275).[29]

Taras Bul'ba is Gogol's transformation of male bonding in *Mirgorod* and all of his work. Andrii dies from his association with a woman, but the Cossacks themselves persevere; their world is not destroyed, but endures forever in myth. And although their fraternity is built on the principles of war and brutality, as Karlinsky points out in his analysis of this story, Gogol glorifies and does not condemn his heroes for their violence. The reasons for this are not unique to Gogol, and are in fact central to the Cossack myth as a whole, as the next chapter will demonstrate in its analysis of the topos of woman and violent creation.

FOUR

Death Transcended and
the Female Threat

MORDOVTSEV'S COSSACK novel *Sagaidachnyi* introduces us to a
Cossack expression of disbelief. Warriors gather at one point in the novel to
witness the marvel of an aurochs dancing at the end of its tether.[1] "Perhaps,"
speculates one Cossack, "the Muscovites have taught it to dance, as if it were
a dancing bear." "Huh!" responds another skeptically. "Like you could teach
a woman to be a Cossack!"[2]

The retort reflects a basic premise of mythic Cossackdom: women do not
make Cossacks. Cossacks are male. No women, in fact, are allowed in the
Sech at all. Even thoughts of women are dishonorable and must be excluded
from the camp, often together with those who bore the thoughts. A good
unit is one from which no Cossack has run off to marry,[3] for, as Gogol tells
us, "a Cossack is not intended to hang around with womenfolk" (Kazak ne
na to, chtoby vozit'sia s babami, II:43). Mordovtsev repeats the precept in
Sagaidachnyi: "The feminine sex, according to Zaporozhian custom, was
not supposed to be in the Sech."[4]

Pushkin writes in *The History of Pugachev* of the passionate belief in
bachelorhood of the Cossacks of poetic tradition, and relates how some
Cossacks proposed to murder their own children and abandon their wives.
Mythmaking was not his purpose in the history; Pushkin concludes in favor
of civilization and praises the women for preventing the murder. Gogol and
later mythologizers of the Cossack hero would not be so quick to condemn
such counterdomesticity.

Repeatedly, Cossacks in the texts under consideration declare that the
Sech or the steppe is their mother, or the Dnepr is, or the Volga. For a bride,
the men must take their sword, or their sabre, or their horse, or again the
steppe or the Sech. They wed their way of life and the great expanse that
represents it. Characteristically, their fight itself is called a wedding, and to
die is to marry:

A Cossack has married, he took for himself a little woman,
In the virgin field he took an earthen hut:
And there the free wind will not enter,
And there the sun of the world will not pour.
There in a wine box an ox-cart driver of the steppe
Has buried his brave bones in the earth.[5]

The motifs of marriage to the Cossack lifestyle and the motherhood of the Cossack land clearly originate in folk poetry. The epithet *Volga-matushka* (Mother Volga) is particularly prevalent in songs of the Cossacks, and relates there to the traditional image of the Russian land itself as female: "Damp Mother Earth" and "Mother Russia." And the metaphor of battle as wedding has a long tradition in epics of all nations. The topos in literature about the Cossacks, however, goes further. Its pervasiveness and the variety of its forms require us to look deeper to determine what the frequent repetitions might be saying about the Cossacks themselves. The overriding maleness of the Cossacks, which includes not only their machismo but their rejection of women in favor of the sabre and steppe, points to yet another way in which the Cossack heroes become myth.

It must be kept in mind that, in reality, Cossacks of course had relations with women, whether at home in their villages or on campaigns and raids. Women were taken as booty and frequently married to their captors. More important, many new recruits brought families with them, or married local women. These Cossacks produced heirs and created a nation that obviously included males *and* females. Folk poetry, as opposed to the literary myth, does not fail to glorify the Cossack women as well as the men.

When relations between Cossack men and women are described in the literature of the nineteenth century, however, they almost always lead to disaster, betrayal, and/or death. *Sagaidachnyi* provides an explanation. One Cossack is led to treasonous statements on account of his defense of having "acquired" a Tatar girl during the last campaign. The subsequent teasing by his fellow Cossacks takes the form of a proof that the girl cannot remain in the Sech: "She's a woman, a girlie. And women, according to Zaporozhian customary law, are not admitted to the Sech, just as they can't go near the altar."[6] The unspoken premise is that as the altar is holy, so too is the Cossack community. Priests who serve at the altar are male; therefore males must be holy. Cossacks are male; therefore Cossacks must be holy. And women must therefore be unholy.

Implicitly or explicitly, several texts go even further, and suggest that entrance into the Cossack community resembles tonsure. In fact, certain initiation rituals among the historical Cossacks did bear a resemblance to holy vows. The hero of *The Zaporozhian* by Narezhnyi reminds us that a newcomer abandons all former titles and signs of distinction, takes on a new name, and shaves his head (except for the forelock). And, of course, "not one single woman crossed over the gates of their town." If we still have missed the association with monastery life, he continues, "And in no time at all, this layman becomes initiated into the Zaporozhian mysteries."[7] Not only do Cossack customs resemble those of the Church, but the Cossack community as a whole becomes associated with the unearthly atmosphere of those who have sanctified themselves to a life of God. It is not surprising that the Cossacks reject women *if* they form a holy Christian brotherhood. Sexuality is problematic throughout the history of Christianity, and the attitude toward women in both the Eastern and Western Church has not always been enlightened, despite the fact that Orthodoxy accepts married clergy. What is striking, however, is that the substitute for women should be in that case not the Church, or ideal femininity embodied in the Mother of God, but the elemental earth and the regenerating violence of the Cossacks' relationship to it.

Frequent declarations in Cossack literature of "Mother-Sech" and "Mother-Volga"—*Mat'-Sech', Mat' ty nasha Sech', Sich'-mati* (in Ukrainian), *Volga-mat' rodnaia*—are therefore and significantly more than folk imitations. As a monk vows celibacy and marries the Church, the Cossack also departs from ordinary life with its established heterosexual, maternal, and marital bonds. He unites instead with his fellow male Cossacks and with nature herself. Furthermore, the union is sanctified. The warrior is a holy monk; when he dies he becomes a sainted martyr.

The Cossacks' exploits are repeatedly referred to as *podvigi*, the term for the deeds of saints, and Ostap Bul'ba, for one, prepares for his death like the martyrs of old. The narrator tells us that at his execution he did not bend in the face of torture, and "he was the first to have to drink this painful cup" (etu tiazheluiu chashu).[8] But "Ostap endured the agony and torment like a giant" (II:164). As already pointed out, his final cry is for his father, not his mother; the male bonding is intact through death. (By way of contrast, the traitor Andrii's last cry "was the name of the beautiful Polish girl," II:144.) The Cossack, to be a true Cossack, does not need women.

The depiction of women in Cossack literature brings into focus an interesting contrast between Cossack works on the Western European romantic model, based on Byron, and less derivative, more native Russian works. Byron includes a romantic element that is central to the poem; a girl discovers Mazepa, nurses him to health, and the two fall in love. Ryleev, who was strongly influenced by Western models, repeats the motif in *Voinarovskii*, where a Cossack maiden saves the hero from the brink of death. In most Russian texts, however, instead of acting as innocent saviors, women ally themselves with the devil. And insofar as they are sexually active, they are a threat that must be kept from possessing the Cossack world.

This topos of woman-as-devil appears most explicitly in Gogol's stories from *Evenings* and in "Vii" from *Mirgorod*. The stepmother from "A May Night or The Drowned Girl" turns into a cat, a traditional symbol of black magic, and female witches test a Cossack at cards in "The Lost Letter" and cause him to exclaim about their cheating: "What kind of devilry is this!" (II:189). "Christmas Eve" boasts a witch-seductress, and the Cossack Khoma in "Vii" mounts a maiden/old witch, only to precipitate his own torment and death. Associations between women and the devil emerge quite clearly in typical exclamations such as "the devil sits in an old woman" (I:133) and, about Khoma's sexual attraction/revulsion toward the witch in "Vii": "He felt a devilishly sweet feeling" (II:187). Gogol's stories are notoriously full of references to the devil, many of which unite the images of sex, women, and evil powers.[9]

The strained nature of Gogol's own relationship to women and sex has been amply covered in previous studies, and need not be discussed here. The Cossack myth seems tailored to justify his sexual attitudes. But psychological speculations aside, the treacherous females in Gogol's Cossack tales are symbols of the non-Cossack or the anti-ideal, and by no means unsuccessful attempts at realistic portrayals of women. Female eroticism endangers the Cossacks' mythic unity and their "wholesome" marriage to the steppe.

In *Taras Bul'ba* Gogol develops the topos of woman-as-devil more subtly than in the obviously fantastic stories, beginning with his first description of the Polish girl. Her laugh turns Andrii to stone. Her beauty and specifically her eyes are blinding, suggesting an association between the girl and the gnome in "Vii" who destroys Khoma once its eyelids are lifted. In that story, the Cossack Khoma is bewitched into a nocturnal flight with an old woman astride his back. He eventually overcomes his tormentor and climbs atop her, in an obviously sexual posture, only to discover that she has transformed herself into a beautiful girl. Having beaten her almost to death, Khoma disappears. The girl's last request is that the Cossack should be found and compelled to recite blessings for the dead over her body. He is brought in, scared almost to death himself, yet manages to keep the evil powers that band with the witch-girl at bay until the last night, when Vii is called. Vii is an androgynous chthonic gnome—male by its name, but associated with both the female corpse and the female earth from which it emerges. The Cossack dies when Vii sees him and he sees Vii. Enchanted into a sexual encounter with the girl, Khoma had, as it were, provoked the encounter with the underworld and his own consequent death. In *Taras Bul'ba*, Andrii's "enchantment" is just as deadly.

The Polish girl in *Taras Bul'ba* bewitches Andrii again on their second meeting, but only after Andrii has walked through the eerie monastery crypt with its open caskets and exposed human bones, and then through the cathedral where "women knelt, resembling ghosts" (II:96). Andrii has entered the world of the dead. The description of the square before the girl's house similarly provokes associations with death: "The square seemed dead. . . . [He saw] the dead body of a woman. . . . Beside her lay a baby. . . . It no longer cried or wailed, and only by the quiet rising and falling of its stomach could one tell it had not yet died or, at least, was still preparing to let out its last breath" (II:97–98). On the square Andrii meets a man about whom the narrator uses the word "mad" three times: *(besnuiushchiisia, beshenstvo, kak beshenaia sobaka)*, a word derived in Russian from the root *bes*, or devil. When describing both the square and the girl's chamber, Gogol fills the pages with the verb "to seem," suggesting again the eerie, otherworldly quality of Andrii's encounter with the girl. Although merely metaphorically, the girl herself is witchlike enough to charm *(pricharovat')* Andrii; to cause him to offer to kill himself, to relinquish all, and finally to deny his Cossack blood.

In discussions of gender in Gogol's works, critics usually cite the confusion of the distinction between male and female characters or symbols. The analyses often conclude that in the struggle between male and female values, the men and all they represent are stifled, overcome, and emasculated.[10] Yet *Taras Bul'ba* must then be relegated to the status of anomaly, for although Taras dies at the end, the Cossack spirit, in all its maleness, is clearly not suffocated.[11] Gogol worked on *Taras Bul'ba* throughout most of his creative career (1835–42), and references to its mythic themes or inversions of them can be found in many of his other stories. The Cossack novel is not at all a total oddity, but rather is central to all of Gogol's oeuvre, as it is to the Cossack myth as a whole. The question of women and sexuality in Gogol's work perhaps has another answer.

Sociological explanations can be ventured: the topos of the threatening woman in Cossack texts may express Russian gender biases, or more broadly, xenophobia, if women are symbolic of any aliens in the male-dominated Russian society. Psychological answers can and have been offered as well: Cossack characters give vent to sexual fantasies of male dominance and machismo.[12] A mythic analysis, however, presents deeper options. The blurring of boundaries between male and female can be read as another example of the transcendence of all barriers in mythic beings. Cossacks do not so much fear or reject women as represent self-sufficient and, most important, self-regenerating individuals. Their union with the feminine land—and conveniently Sech, steppe, and sabre are all feminine nouns in Russian—is an interpenetration of their own essence. Far from representing suppression of the male principle, the Cossacks of Russian literature recover the earth for men. They repossess the land as they become one with free, barrierless, and "womanly" space. They thus reconcile male and female qualities within themselves, and like male Amazons can further their own kind without recourse to women.

Gogol tells us: "It seemed that the existence of this nation was eternal. Its size never diminished, for new [Cossacks] replaced those who left, were murdered, or drowned" (VIII:48). The reference to eternal existence is more telling than the historical fact of a constant supply of new recruits to swell the host. It emphasizes the mythic aspect and ignores the logical one; Gogol gives us perpetuity without female interference in the process of creation. In fact, Cossacks did marry and have children, who themselves became Cossacks by birth rather than choice. It is the choice itself, however, that makes a Cossack authentic.

This is not to imply that sexuality has no part in the Cossack world. The physicality of the Cossacks, their male comradeship, their bonding itself, all create a picture of highly charged relationships that we would normally associate with sex. The implication is merely that true Cossack sexuality expresses itself in ways grander, again holier, and more mythic than that of ordinary mortals.

The Cossacks' sexual energy emerges most of all in their violence. This too is not unfamiliar to experienced readers; the warrior is male and his masculinity is tested in war. What is particularly interesting in terms of the Cossacks is the association between their violence and their consequent resurrection. With amazing regularity, Cossack characters undergo some sort of death-in-life experience, whether by apparently dying themselves, or by causing the death of another, from which they emerge renewed, refreshed, and reborn.

We will find the topos of rebirth through violence particularly widespread in Cossack literature of the twentieth century, and the reasons for its popularity then will be suggested in Part 2 of this study. The nineteenth-century antecedents, however, are equally compelling. The death of a Cossack repeatedly represents not an end but a renewal of life. And the new life given to him derives not from a woman, but from the Cossack's exuberant exploits alone.

The imagery of rebirth can be found already in Byron's *Mazeppa*—the Cossack almost dies tied on the back of a wild horse, but is nursed back to life to become a great hetman—as well as in works influenced by Byron, such as Słowacki's *Mazeppa*.[13] In this Polish example, the hero remains walled up in a shrine, referred to as a "tomb," only to emerge in the next scene as "a very Lazarus."[14] In *Voinarovskii*, the hero's horse collapses by a mass grave in the steppe *(stepnaia mogila)*, itself evocative of death, where even his voice dies out: "having barely been born, it was dying" (edva rodias', on umiral). The hero recalls: "already it seemed, I was dying." Like Byron's Mazeppa, however, he is resurrected: "I arose renewed from my deathbed."[15]

The imagery of death-in-life in Cossack works extends well beyond the works directly derived from Byron's poem. Palei, the hero of Bulgarin's *Mazepa,* remains imprisoned in a coffin in a basement in a monastery—a triple-walled tomb; Neon in Narezhnyi's *The Seminarist* sleeps unnaturally deeply because of a serious wound, but eventually awakes to hear the chirping of birds, a sign of spring and renewed life.

Gogol too has the Cossack Petro in "St. John's Eve" fall into a "deathlike sleep" only to awaken on the third day—a direct reference to Christ's resurrection; Vakula in "Christmas Eve" is rumored to have committed suicide, and to have been "resurrected" when he reappears; the monk in "A Terrible Vengeance" sleeps in a coffin; and Taras Bul'ba receives a mortal wound—"And he crashed to the ground like a felled oak. And mist covered his eyes"—from which he could have "fallen asleep . . . perhaps forever" (II:146). He is, however, nursed back to life by his male companions, and resumes his Cossack role as though reborn.

Later in the novel Taras undergoes a metaphoric death and resurrection as well. In order to see his son he agrees to capitulate to the Jews and Poles, that is, to those who represent the antithesis to his own mythic essence. Taras rides to Warsaw enclosed in a tomblike pile of bricks; he offers to make a contract with the Jews; he dresses in German clothes; he bribes the Polish guards at the prison where his son is incarcerated—all "non-Cossack" behavior. As a consequence, it seems that his Cossack spirit dies: "He no longer resembled his former self, steadfast, unbending, as strong as an oak; he became cowardly and weak," until finally, "the heart of Taras stopped beating" (II:156). Taras recovers after this death of his Cossack heart, however, stronger than ever, and sets out to avenge the death of his son with more vigor than his younger compatriots. And the elevated figure of the Cossack leader presides over the end of the novel, with his hands nailed to a tree trunk that has been "cleaved at the top by thunder," (II:170). We are conditioned to see this "crucifixion" as an implication of Taras's imminent resurrection.

Interesting inversions of the motif occur in "A Terrible Vengeance," where corpses rise from their graves and the wizard opens his eyes after death, and in "Vii," with its female corpse that will not completely die. These figures represent life-in-death rather than death-in-life followed by reinvigoration. The inversion of the imagery parallels an inversion in the characters: both the wizard and his ancestors are demonic, not divinely mythic like the Cossacks. And the girl in "Vii" who refuses to sit still in her coffin is of course antithetical to the Cossacks: she is a sexual female. Vii itself, with the earth that still clings to it after its ascent from underground, is an excellent symbol for life-in-death. And the gnome brings destruction, not vitality, to the Cossack Khoma.

Typically, the Cossack custom that most fascinates Andrii, the son in

Taras Bul'ba who is destined to betray his true self and comrades, is the punishment for murder. "They dug a pit, placed the living murderer into it, placed over him the coffin containing the victim's body, and then sprinkled earth over them both" (II:67–68). This practice again suggests a cruel life-in-death experience rather than the positive death-in-life/rebirth imagery associated with the Cossacks. It is fitting that Andrii, who does not share the Cossack ethos, singles out this particular custom.

Birth, or rebirth out of violence, is well known in myth: Dionysus is born from the flames of his mother's destruction. Creation is thus inextricably linked to death, for violence is not only destructive. Out of its ashes can emerge great heroes.[16] By insisting on the creative and thus positive aspect of violence, moral structures are evaded. This is very evident in Gogol, for though many readers express indignation at the Cossacks' wanton violence, Gogol himself does not judge. In fact, for him there seems to be something highly positive, even marvelous, about the Cossacks. Their battle is a feast (a typical epic reference); their fight is music; their murdering is dance.

Gogol's admiration of the Cossacks' violent strength and activity can be seen in his vocabulary as a whole. He develops a pool of images to convey certain positive qualities referring to the Cossacks that he employs in other works as well. To describe the Middle Ages—the time, he claims, that transformed the world, united ancient and modern, and appears in history like the heart of the human body (VIII:14)—Gogol employs the terms variety *(pestrota)*, lively activity *(zhivoe deistvie)*, sharp contrasts *(reskie protivopolozhnosti)*, and strange brightness *(strannaia iarkost')* (VIII:16), all of which relate to his Cossacks as well. He claims that the Middle Ages possess a "gigantic, almost miraculous colossal nature" *(kolossal'nost' ispolinskaia, pochti chudesnaia,* VIII:17). Gogol uses a similar image when he writes of the colossal grandeur *(kolossal'noe velichie)* of history (VIII:27), or again of the gigantic colossal nature *(ispolinskaia kolossal'nost')* of subterranean geography (VIII:102). The writer could and does use the same words when describing his Cossacks, who attain a giant stature in battle. The Cossacks embody variety, activity, and magnitude.

Even more telling is his article "Sculpture, Painting, and Music," the introductory piece to *Arabesques*. Gogol ranks these three artforms on various scales. He sees a Hegelian-like historical progression from pagan (sculpture) to Christian (painting) to modern (music); from stasis to movement; and from passive reception by the viewer to actual participation, in fact to the interpenetration of music and the human soul. Painting, the middle stage, crosses borders as do the Cossacks: "It does not merely capture a single quick moment the way marble does; it prolongs that moment, it continues life beyond physical barriers; it abducts phenomena from another limitless world. . . ." In fact, it unites the physical with the spiritual (VIII:11).

Gogol's description of music, the highest stage, sounds even more familiar from our understanding of the Cossack topoi. Music evokes many opposing images (he cites, for instance, weariness and storm), and all of the vocabulary used to explain it shares a violent, powerful quality:

> But effervesce more strongly, my third goblet! Resounding foam, sparkle more brightly and splash against the golden rim—you sparkle in honor of music. She is more effusive, more impetuous than her two sisters. She is nothing but a gust of energy. Suddenly and instantaneously she rips man from his earth, deafens him with the thunder of mighty sounds, and immediately plunges him back into his world. Commandingly, she strikes his nerves, as on a keyboard, and turns him trembling. He no longer simply enjoys [as he did with sculpture], no longer simply feels compassion [as with painting]. He is himself transformed into suffering itself. His soul does not passively contemplate incomprehensible phenomena, but lives itself, lives its own life, lives violently, crushingly, rebelliously. . . . (VIII:11–12)

Gogol's aesthetic, we note from this passage, is generically feminine. His third goblet, music, is one of three sisters.[17] Yet her actions all derive from a stereotypical male pool. She rips, she thunders, she strikes powerfully. And, in turn, she causes the soul of the male viewer to act similarly: to live violently, crushingly, and rebelliously. She causes others to be reborn in her image. The highest form of art, in other words, acts like a Cossack. But it is female as well. If we recall the frequent musical references used in conjunction with the Cossacks in *Taras Bul'ba,* and the contrasting static, pictoral descriptions of the enemy Poles, we can begin to recognize a relationship between violence, art, and our heroes. True art is destructive, yet it creates. Cossacks, too, destroy, yet their violent spirit participates in Gogol's aesthetic.

In "A Glance at the Composition of Little Russia," Gogol calls the Cossack era "a poetic time," marked by unity, activity, and growth, when "the sabre and the plow made friends and could be found by the side of every peasant" (VIII:49). This formulation is nothing short of a Gogolian transformation of the biblical passage: "And they shall beat their swords into plowshares, and their spears into pruning hooks" (Isaiah 2:4, Micah 4:3). For Gogol, the Cossack destruction is not transformed into domesticity. Rather the violence of the sabre and the creative potential of the plow exist in organic unity within the Cossacks' wondrous mythic aura. And this is a way that the feminine principle has a place in the Cossack world: not women, but violent creativity.

Gogol clearly does not simply ignore aggressive aspects of the world, the Cossacks included, but rather raises them to an aesthetic ideal. He does not condemn the Cossack violence, nor does he contrast it to their or others' potential for good. In fact, despite the ethical tenor of many of his Cossack stories, evil and good do not appear as a contradictory pair. Like other opposites, the two are reconciled within the heroes. The Cossacks can destroy, and do so in a major key, because they can transcend traditional moral boundaries. They become amoral music or poetry itself. Ethics in the Cossack myth gives way to aesthetics.

FIVE

Space and Time Unbounded

In a famous essay, Dmitrii Chizhevskii suggests that Gogol makes extensive use of *coincidentia oppositorum,* a patristic concept by which opposites are said to unite in any true being.[1] Chizhevskii is here speaking of Gogol's parodic technique of investing trivial characters with absurdly grandiose significance. The device works directly instead of parodically, however, in the case of *Taras Bul'ba.* The authenticity of the Cossacks derives from their ability to cross boundaries and thus reconcile opposites.

When a newcomer joins the Cossacks, he must wholeheartedly abandon all ties to his past. The narrator of *Taras Bul'ba* informs us:

> Every new arrival here would forget the past and discard anything that had once occupied him. You might say that he would spit upon his past, and with a light heart give himself up to the will and comradeship of those like himself, a roamer with neither relatives, nor home, nor family. He had only the free sky and the eternal feast of his soul. (II:65)

In *The Zaporozhians,* Nestor Kukol'nik (1809–68) similarly suggests that bonds to a former life are eliminated when any newcomer joins the host; we are reminded that it is an infraction of Cossack law to ask where a fellow warrior hails from.[2]

Such radical severence from the past suggests that the Cossack host exists *permanently* in a liminal realm, and not only when electing its officials, as suggested in Chapter 1.[3] Entrance into the Cossack brotherhood involves movement out of our restricted world. Cossacks grow young, and adults act like "schoolboys" (*Taras Bul'ba* II:65), as they disregard the rules of civilized society. No physical bonds tie a Cossack to the host: "We keep no one forcibly; the [Cossack gathering place] is always unlocked."[4]

This chapter will further examine topoi that emphasize the liminal nature of the Cossack heroes, in particular their fluid relationship to space and time. Association with the frontier, with epic, with the fantastic, and with a temporally ambiguous narrator all suggest that the Cossacks live here *and* there, then *and* now, free of the restrictions that hinder other earth- and time-bound individuals.

The Boundless Frontier

Mordovtsev's *Sagaidachnyi* presents a central motif of spatial boundlessness: "Cossacks did not like to live in the unit huts; their free Cossack souls felt crowded under a roof or any kind of covering. Summer, spring, or in the dry fall they loved to sleep under the open sky. . . ."[5] Cossacks are always more comfortable on the open steppe that is a "mysterious distance," "something inscrutable, immense," and "a boundless desert [that] leads to there, where the earth ends, leaning on the sky."[6] The sea, too, on which the Cossack rows, "has no end, no edge." A Cossack lives in this endless world, upon the

> unbounded mass of water with its unprecedented color. . . . No matter how far you look your glance seems to drown more and more in this endlessness. . . . You feel a terrible helplessness, an isolation from the whole world. You are no longer between heaven and earth, but rather between heaven and an abyss that has no limit, an abyss that has swallowed the earth itself, that is dumb and deaf like the grave, like death.[7]

The endlessness of the Cossack land and waterways evokes terror, but it is also "God's steppe," "a paradise,"[8] and as empty as it was in Adam's time.[9] Cossack space is Edenlike—primal, pure, and unrestricted.

Gogol again most clearly of all the authors of Cossack texts suggests the heroes' existence outside any fixed spatial realm, and he does so largely by associating them with the emotionally laden concept of the frontier. Literally, frontier *(granitsa)* means barrier or border, generally the demarcation between two states. Yet the analogy of the American frontier suggests that the associations extend much further. Both Russia/Ukraine and America are countries so large that to eighteenth- and nineteenth-century citizens they seemed to stretch on forever. In other words, the frontiers moved infinitely outward. Thus, those inhabitants of the frontier lands—the American pioneers and Indians on the one hand, the Cossacks on the other—paradoxically lived in areas with *no* frontier, in a place of unbounded space.

Historically, frontierlands attracted people of a certain temperament. A colonist in early America, for instance, may have left the civilization of the eastern colonies, with its European values, and set off in a wagon or canoe for the wilderness. He may have at first been overcome by the new, open world he encountered, but, assuming he survived, both he and the new world changed.[10] The two contradictory states of savagery and civilization meet at the frontier,[11] and the meeting shapes the people who live in it, just as the people come to shape the land. This was as true for the Cossacks as for the American settlers.[12]

As for the Western European countries which have no frontierland to speak of, a profoundly different worldview emerges.[13] The European of the late eighteenth and early nineteenth centuries faced confusion in his society, shaken as it had been by the French, Napoleonic, and rising industrial revolutions. Looking around for a way to rebuild his home, he grasped the romantic but conventional image of a hero drawn from mythic tradition in order to invoke traditional values and reaffirm a vision of order. For him, the American frontier (or the Russian one, as in the case of Byron and Hugo's Cossack poems) was an exotic setting for a drama of reason versus passion in which the man of reason, and thus traditional European cultural values, could continue to survive and usually dominate. Nonetheless, passion too could exist in this vision—confined within its proper realm of art and distant exotica.[14]

For the Russian or American writer who lived closer to the so-called savage frontier, however, the situation looked more complex. And the borrowing from, and often imitation of, European literary models takes on an element of bravura. Here, in fact, we might find the clue to surprising similarities between Russian and American literature as a whole (could Dostoevskii and Melville harbor "savagery" even within their urban libraries?), and the challenge they pose to the "civilized" Western European literary tradition out of which they grew. The propensity toward religious themes in these "frontier" literatures may well grow from the tendency to see that frontier as a type of sacral space, to see the land itself as an embodiment of the national holy soul, and its inhabitants as holy soldiers in a rebellion against a dominant European culture that could no longer represent the New Adam's experience.[15]

The nineteenth-century American writer could not rest upon a fixed, value-confirming image, or could do so only with irony. Instead, his heroes take on apocalyptic characteristics. Natty Bumppo, the hero of James Fenimore Cooper's Leatherstocking tales and perhaps the most representative American hero, was at heart a deeply enigmatic character, by no means an unambiguous symbol of natural impulses as some would want to cast him. A white man raised by Indians, he assimilated the traits of both civilization and wildness. Not a simple foil for his opposite, the educated European or city dweller, he combined traits of the civilized world with others borrowed from his Indian soul brother. The Russian frontiersman, the Cossack, also evades easy classification as a noble savage familiar to us from European romantic literature. Taras Bul'ba, after all, could quote Horace. The frontier hero is neither savage nor civilized, but the mediator between the two opposing realms of civilization and wilderness. In American literature, he bridges the gap between European past and Indian present.[16] The Cossack, we might say on the other hand, unites European present with old Russian and/or even Tatar past. He himself is on the threshold.[17]

Gogol draws on the historical association of the Cossacks with the frontier to remind us constantly that his characters live in unbounded space.[18] Like other Cossack characters already quoted, Taras informs us that Cossacks "need no bed. We will sleep outside" (II:49). In "The Hetman," Ostranitsa states, "Well then, let's go to sleep! Only not in a stuffy hut, but on the free, unfettered [*vol'nyi*] earth, under the sky" (III:295). Similarly, in "A Terrible Vengeance" we read: "But it is better for a Cossack to sleep on the smooth earth under the free [*vol'nyi*] sky" (I:250). The Cossacks' natural habitat, the steppe, is similarly free: "Then the whole south, all that expanse . . . to the Black Sea itself, was a green, virginal wilderness" (II:58). It is called a "many-colored expanse [*pestroe prostranstvo*]" and "all the same limitless, unfettered, beautiful steppe" (II:59–60).[19]

The Cossack camp or Sech is an ambiguous term, signifying both the organization of Zaporozhian Cossackdom and the place where the Cossacks camped. Gogol used this ambiguity to personify the Sech, thus denying its role as a fixed geographic entity:

> [The surrounding area] fed and clothed the Sech, since it [she] knew nothing but how to carouse and fire its [her] rifles. (II:62)

> The Sech did not like to trouble herself with military exercises and to waste time. (II:64)

> . . . and the entire Sech fell asleep. (II:73)

> When the transport started up and pulled away from the Sech, all the Zaporozhians turned their heads back. "So long, our Mother!" they said almost in a single voice. "May God protect you from any harm!" (II:81–82)

The Sech is a place that accepts all comers, "as though they are returning to their very own home" (II:66). Yet it does not hold them there; it is "the nest *from which* the proud and free [Cossacks] fly out like lions! *From there* freedom and Cossackdom flow into the entire Ukraine" (II:62, emphasis mine). The Cossacks behave like schoolboys, yet Gogol tells us that instead of a playing field they have "the unprotected, carefree frontier [and] instead of the oppressive power which bound them to school, they themselves had cast off their fathers and mothers and escaped from their parents' homes" (II:65).[20]

Gogol's description of the physical plan of the Sech further emphasizes its lack of enclosing walls: "Nowhere could you see either a fence or those low cottages with awnings on short wooden posts which were found in the surrounding area. A small rampart and barricade, guarded by absolutely nobody, demonstrated a frightful carelessness" (II:62). By contrast, the description of the Polish town is replete with images of enclosure: "A tall earthen rampart surrounded the city; a stone wall jutted up where the rampart was lower, then came a building which served as an arsenal, and finally, an oak paling" (II:85).

As Andrii enters the Polish town before his betrayal, he must leave the open camp and first climb into a ravine so deep that the field is blocked off from sight. Beyond, more enclosures are either described or suggested: Andrii and his guide are blocked from sight; they hear nothing; the bank rises up like a cliff; at this point the fortification is strong; no one peeks over the earthen wall behind which the thick monastery wall rises; the top of the bank boasts the remains of a fence that once enclosed a vegetable garden. Finally, Andrii must walk through an underground passage so confining that he "scarcely moved in the dark and narrow corridor" (II:93–94). His transition from Cossack to foreigner is clearly directed by these walls and cliffs. Gogol marks the transition by repeating the term *pereshel* (crossed over, as over a barrier) seven times in the course of a brief dialogue relating Andrii's betrayal (II:112–13). Once inside the Polish walls, Andrii becomes metaphorically enclosed as well, and can no longer express himself freely: "He felt as though something obstructed his lips" (II:102).

The description of the siege of the fort of Dubno—the Cossacks free to carouse in the surrounding fields while the Poles remain trapped within their walls, too weak to venture out and preferring to starve rather than open their doors—suggests the barrierless quality of Cossackdom by contrasting it to Polish enclosures. Cossacks both live in and share essential qualities with the paradoxically unending frontier. The association of the Cossacks with their boundless environment found in *Taras Bul'ba* is particularly telling in light of the relationship Gogol believed existed between a people and its geography already discussed. In a number of Cossack texts we are told that not only do the Cossacks share the openness of the steppe, but the steppe takes on something of Cossack nature as well: nature occasionally *kazakuet*, or "acts like Cossacks."

Timeless History

The Cossacks' relationship to the endless space in which they live explains only part of their permanent liminal nature. Restrictions of time, as well, are eliminated. An inordinate amount of attention is paid in Cossack texts to claims of historical accuracy, and most include references to or depictions of known events and historical personages. Gogol, as we noted, did considerable research for his Cossack articles and stories. But the more factual historical material incorporated in his fiction, often the more unreal become his Cossacks. Confusion of chronology, for which Gogol the historian has often been criticized, may in fact be the fault of inaccuracies in Gogol's sources,[21] but Gogol's juxtaposition of different eras in his fiction seems definitely an artistic decision. While producing the sensation of historicity, he actually destroys any historical grounding in his work whatsoever. This temporal or historical aspect ultimately associates the Cossacks not with time, but with epic, or rather pre-epic, mythic timelessness.

The history of the Cossacks takes the form in Cossack texts of dialectic usually between images of the past and the present (or less distant past), but also of rich versus poor Cossacks (reminding the reader of socio-economic elements in history), old versus young Cossacks, and Cossack versus ex-Cossack who has betrayed his heritage. In all the examples the contrast is not simply between Cossack and non-Cossack, but between "true" Cossacks and those who do not live up to their potential to be as true.

The Zaporozhian by Narezhnyi ends with a prophecy by the protagonist that the Sech will collapse, and a time will come when geographers alone remember its location. The age foreseen obviously refers to the present (or the author's present), and Narezhnyi thus reminds us that the Cossack nation no longer exists. The reference to dying glory, spoken in this case by a Cossack on his own deathbed, recurs throughout Cossack texts. Gogol resorts to a narrator in *Evenings* (Rudyi Pan'ko) who relates tales told to him by another (Foma Grigor'evich) that have been told to the latter by his father's father, thus distancing the Cossack narrator from the "true" Cossack characters by at least two generations.

Bulgarin in his *Mazepa* sets up a very clear contrast between the older Cossack Palei and both his son and Mazepa, the father of his son's fiancée. Palei defends the Cossack nation, the poor peasants, and the Orthodox Church. Mazepa, however, who has spent his youth in Poland and continues to nurture his Polish ties, calls for reconciliation with, if not actual betrayal to, the Poles. Palei's son, too, has connections with the Poles. The father bemoans:

> If only I had brought you up in the Zaporozhian camp and not given you over to the accursed Poles for your education, then you wouldn't now be running after girls like a madman and you'd know nothing but Cossack affairs! Oh such times! The Cossacks have begun to pamper themselves like gentlemen's sons. Nothing good will come of it.[22]

This last example suggests that the Cossack association with historical development has a political aspect. Not only have times changed, but true nationalist spirit, represented by the Cossacks of old (or the older Cossacks), has been perverted in the process. Such a corollary allows the Cossack texts to be read simply as political propaganda, for the Cossacks can be associated with the good party or nation, the betrayers with the bad. Yet the Cossack characters can represent opposing sides of any given political conflict, depending on the author's orientation.[23] The Cossack myth is concerned not with specific conflicts but with history as a whole.[24]

Gogol makes extensive use of the historical dimension in all his Cossack stories. Not only did he claim to be writing a three-volume history of Ukraine,[25] and avidly reading other historical works, but even after abandoning his scholarly pursuits, he continued to cite specific—though often inaccurate—events, dates, and names.[26]

The inaccuracy stems from Gogol's association of history, ethnography, and literature, and contributes to the blend of genres so characteristic of myth. As he wrote to his friend Pogodin, presumably in response to criticism of his research: "My Little Russian history is extremely wild; it could not be, however, any other way. I am reproached that its style is too fiery, that it is unhistorically burning and alive. But what kind of history would it be if it were boring!?!" (Jan. 11, 1834, X:294).

Interest, excitement, and variety played a large role in Gogol's pedagogical philosophy in general. He instructs teachers of geography, for example, to show their students the world as "a whole, bright, picturesque poem" (odna iarkaia zhivopisnaia poema, VIII:99). And he demands of historians that their words be alluring and fiery (uvlekatel'nyi i ognennyi, VIII:27–28).

Gogol's history of the Ukraine never materialized, less because of academic inadequacy (though there is no dearth of scholars who support this reason for Gogol's failure) than because he found belles lettres a better vehicle for the expression of his ideas. He set out to write history, wound up writing literature, but saw no fundamental distinction between the two.[27] Factual research into the Cossacks' history no doubt preceded the writing of his stories (though the revisions in *Taras Bul'ba* show that the opposite was also often the case), but there can be no question of cause and effect. In all of his writing on Cossack themes, fiction and nonfiction, Gogol was searching for the same expression of life and vitality.

For literature about Cossacks, the use of historical data ironically accentuates the lack of real indices of time in the Cossack myth. Many aspects of the hero in *Taras Bul'ba* suggest the Cossack Khmel'nitskii, a real historical figure of the mid-seventeenth century. Yet Gogol juxtaposes events which could have occurred in the previous and subsequent centuries and at one point calls Taras "one of those types who could only have arisen in the difficult fifteenth century" (II:46). The end result is a loss of grounding in any century whatsoever.[28]

A second example, this time from Gogol's fragment "The Bloody Bandura Player," shows historical references so intertwined with folk motifs as to destroy totally any factual index. The story is explicitly set in spring 1543, and its association with other fragments from "The Hetman" suggests its relationship to the events surrounding the career of Hetman Ostranitsa. Yet the fragment breaks off after a mysterious, disembodied voice echoes from the depths of the dungeon and a man, skinned and dripping with blood, marches out with his bandura slung over his shoulder.

On a larger scale, Gogol's juxtaposition of stories in *Evenings* anticipates historicity at the same time as destroying any firm footing in historical reality at all. He features Cossacks from different eras, and presents narrators who lived earlier than the author (supposedly during Gogol's childhood in Ukraine), telling stories heard in previous years about Cossacks who lived at a still earlier time. "The Fair at Sorochintsyi" supposedly takes place in the early nineteenth century; "The Lost Letter" is clearly placed during the reign of Elizabeth; and "A Terrible Vengeance" unfolds "in ancient times" and includes a description of events from a still earlier era. Yet Cossacks are featured in all the stories with no explanation about their historical relationship to each other. The term "to be Cossacklike" (*kozakovat'*) appears twice in the first two stories of *Evenings,* and Gogol implies in both cases that to behave like a Cossack is somehow different from the way the Cossacks to which it refers actually act. The intended contrast is evidently between the Zaporozhians and the peasants, or between the heroes of old and the domesticated contemporary Cossacks, but Gogol calls both contrasting groups by the same name.

Gogol makes further use of these historical references that ultimately evade historicity by repeatedly contrasting the old ways with the new, the true Zaporozhian with the peasant, the "real" Cossacks with those who have compromised themselves by association with foreigners. The narrator often reminds us that "those days" differ greatly from our own: "There's no comparison between our weddings and those in the old days" ("St. John's Eve" I:147); "Inns at that time weren't like those today" ("The Lost Letter" I:184).

When contrasting Taras Bul'ba to the younger Cossacks, the narrator tells us:

> Taras belonged in the ranks of original, old colonels; he was created for martial unrest alone, and distinguishable by the crude simplicity of his nature. At that time the influence of Poland had begun to show itself on the Russian nobility. Many had already taken on Polish customs, acquiring riches, magnificent servants, falcons, huntsmen, dinners, and courts. None of this fit Taras well.

He loved the simple life of the Cossacks and quarreled with those of his comrades who tended toward the Warsaw side. (*Taras Bul'ba* II:48)

And Danilo tells Katerina in "A Terrible Vengeance":

Something grievous is happening in the world. Evil times are coming. Oh, I can remember the years that have passed, they will surely never return. . . . That was a golden time. . . . Now our nobility has all taken on Polish customs, adopted crafty ways. . . . They sold their souls and have taken up the Uniate religion. The Jews are oppressing the poor folk. Oh, the past, the past! (I: 265–66)

The message seems clear, on the surface at least, that history is a degenerating process. The purity of the past is corrupted by the modern world, often in the guise of the Poles, but, in the works set in periods closer to Gogol's own, by the non-Cossack, northern Russians as well. What suggests that Gogol does more than repeat sentimental conventions about the loss of an idyllic past is his repeated insistence that historical change is not a linear progression leading to our day, but a more complex phenomenon in which the present, or at least something which is not like the past, occasionally creeps—or bursts—into the past. Gogol contrasts the past to the present by painting a picture of the former Cossacks contrasted to each other and split among themselves. The past is contrasted to itself, or a more distant past. Danilo, in the example cited just above, is actually a rather young man, lamenting the passage of time as though he were much older. His rhetorical address to the past loses its weight as a declaration about history when we realize that the speaker had little historical perspective himself. Ultimately the message becomes one of a transcendent problem, discussed in historical terms but essentially existing outside of any historical progression (or regression) whatsoever.

An interesting example occurs in a fragment of "The Hetman." The narrator digresses from the plot in a lengthy description of a particular dwelling; the room is "a very remarkable monument in that country where there was almost no antiquity at all" (III:293). Apparently, the room has survived much turbulence that should have wiped out all traces of the past. "Its existence should have been ephemeral, but . . . it remained standing for nearly fifty years." In this room hangs a portrait of Ostranitsa's grandfather, already yellowed with age, which the narrator describes in great detail. Having told us that the Cossack land has no memory of the past, the narrator presents a picture of just that, of a historical person, older still than the historical period in which the action takes place. The reader cannot help but be confused about this bit of history in a historyless place.

All of Gogol's Cossack works encourage the reader to choose a certain time structure as reference point only to take the story outside of that structure altogether. Paradoxically, then, the historical motif contains its own opposite. Recurring references to epic further suggest that the Cossacks live outside recognizable human time, as well as firmly planted within its dialectical progression. These include specific references to Homer, such as when the Cossack warriors are said to fall like oaks in *Taras Bul'ba*,[29] and the frequent references to birds, which so characterize the medieval text *The Lay of Igor's Campaign*. As in the *Lay*, birds of flight and song vie with "evil" birds, usually carrion eaters, to correspond to the positive or negative characters in the narrative.

The association can be found throughout the Cossack myth. Ryleev has a raven hover over the Cossack hero as he lies dying in *Voinarovskii* ("Already, it seemed, I was dying; / Already, staring me in the eye, / A predatory raven flew above me . . ."),[30] and compares Jews, Poles, Lithuanians, and Uniates (i.e., all non-Cossack characters) to bloodthirsty crows. Bulgarin likewise shows Palei, the true Cossack, overlooking Mazepa's feast with the Poles, "like an eagle at a feast of ravens" (kak orel na pir voronov).[31]

Birds are also conventional harbingers of spring and thus representatives of cyclical time. By associating Cossacks with birds who return faithfully each year to soar freely through the boundless sky, authors underscore the endurance of their warriors outside of linear history.

Some writers extend the bird motif to more complex applications as well. Gogol in *Taras Bul'ba* describes non-Cossack characters (Iankel the Jew, and the Bul'ba mother) as chickens, or birds that cannot fly, and the Polish jailer as a cat, or an animal that catches birds. The final metaphor for the citified Poles, that is, for those whose characteristics are the antithesis of the Cossacks, is a falcon that hangs confined in a golden cage. The non-Cossacks somehow trap and are trapped, while the heroes soar in freedom.

The evocation of an epic bard parallels the use of bird metaphors described above to associate the Cossacks with epic. Gogol evokes a bandura player who is

> still full of ripe courage, though already a white-haired old man, inspired by prophetic spirit. He will utter [about the Cossacks] his thick, mighty word [*gustoe, moguchee slovo*—perhaps referring to a *slovo*, or lay, as in *The Lay of Igor's Campaign*]. And their glory will gallop throughout the entire world, and all who are born in the future will speak of it. (II:131–32)

In case the reader misses the parallel between this bandurist and the narrator who "sings" *Taras Bul'ba* in order to preserve the spirit of the Cossacks for posterity, Gogol concludes the passage with an epic simile, reminding us that his narrator, too, can speak like Homer:

For the mighty word will resound far and wide. It is like the copper of a ringing bell into which the master has poured much dear, pure silver, so that its beautiful ring would resound farther throughout towns, shacks, palaces, and villages, calling everyone alike to the holy service. (II:132).

Bards like this one, and particularly proverbial blind ones, are extremely common in all of these Cossack texts, along with their claims to enduring, eternal epic glory (*slava,* the Russian translation of the Greek *kleos*).

The hubris of the narrator's self-professed epic stance in *Taras Bul'ba* cannot escape the reader. Yet the story is not a true epic, but rather uses epic techniques along with other references to the past in order to turn the Cossacks into historyless myth.[32] The epics of Homer stand on the borderline between purely oral literature with its mythic consciousness and the linear narrative of later art. Gogol tries in *Taras Bul'ba* to return back before the break and reevoke mythic timelessness, losing specific references to both time and space.[33]

Gogol further mythologizes his Cossacks by refusing to create either a narrative or a metaphoric resolution to his story. Taras hangs above the earth, chained and nailed to a tree trunk "cleaved at the top by thunder" (II:170) (and thus a natural crucifix), aiding his comrades with his last breath. Yet even as flames embrace his legs the narrator interrupts to assure us, rhetorically, of Taras's immortality: "But would it be possible to find any flames, tortures, or power on this earth that could overcome the Russian might?" (II:172).

Meanwhile, Taras's fellow Cossacks save themselves from their enemies by leaping into the Dnestr River. They miraculously escape while the pursuing Poles stop short at the cliff or plunge to their death in the river below. Gogol thus creates a scene in which the Cossacks escape safely into a watery infinity:

> The Dnestr is no small river, and many are its backwaters, thick river reeds, shallows, and depths. The mirror of the river glistens, deafened by the ringing voices of swans. A proud goldeneye duck glides quickly along, and snipes, red-cropped sandpipers, and birds of all sorts abound in the reeds and on the banks. The Cossacks were vigorously rowing their narrow, double-ruddered boats, plying the oars in unison, carefully avoiding the shallows, startling the soaring birds, and speaking of their leader. (II:172)

The imagery—including the opposites of shallow and deep, the mirror which can reflect the whole, infinite sky,[34] and the abundant life—evokes a world of plenty, a world unobstructed and enduring.[35] In this final passage of *Taras Bul'ba,* Gogol again sets the Cossack events in the past *(plyli, grebli, minali, govorili)*, but places them in a present-tense setting (*blestit, nesetsia,* the implied present tense of the verb *to be*). The much more fluid relationship of tenses in Russian grammar must be recognized, of course. Yet the strong contrast and repetition in this passage cannot be ignored. The Cossacks speak of the past as they row off toward more adventures in the future, like the American cowboy who disappears into the sunset.

The use of past imperfective verb forms in this last paragraph of the novel further opens up the narrative beyond the bounds of simple past time, for it suggests the opening of a story, not the ending. In general, imperfective verbs require some explanation or continuation, as in: "The Cossacks were rowing when suddenly. . . ." To leave off narration at this point thus implies a continuation through time, or lack of closure on the past, historical event.

Gogol significantly changed the imagery at the end when he rewrote *Taras Bul'ba*. In the 1835 version, the Cossacks come to a precipice that "they could have gone around." This description does not allow for an interpretation of the precipice as a sort of cosmic space crossed by the Cossacks, for it is small enough to be circumvented. The only water mentioned in the 1835 version is "the dying murmur of some stream rushing down to the Dnestr," not the broad Dnestr itself. Furthermore, the Cossacks in the 1835 edition safely leap across from one side to the other and then ride to the river, where they escape. "The Dnestr is no small river," the narrator states, but does not continue with the lyrical passage evoking a world of plenty and infinity as he does in the later version (II:354–55). The first edition lacks the image of escape into a wholly new realm that so marks the latter. The Cossacks' escape is not miraculous as in the final version, but simply skillful, for they leap from space to space, not out of our world altogether.

The Cossacks' escape by water in the final version recalls the prototypical myth in which the children of Israel evade the Egyptians by fording the Red Sea. In the two cases the enemy army remains fettered on shore or drowned in the waves. The Cossacks thus participate in a "new Exodus."[36] The impact of the new myth, however, reverses its prototype. The Jewish people enter history with their exodus from Egypt; the Cossacks leap out of history, and out of time altogether at the end of *Taras Bul'ba*.

Narrative Strategies: Boundaries Blurred and Transcended

Perhaps Gogol's most important innovation from the point of view of the development of the Cossack myth is his use of multiple narrators. By rapidly shifting between various voices, he was able to destabilize the boundary between reader and character, thus enacting on a narrative level the self/other paradox seen up to now in terms of character, scene, or theme.

In later works, Gogol skillfully combined a number of narrative stances within a single story, but in *Evenings* he was still experimenting with the distribution of various voices among identifiable narrators in different stories or within a partial frame structure. Yet, Gogol intentionally published the stories of *Evenings* as a two-part whole.[37] And he attempted to include *Mirgorod* in the collection by subtitling it "stories serving as a continuation to *Evenings*." The various narrators may arguably serve as different voices and not necessarily as unconnected, erratic storytellers.[38]

A catalogue of the narrators in *Evenings* reads as follows: the introductions to both the first and second parts begin with the half-literate, native Ukrainian small village dweller *(khutorianin)* Rudyi Pan'ko, who dares "to stick his nose out of his backwash into the wide world" (vysunut' nos iz svoego zakholust'ia v bol'shoi svet, I:103). Gogol then presents an impersonal, more literary narrator for "The Fair at Sorochintsyi," but has Rudyi Pan'ko reenter briefly in "St. John's Eve," only to introduce Foma Grigor'evich as the storyteller. The latter, in turn, retells not his own story but his grandfather's. The literary narrator returns in "A May Night," gives way for Foma to narrate the "true story" *(byl')* titled "The Lost Letter," but comes back, slightly altered, in the first story of part 2, "Christmas Eve." "A Terrible Vengeance" is then told by an ambiguous narrator related to the one or many we will find in *Taras Bul'ba,* but with closer ties to the literary narrator of the earlier stories than to Foma or Rudyi Pan'ko. It is concluded by yet another narrator, a "blind bandura player," who tells tales of former Cossack heroes— Sagaidachnyi and Khmel'nitskii—as well as "one very distant deed," the story of Petro and Ivan. "Ivan Shpon'ka" supposedly has an oral-style narrator, presumably Rudyi Pan'ko himself, who claims to have heard the story from yet another source, one Stepan Ivanovich Kurochka. Yet his tale is not really oral at all, but shares many of the traits of the more literary tales discussed below. Finally, "An Enchanted Spot" is again labeled a "true story" told by Foma, like "St. John's Eve" and "The Lost Letter." Foma here claims he is sick and tired of storytelling (uzhe nadoelo rasskazyvat'! I:309) and this, in fact, is his last story.

The result of Gogol's multiple voices, whether juxtaposed from story to story or combined within a story as is the tendency in part 2 of *Evenings,* is to set up a paradigm of fluctuating distances between the narrator, the characters, and the reader. The oral-style narrator, Rudyi Pan'ko or Foma, often speaks directly to his audience, yet places himself at a distance by his knowledge of details of Little Russian life, his use of Ukrainian or Ukrainianisms, and his often substandard speech.[39] Furthermore, Rudyi Pan'ko requests that we not be angry that a lowly beekeeper dare address his "dear readers" so intimately (I:103), suggesting he considers himself separated from his Russian audience by more than geographic boundaries. In fact, he often distances himself twice, either by introducing Foma to tell the tale or, as in the case of "Shpon'ka," by informing us that "a story happened with this story" (I:283) and claiming (1) he heard it from another storyteller, and (2) his memory is poor in any case. Despite the narrator's direct appeal to us, his readers, he destroys his own credibility and forces us to view him from a skeptical distance. He seems "other" to us, more like the characters he describes than like ourselves. And because the characters he describes are so varied, the picture is further confused. He resembles Cossacks and Cossack descendents from several different eras.

We feel more familiar with the so-called literary narrator of "The Fair at Sorochintsyi" and "A May Night." We can identify him by his consciousness of literary form, including his division of the tales into chapters, each numbered and titled. Before each chapter of "The Fair at Sorochintsyi" he further includes epigraphs from other literary works, notably the Ukrainian Kotliarevskii's *The Aeneid* and Artemovskii-Gulak's *Master and Dog,* and from folk sayings or songs. "A May Night" has an epigraph only in the beginning, but is replete with quotations from other works or genres, mostly folksongs. These distinguishing literary characteristics appear also in "Christmas Eve" (quotations), "A Terrible Vengeance" (chapter divisions, quotations), and "Shpon'ka" (chapter divisions and titles), a story superficially noted for its oral character.

Yet this literary narrator also distances himself from his audience in subtle ways. His narration is largely impersonal, but he occasionally lapses into speech patterns which associate him with the Cossack characters. These include highly lyrical or rhetorical passages, often punctuated with exclamation points and marked by a large number of poetic devices including inverted word order and parallelisms. He also frequently employs present-tense narration, suggesting that he lives contemporaneously with the events of his tale, and addresses the Cossacks directly at several points. Compare, for instance, the narrative passages from "A Terrible Vengeance" below with examples of the Cossack Danilo's speech which follow:

> It resounds, it thunders, the edge of Kiev: Captain Gorobets is celebrating his son's wedding. (Shumit, gremit konets Kieva: esaul Gorobets prazdnuet svad'bu svoego syna, I:244.)

> Chop away, Cossack! Carouse, Cossack! Amuse your young heart, but without glancing at the golden harnesses and Polish jerkins! Trample under your feet the gold and stones! Stab away, Cossack! Carouse, Cossack! But take a look behind. . . . (Rubi, kozak! guliai, kozak! tesh' molodetskoe serdtse; no ne zagliadyvaisia na zolotye sbrui i zhupany! topchi pod nogi zoloto i kamen'ia! Koli, kozak! guliai, kozak! no oglianis' nazad . . . , I:267.)

> But who is riding on a huge raven-black horse through the night, whether the

stars shine or do not shine? What kind of a knight of inhuman size leaps under the mountains, over the lakes, who is reflected with his gigantic steed in the motionless waters and whose endless shadow flickers frightfully on the mountains? (No kto sosredi nochi, bleshchut ili ne bleshchut zvezdy, edet na ogromnom voronom kone? Kakoɪ bogatyr' s nechelovech'ɪm rostom skachet pod gorami, nad ozerami, otsvechivaetsia s ispolinskim konem v nedvizhnykh vodakh i beskonechnaia ten' ego strashno mel'kaet po goram? I:272.)

We should note especially the parallelisms *(shumit-gremit, rubi-guliai, bleshchut ili ne bleshchut);* the rhythmic speech of the first passage particularly; the use of archaic or highly poetically marked vocabulary *(kon', bogatyr');* and the emphatic punctuation. The Cossack speaks similarly:

"And my head is pained and my heart is pained." (I golova bolit u menia, i serdtse bolit, I:265.)

"Amuse yourself then, Cossack soul, for one last time! Carouse, fellows, our festival has arrived!" (Natesh'sia zhe, kozatskaia dusha, v poslednii raz! Guliaite, khloptsy, prishel nash prazdnik! I:266.)

"The world is somehow turning sad. Evil times are approaching. Oh, how I remember, remember the years gone by!" (Shto-to grustno stanovitsia na svete. Vremena likhie prikhodiat. Okh, pomniu, pomniu ia gody! I:265.)

In these passages there is often no clear verbal distinction between the narrator and the characters whose speech he reports. In these instances the reader perceives the narrator as in the Cossack camp, temporally and physically, in contrast to the times he, like us, views the Cossacks from a literary distance, as well as a historical and cultural one. In other words, the narrator in *Evenings* jumps back and forth across temporal, geographic, social, and educational barriers. To use the terminology of the myth, he is sometimes "self" and sometimes "other."

The multiplicity of narrative voices serves to disorient us, the readers, so that eventually we become unsure of the place, century, or any other fixed reference point within the stories. The reference we are searching for most of all is the position of Gogol himself, the implied author behind his storehouse of narrators. Yet the sense of security a known point of view would provide constantly eludes us. Gogol specifically chooses a narrative voice that is many voices at once, a stance that ignores the distinctions between different stances. The readers, abandoned without a fixed reference point, are forced either to choose their own and claim it to have been Gogol's intent (as sociologically oriented critics have done for a hundred fifty years), or to understand the technique of an ambiguous narrative viewpoint as an intentional aspect of Gogol's art, as part of his effort to associate the Cossacks with the idea of temporal and spatial barrier crossing.[40]

The shifting stylistic levels of Gogol's narrators emerge as an important element in the growth of the Cossack myth. Some of the narrative stances have been relegated to the catchall *"skaz"* that most critics see as serving only a comic purpose. In *skaz,* a narrative imitates an oral tale and creates the illusion of its narrator's presence not through his acts but through his speech itself.[41] In conjunction with the other narrative stances, *skaz* narrators actually serve a vital function of underlining the fluidity of barriers of all kinds in Cossack works. Up until Gogol's work, narrators of Cossack stories viewed the Cossacks from a cultural and/or historical distance, or they pretended to speak from the Cossack camp itself, as in folk imitations. In Gogol, even in his early Cossack stories, the narrator travels between the two points. We readers follow the narrator, having no other authority, and thus find ourselves on a moving reference frame unaware, like a passenger in a train, that we and not the scenery are in motion.[42] But in this case, Gogol's train does not draw its passenger along in one direction, nor does its progression in space correspond to progression in time.

The narrator of the first chapter of "A Terrible Vengeance," for example, begins in present tense, making a general statement to set the scene. He then switches to past and indicates his position firmly in our present with the phrase "in olden times" *(v starinu).* The remainder of the chapter is related in the past or as quoted material from actors in the past, except for one rhetorical interjection when the narrator seems to speak the thoughts and emotions of the Cossacks: "And how could one not tell stories, having been so long in a foreign land! There all is not right, and the people are different, and there are no Christian churches" (I:244). This type of interjection will become very familiar to the reader of *Taras Bul'ba.* The device pulls the narrator out of a fixed position alongside the reader by making him, momentarily, contemporaneous with the heroes whose actions he describes.

In the last chapter of "A Terrible Vengeance," the narrator introduces a secondary narrator who offers to sing to the gathered crowd about events in a more distant past. Gogol suggests that the reader hears this new narrative style too, by graphically dividing the chapter into short passages separated by special markings, unlike a straight narrative text. Gogol also eliminates quotation marks in this section, so that the reader begins to associate the narrator with the original one located—usually, but not always—in the present and looking back. The reader then looks still further back, almost as though he has joined the crowd around the bandurist. Yet the first narrator returns in the last paragraph, jolting the reader back to his safe distance.

Ultimately, we must understand that the fluctuating relationships between the narrator and his heroes and the narrator and ourselves have become our own relationship with the Cossacks. We at times feel far from them—as in the descriptions of "quaint" old Ukraine and its folksy practices—but at the same time closely associated with them, sharing a common point of view. Yet we tend to see the heroes as though they are moving toward or away from us, and not we from them.

The destruction of barriers of all sorts is further suggested in Gogol's first collection by his use of the fantastic to create a carnival atmosphere. Fantasy obliges the reader to hesitate between two contradictory realms, between a natural and supernatural explanation of the events described.[43] In Gogol's story "The Fair at Sorochintsyi," mere mention of the "red vest" produces concrete experiences of the devil's power, suggesting the penetrability of the limit between the physical and the mental, word and thing.[44] And in "A May Night" the distiller tells a story about his mother-in-law in which the latter grumbles to herself about a voracious eater: "You should just choke on those dumplings" (I:167). No sooner said than done; the man chokes, falls to the floor, and dies.

Time and space are both transformed in the fantastic.[45] In "St. John's Eve" the narrator exclaims: "How time has been stretched! Somewhere God's day has obviously lost its end" (I:40). Grandpa in "The Lost Letter" sits down to a table "as long, perhaps, as the road from Konotop to Baturin" and uses a fork "not much smaller than those used by a peasant to pitch hay" (I:188). We also find the following description of night in "A May Night": "Do you know the Ukrainian night? Oh, but you don't know the Ukrainian night! Take a look into it. The moon gazes out from the center of the sky. The boundless heavenly vault has stretched out, expanded to be more boundless still" (I:159). When the truly fantastic section of this last story begins, the reflection in a pond of a manor house reveals dark shutters turned to transparent glass, suggesting a break in the solidity of the walls. The hero, glancing into the pond, "seemed to pass right into its depth" (I:174). The water then begins to shake, the window shuts, and he finds himself back on the bank. But he feels "some kind of sweet tranquility and a feeling of free space [*razdol'e*] in his heart" (I:175). He finds himself in a world where girls flit about in the mist "like shadows . . . whose bodies were formed as though from transparent clouds and through which shone the silvery moon" (I:176) The hero has evidently passed into a realm where the walls of an abandoned house, the surface of a pond, or the bodies of maidens are no longer impenetrable barriers.[46]

"Vii," a story from *Mirgorod* whose clearly fantastic elements unite it to *Evenings,* blurs the boundary between internal (sexual) fantasies and external reality.[47] In Khoma's case, his fears become so real as actually to cause his death. Yet Gogol's hand continues to hesitate between fantasy and reality on the last page of "Vii," so that neither clearly dominates. A character confuses inner psychology and its external rationalization in the following lines:

> I know why he [Khoma] was done in—it was because he was afraid. If he hadn't been afraid then the witch couldn't have done anything with him. He would have had only to cross himself, spit on her tail and then nothing would have happened. I already know all about it. Why, all the women who sit in the bazaar in Kiev are witches, all of them. (II:218)

The reader of *Evenings* constantly confronts the theme of boundary crossing, yet limits here are not unequivocally transcended.[48] Gogol actually emphasizes the fact that boundaries *do* exist. *Evenings* thus introduces the issue of barriers and potential crossing of thresholds in relation to the Cossacks, but does not yet eliminate all distinctions in a mythic sense. This is left for *Taras Bul'ba*.[49]

Taras Bul'ba, like *Evenings*, boasts a temporally ambiguous narrator who views events alternately from our standpoint and from the heroes'. He begins by merely observing the action in *Taras Bul'ba*. He watches as the two sons return home from Kiev, as Taras taunts them and their mother embraces them. He is conscious of his role as literary agent, for he interrupts a speech of Taras's which he is reporting with the explanation: "Here Bul'ba interjected into his line [*prignat' v stroku,* as though Taras, too, was not speaking but writing] a word that could not be used in print" (II:43).

The narrator continues to demonstrate his formal association with the reader and consequent distance from the Cossacks by describing Cossack customs as a historian:

> The room was decorated according to the taste of that time, about which living hints remain only in the songs and native *dumy* that bearded, blind old men no longer sing in the Ukraine to the gathered people, accompanied by the quiet strumming of the bandura. (II:43–44)

At this point, the narrator clearly resides in the reader's present. He describes the windows as ones which are found "today" only in old churches and speaks of "those daring times" using past-tense verbs. Furthermore, he reinforces his bond with the reader by calling the Cossack sons "our two youngsters" (II:44), as though we are somehow in alliance with him.

Yet the narrator knows the intimate thoughts of his characters. At a point early in the story he begins to talk like the mother. He opens the passage with a literary description in which he employs a poetic simile, but quickly falls into indirect speech or *erlebte Rede:*

She hovered over her children with fervor, passion, and tears, like a gull of the steppe. They are taking her sons, her dear sons, taking them from her so she would never see them again! Who knows, maybe a Tatar will chop off their heads in the first battle and she would not know where their discarded bodies lie, pecked to pieces by a wild bird of prey. . . . (II:50)

Only later in the paragraph does he resort to actual quoted speech.

The narrator speaks Taras's thoughts as well later in the story: "Walking off toward his regiment, Taras wondered vainly where Andrii could have gotten off to; was he taken captive along with the others and bound while sleeping? But no, Andrii wasn't the kind to be taken prisoner alive . . ." (II:110).

Taras's and his fellow Cossacks' speech patterns are easily identified by their emphatic, almost urgent quality, mixed with a strangely lyrical rhetoric:

I would like to tell you, my men, just what a thing is our comradeship. You heard from your fathers and grandfathers how all nations honored our land: she let the Greeks know who she was, she took tribute from Tsargrad, and her cities and churches were rich. And the princes were native Russian princes, our own princes, not Catholic heretics. But the infidels took it all; all of it vanished. Only we old men are left, yes, like a widow after a strong husband, and our country is just like us! That is the kind of time in which we comrades clasped hands in brotherhood! That is what our comradeship stands on! There is no bond holier than comradeship! (II:133)

The narrator adopts these patterns in *erlebte Rede* more and more frequently as he becomes involved in the Cossack exploits. He seems to become excited as he falls into the lyrical, hyperbolic speech patterns of the Cossack characters, marked especially by the use of exclamation points. At these moments he also often switches from his usual simple-past-tense narrative into the present or future:

Everywhere, around the whole field, a brightly colored mixture of people gathered in picturesque bunches. It was obvious from their ruddy complexions that they were forged in battle, and had experienced all sorts of adversity. Yes, that it is, the Sech! [N. B. the switch to present tense] There is the nest from which the proud and free fly out like lions! From there freedom and Cossackdom flow out onto the whole Ukraine! (II:62)

Eagles will swoop down [upon the dead warriors] to tear at and pluck out their Cossack eyes. But there is a great good in such a wide, freely sweeping deathbed! Not one generous deed will perish, and the Cossack glory will not disappear like a bit of powder from a rifle's barrel. . . . (II:131)

89

How the Cossacks threw themselves into the fight! How they all came to blows! How Ataman Kukubenko boiled, seeing that the better half of his unit was no more! (II:136)

The narrator even begins to speak directly to the Cossacks, as though he, too, were on the battlefield: "Cossacks, Cossacks! Do not give up the best flower of your troops . . ." (II:140).

The use of *erlebte Rede* and the confusion of tenses that accompanies it serves, again, to suggest the narrator's—and the Cossacks'—ability to transgress temporal barriers. We the readers can no longer identify the time frame in a paragraph such as the following:

> And a Cossack perished! He vanished for all of Cossack knighthood! No longer to see the Zaporozhian Sech, nor his father's villages, nor the church of God! Nor will the Ukraine see the bravest of her children who undertook to defend her. Old Taras will tear out a gray clump of hair from his forelock and will curse the day and hour when he, to his shame, gave birth to such a son. (II:107)

Taras has clearly already torn his hair at the time of writing, yet the foreshadowing suggests that the narrator's stance is somewhere between the events of Andrii's perishing and Taras's tearing. Perhaps, he seems to indicate, Taras lives sometime *after* the time of writing, even after our own time. In fact, he lives outside of time and ordinary space altogether, in the mythic world of the Cossack. This is the world Gogol bequeathed to writers for at least one hundred more years of Russian literature.

SIX

Conclusion: The Ambivalent Tolstoi

Though it is perhaps the best known of nineteenth-century works with Cossack characters, Lev Tolstoi's (1828–1910) short novel *The Cossacks* (1863) does not fit securely within a study of the myth. Tolstoi describes a Cossack community with which he had personal contact during his military stay in the Caucasus in the early 1850s. Like Pushkin in *The Captain's Daughter,* he begins his tale with the departure of a Russian character from "civilized" Russia en route to the Cossack territory. We assume that the story will again be a romance on the model of Walter Scott; a fictional hero will interact with famous (or infamous) characters against a background of historical and ethnographic detail. In a Scottian historial novel, we expect that the Cossacks will provide the local color rather than stand out as the story's heroes. And, in fact, *The Cossacks* seems to employ the Cossacks for little more than backdrop to the main character's spiritual state.

Tolstoi tends to set his fiction in wide-ranging locales—a Cossack cordon, Petersburg drawing room, Western spa, or peasant village—but the scenery reflects only the heroes' inner quests, heroes who are for the most part wealthy Russians like Tolstoi himself. Tolstoi's approach to background distances the novel from the Cossack myth as much as does Pushkin's fictional editor at the end of *The Captain's Daughter* or the self-conscious quotations from folk poetry that head its chapters. And with both authors, the distance tends to create irony, not exultation.

Tolstoi's interest in the noble soul and his attempts to understand the secrets of love and death, however, distance him from Pushkin as well, and make his short novel more typically romantic than its predecessor.[1] The Cossacks for Tolstoi are milestones on an individual and profoundly private journey. For Pushkin, they are objects in a social setting. While love in Pushkin is a question of loyalty or nobility, in Tolstoi it marks emotional purity. And violent rebellion in the former is of historical interest, of spiritual significance to the latter. But in neither case is the involvement—be it individual or social, aesthetic or spiritual—of Cossacks in the setting a necessary mark of myth. The Cossack backdrop enables Pushkin to take an ironic look at romantic literature; for Tolstoi it is an excuse for, if anything, a counterromance.

The story might be better understood in terms of the tradition of the Caucasus in Russian literature.[2] The original musings of Olenin, the protagonist, concern the mountains and the mountain peoples much more than the Cossacks. His dream of marrying and educating a Circassian (not a Cossack) woman is far indeed from the topoi of the Cossack myth.[3] Here Tolstoi draws from and parodies the Caucasian tales of Mikhail Lermontov and A. A. Marlinskii, as a direct reference to the latter's novel *Ammalat-Bek* suggests (VI:11).[4] Those stories keep the Caucasus at an exotic distance and do not assume that the alien other and known self merge in the mountain people, as they do in the mythic Cossacks.

Nonetheless, important reminders of the Cossack myth do appear. Tolstoi began *The Cossacks* a full decade after Gogol's most explicit enunciation of the myth in *Taras Bul'ba,* and did not finish it for another ten years, yet his variation of the Cossack harks back to the earlier portrayal in *The Captain's Daughter.* If Pushkin can be said to gather the elements of the Cossack hero that Gogol then makes mythic, Tolstoi recapitulates those elements, commenting sometimes ironically on the hero developed in the interim. In fact, *The Cossacks* ultimately if ambivalently propagates Cossack topoi by foregrounding, but in its case *not reconciling,* the contradictory aspects of the heroes which, decades earlier, grew out of the romantic movement and into myth. If in Gogol myth simplifies, then for Tolstoi it complicates. The conflicting ways in which its characters and narrator relate to the Cossack myth prove *The Cossacks* to be another example of Tolstoi's refusal to aggrandize or generalize, whether about history or psychology, national or individual. For Tolstoi, the world that really matters is made up of ordinary and undramatic events. It is essentially systemless, or "messy," as Gary Saul Morson has claimed,[5] and the contradictions which comprise it turn out to be the real "stuff" of life.

Tolstoi substantially revised *The Cossacks* a number of times, experimenting with verse, prose, letters, first- and third-person narratives, and epic.[6] He apparently began with a vision of character, rather than plot or genre. Tolstoi wrote in his diary: "The Cossack is something different— wild, fresh, like a biblical legend," and one critic asserts, "he was referring here not to any particular writing but to a national character."[7]

Olenin interacts with Tolstoi's version of this "wild, fresh legend" in both revery and reality. Like many of Tolstoi's characters, he is literally an orphan (we are told that he lost his parents at an early age, VI:7), and figuratively in search of a spiritual home where he can feel the love and security that elude him in high society.[8] Leaving the glitter of Moscow behind, he arranges to be stationed in the Caucasus, where he is billeted in the home of a Cossack couple and their beautiful daughter. Predictably, Olenin falls in love, but not without continual confrontation with the rest of Cossack society, as it is and as he still imagines it to be. Despite his attempts to dress like the Cossacks, and to assimilate their, as he sees it, natural attitudes toward love and death, he fails to understand the Cossack community, leaving the Caucasus as "orphaned" as he arrived.

Even a brief moment of spiritual communion with the world around him, experienced while out hunting (chap. 20, VI:75–79), does not bring to Olenin the permanent sense of security he seeks and assumes that the Cossacks possess. A reference to James Fenimore Cooper's *The Pathfinder* that immediately precedes the description of his solitary hunt (VI:74), and, culminating the experience, an overintellectualized decision to renounce his own ego (VI:78), suggest that Olenin can do no more than play at being a "literary" noble savage.

But Olenin's failure to transform himself into what is, in his case, only an imaginary construct does not necessarily mean that *The Cossacks* proclaims the failure of the Cossacks as myth. In fact, although the story itself does not always glorify boundless and creative heroism, as we found in Gogol or Mordovtsev or Danilevskii, the irony of its stance toward the Cossacks nonetheless does not destroy the myth. Olenin's romantic and mistakenly simplified view of the Cossack clashes on the one hand with the more realistic picture revealed through the narrative, but also with Tolstoi's guarded admiration of the Cossacks in their more complex portrayal.

The first description of the Cossacks given in a historical aside in chapter 4 calls them a "warlike, beautiful, and rich Russian population of the Old Believers' sect [with] love of freedom, leisure, plunder, and war" (VI:15–16). Regardless of the fact that the account of the Cossacks' presence along the Terek River that accompanies this description is apparently factual, the epithets "warlike," "beautiful," and "rich" and the references to freedom and war rely more on myth than reality. Cossack society may indeed have been more militaristic than was that of the nobles in St. Petersburg, and there may have been great beauty in the physicality of Caucasian Cossack life and dress, but the proliferation of specifically these adjectives erases the complexity that in fact describes societies. That the account comes before Olenin actually reaches the Cossack village, and immediately follows his romantic reveries about potential future adventures, is further indication that the description cannot be read as realistic.[9]

A parodic reading, of course, is possible; Olenin's dreams, whether of Cossacks or Caucasians, are further indications of his spiritual immaturity. But the passage is not delivered in *erlebte Rede,* as is the end of the preceding chapter, with Olenin's enraptured thoughts about the mountains he is approaching (VI:14). Instead, the narrative voice itself turns to mythic praise at this point in *The Cossacks,* relying on traditional Cossack topoi. The lengthy digression stands out in the narrative, both structurally and stylistically. The description purports to be "true," as it is couched in historical and sociological language, but key words evoke an atemporal image of unbounded martial freedom. The reader recalls THE COSSACK.

In his description of Cossack society, the narrator stresses the closeness of the mythic Cossack to his untamed neighbor, the Chechen, and his consequent distance from the Russians. Although a river separates the two mountain communities, it is a river that is repeatedly crossed. And later in the novel one character explicitly mentions that an actual bridge is to be built over the Terek River (VI:51). The expanse from the Cossack homeland to Moscow is not as easily bridged; Olenin's initial trip takes several uncomfortable days by sleigh and cart.

The narrator further mentions the Cossack practice of intermarriage with the surrounding tribeswomen and the adoption of their customs, and claims that "[the Cossack] respects his mountain-dwelling enemy, but despises the [Russian] soldier who is for him a foreign oppressor" (VI:16). Tolstoi here sets up the Cossack as other than the Russian. Yet he also has his anthropologically minded narrator mention how the Cossacks preserve the Russian language and faith "in all its former purity" (VI:15), and speak of their high level of civilization. He seems here to suggest their close relationship to the Russians, not distance from them.[10]

Only the Cossack character of Eroshka is sufficiently well drawn in the novel to present a counterpoint to Olenin, like Pushkin's Pugachev to Grinev. The other Cossacks—Mar'ianka, with whom Olenin falls in love; Lukasha, her fiancé; her parents and the other villagers—are little more than shadows interacting in the background. Eroshka is a highly contradictory character, a former hero now mocked by the younger Cossacks, who acts as an epic bard for the tales of his own past. He can speak the language of the Chechen as well as that of the aristocratic Olenin, and feels comfortable in either society. He alone of the Cossacks displays the mythic ability to reconcile opposites, Russian and exotic. In fact, the other Cossacks of the story turn out to be more mundanely like Olenin than he (or they) imagine.

But Eroshka is an outsider in his own community. Too old to fight, he spends his days drinking, hunting, and reminiscing with the Cossack girls and the Russians stationed in his village. Tolstoi gently pokes fun at Eroshka's drunken nostalgia, at his character's own evocation of the heroic past. Like Mariia in Pushkin's "Poltava," Eroshka is under sway of the Cossack myth, a myth that he himself personifies. Despite the old Cossack's charm, his idealism is anachronistic and unattainable. The world he represents is immensely attractive but it exists only at a distance, like the mountains in which Olenin exults as he approaches the Cossack village. It is as out of place as the narrative digression on the "warlike" and "beautiful" Cossacks in the beginning of the novel.

Ultimately we are faced with Tolstoi's ambivalent attitude toward Eroshka and the Cossack. He, like his readers, is simultaneously attracted and repelled by the coarse and amoral hero.[11] Critics often read *The Cossacks* as a work that debunks the Cossack myth, for Olenin arrives with a romanticized view of the heroes and leaves with a supposedly more realistic one. But Tolstoi's novel in fact betrays a much subtler understanding of the development of the Cossack hero. What changes is not the Cossack character, but Olenin's initial understanding of him as a one-sided, romantic noble savage, alien to Russian man. The readers, and even Olenin to a partial degree, eventually adopt a fuller view of the Cossack as at once self *and* other, brother *and* stranger, thus underlining, not undercutting, the complexity of the myth.

But the myth itself is ambivalent, and Olenin cannot fully assimilate it, for he wants answers and codes, not boundless freedom. Olenin's view of life is thus too doctrinaire and one-dimensional to allow assimilation of the contradictions that myth glorifies, and that, Tolstoi tells us, comprise life. Olenin cannot do what the writer himself wants: to accept and delight in the multiplicity of the world around him and in the disjunction between revery and reality.

In the final analysis, Tolstoi's use of the Cossack, like Pushkin's almost thirty years earlier, is a comment on mythmaking rather than a mythic glorification of the hero. Unlike Pushkin, however, Tolstoi uses irony only to question, not to discard, the myth. Eroshka is vital to Olenin's spiritual development in the story; only through the Cossack and the world he claims to represent can Olenin glimpse the richness of life. But the glimpse is only that, and at the end of the story Eroshka does not bother even to wave goodbye as Olenin leaves the Cossack village.

In his short novel, Tolstoi's choice of the Cossacks as heroes may indeed have been arbitrary, and no doubt not motivated by a Gogolian desire to define the Russian "soul." In fact, a later story, "Khadzhi-Murat" (1912), which concerns the life of a violent Chechen instead of a Cossack, tackles many of the same themes as his Cossack story, but less ambiguously. *The Cossacks* instead betrays Tolstoi's more general yearning for a mythic world devoid of the agony over questions of love and death that so plague his noble heroes. The ambivalent portrayal of Eroshka suggests Tolstoi's inability to convince himself that such an emotionally uncomplicated world can ever exist. But the interplay of contradictory pictures of the Cossacks, whether in Olenin's fantasy, Eroshka's self-congratulatory tales, or the narrator's supposedly objective presentation, also proclaims that myth exists as a real element in people's lives. Our dreams and desires, and the myths we construct in order to organize the chaos of our experiences, only add to the contradictory and messy "stuff" of life.

Although Tolstoi does not accept the Cossack myth whole, by ironic contrast he in fact highlights the many and contradictory images that readers assimilated through nineteenth-century Russian literature. The Cossack is outlaw and frontiersman, warrior and monk, destructive anarchist and maker of myths. Ultimately, the Cossack hero in full form allows the Russians to present themselves as free and bold, in touch with creation itself. That these traits contrast strongly with the dandified, European-educated superfluous man of much nineteenth-century Russian literature does not negate but rather reinforces the potency of the Cossack myth. We may not look like proud warriors now, Russians can say, but it is how we *really* are; our freedom and energy know no bounds.

The historical Cossacks seemed exotic, so romantic writers made them superhuman; they had been politically freer than nineteenth-century Russians, so the writers made them ontologically free of all mortal restrictions. They had lived in the territory of old Rus', and therefore became heirs to Kiev's allegedly pure Slavic spirit. Most of all, the Cossacks were self-sufficient and able to create their world in the manner they deemed worthy. So the hero of literature is not troubled with the contradictions of our daily world, but reconciles them within his vibrant whole. Is he European or Eastern? He is both. Does he live within the Russian state or on the liminal frontier? He does both. Is he grounded in a particular historical period or does he live in mythic time? Again both.

The nineteenth-century Cossacks became THE COSSACK, to return to our initial formulation, through a process of purification, amplification, and ascription to them of traditionally accepted myths of the Russian soul. They live exuberantly, fearlessly, and in harmony with Mother Russia. In the twentieth century, this mythic image will grow ever farther from any Cossacks actually living in the Russian land. It will survive world war and revolutions, only to die in Stalinist literature at the hands of aesthetic and moral norms of a centralized authority, finally and inescapably bounded.

Part Two

The Twentieth Century

Wassily Kandinsky, "Cossacks," 1910–1911. © 1992 ARS, New York/ADAGP, Paris.
Courtesy of Tate Gallery, London/Art Resource, New York.

SEVEN

Introduction: From Myth to History

THE NINETEENTH century left a rich legacy of literary types to twentieth-century Russian writers. In the case of the Cossacks, it bequeathed a character ripe with the possibilities of myth and still replete with the paradoxes and contradictions that gave it depth. The paradoxes were further strengthened by the contrast between the mythic hero—free and independent—and his suppressive military role at the turn of the century, including anti-Semitic pogroms and the quenching of revolutionary activities in 1905. In fact, the public profile of the Cossacks had undergone a major reversal— from freedom fighter to wielder of the knout of oppression.

Already in the nineteenth century, the Cossacks had come to resemble their mythic prototypes in little more than name. Self-rule was virtually denied to the hosts by the middle of the century, and the Cossacks were designated an official hereditary caste, with entrance into or marriage out of it strictly controlled.[1] Agriculture, not raiding, was by then the principal livelihood of the Cossacks, and the legendary warrior-rebels demonstrated their fighting acumen within the confines of the Russian army alone, for which they were subject to special regulations of conscription and service.[2]

Cossack males served as imperial guards or in the army's cavalry, and were relied on for internal as well as external security. Assumed to be loyal supporters of autocracy and Russian nationalism, they were called to suppress the increasingly frequent rebellions within the empire and occasionally required to stand against their fellow soldiers during times of mutiny.[3] But the Cossacks in fact sometimes abetted the mutineers, passively refusing to oppose them if not actively participating. In the Revolution of 1905 and subsequent worker strikes, some Cossack reserve regiments resisted mobilization and mutinied themselves.[4]

Revolutionary propaganda filtered into Cossack villages in the years preceding World War I, and attracted some of the poorer elements and the *inogorodnye*, or non-Cossacks living in Cossack territory. During the nineteenth and early twentieth centuries, the disparity had increased between landless and prosperous Cossacks, so that class differences marked Cossack society no less than Russian society at large. Struggling Cossacks found they had more in common with their poor neighboring peasants than with their own ruling elite.[5]

Still, the nature of the traditional Cossack communities—close-knit and hereditary—insulated them somewhat from revolutionary disaffection.[6] When it came to the threat of losing inherited family property, Cossack unity ran higher than either tsarist loyalty or proletarian fervor. Well into the Civil War following the Revolution of 1917, more than one regiment suffered from "'Cossack sickness', an unwillingness to stray far from its home stanitsa [Cossack village]."[7] The Cossacks' reluctance to roam freely contrasts sharply with their mythic legacy. Their ancestors had originally escaped to the Zaporozh'e or the Don steppes to avoid enslavement to the land, and had rejected agriculture in favor of a marauding lifestyle. A reversal in consciousness had clearly taken place.

The beginning of war with Germany rekindled Russian nationalism among the Cossacks. But as they did for the rest of the population, hardships at the front and home turned many against the imperial war policies. When revolution broke out in Petrograd, Cossacks were again called in to suppress it, but in significant instances they refused to intervene. Cossacks began to talk seriously in the next few years of secession from the Russian regime, be it imperial, provisional, or Bolshevik, and of the reassertion of their pre-Petrine independence.[8]

In 1918, a provisional Don government was formed among the Cossacks under Petr Nikolaevich Krasnov as military ataman. Krasnov had been commander of a Cossack brigade in World War I, and involved with A. F. Kerenskii's failing provisional government in Petrograd in the fall of 1917. When the Bolsheviks defeated Kerenskii, Krasnov vowed not to oppose the new regime. He nonetheless formed a hostile army on the Don, where many Cossacks feared for the preservation of their privileges and sought to create an autonomous state. In need of financial support, Krasnov's Cossacks joined with the Union of the Southeast and General A. I. Denikin's anti-Bolshevik White Army. With the eventual defeat of the Whites, Krasnov fled to Europe, where he collaborated with the Germans in World War II. He was returned to the Soviet Union after the war and executed in 1947.

For the most part, Cossacks sided with the Whites in the Civil War, although their regional interests generally took precedence over the aspirations of non-Cossack White generals, and they often did not fight as effectively away from the home territory as for it.[9] Some Cossacks did join the Reds, particularly in the south under the leadership of Semen Mikhailovich Budennyi, a non-Cossack general.

The Civil War devastated Cossack communities; it tore families apart and ravaged crops, for much of the fighting took place in Cossack territory. The destruction of the land aided neither the Whites nor the Reds, and turned many Cossacks against both. It was to take many years for the fertile Don and Kuban regions to reattain their pre–World War I productivity.

By 1920 the Bolsheviks had asserted control in European Russia. Early that year the First All-Russian Congress of Working Cossackdom was convened in Moscow. It declared the Cossacks an integral part of the Russian people—no longer a separate nationality—and officially disbanded the hosts.[10] Cossacks in Siberia and the east, where the Whites were not defeated for another two years, continued to oppose the new Soviet regime, although poorer elements again joined the Reds. A large number of Cossacks emigrated in those early years, and more after the total demise of the Whites. The remaining Cossacks fell victim to the repeated famines of the twenties, as well as to Stalin's forced collectivization policies.

During World War II, Cossack units were restored to the Soviet Army, although as suggested in Part 1, they included as many non-Cossacks as legitimate Cossacks, and were designed solely for patriotic appeal. General Budennyi himself reappeared in 1936 under the label of "true son of the Don," falsely implying actual Cossack heritage.[11] Traditional Cossack reliance on cavalry, however, no longer had a place in modern warfare. The parading of Cossack dress and mount served only to remind soldiers of the myth of bravery associated with the heroes of old. Their actual military use was minimal.

More dramatic, but not necessarily of more military significance, were the Cossacks who fought against the Soviets, many under the command of the now Nazi collaborator Krasnov or the Soviet deserter General A. A. Vlasov.[12] As a whole, however, the Cossacks who still identified themselves as such sided with the motherland, if not the Soviets per se,[13] and were indistinguishable from their fellow soldiers and farmers.

The Literary Hero

It is against this historical background that we must consider both pre- and postrevolutionary writers who chose to glorify Cossack heroes. The actual Cossacks had become largely associated with their own strong regional and agricultural interests and/or with the imperial and White armies. Although not always justly, they became known for their reactionary conservatism, their willingness to obey orders, and their violent oppressive tactics. It is testimony to the strength and appeal of the myth that the Cossack hero of literature remained so strongly dependent on his nineteenth-century predecessor. The ways in which he did adapt to the changing cultural and historical reality around him, however, are significant.

The works in which Cossacks appear as protagonists—leaving aside those in which Cossack units play a role as White enemies but do not enter the main stage of the narrative—fall into two major, and contradictory, categories. On the one hand, some writers and poets adopt the myth in all its splendor. They equate the Cossacks with bold, aggressive spirit, and by extension with their own creative talent. Thus, the Cossacks' mythic energy becomes a symbol of the rebelliousness of modernist poetics, and their contradictory nature is felt to represent the chaotic revolutionary times of which/ in which the poets write. The actual Cossack as oppressor rests in the background for these writers, who include Isaak Babel in his *Red Cavalry* cycle, the Futurists Velimir Khlebnikov and his friend Vasilii Kamenskii, and the iconoclastic poet Marina Tsvetaeva. Their adaptations of the myth, and particularly the ways it relates to poetic creativity, will be discussed in the following two chapters.

The second type must be kept in mind, however, while exploring the former. This adaptation of the myth eventually leads to the numerous and lengthy historical novels of the Soviet period that supposedly report the origins of revolutionary spirit under the guidance of Cossack figures. Rather than strengthening the myth, these works actually represent its death, for they contribute to the wholesale transfer of topoi from the Cossack onto a more politically appropriate hero: the Bolshevik. Razin and Pugachev in these novels, by the Soviet writers Stepan Zlobin, Viacheslav Shishkov, and Dmitrii Petrov, are Cossacks in name only. They have become allegorical symbols of the "new man," lending their Cossack characteristics and sometimes their titles, but not their contradictory mythic attraction.

This movement is particularly apparent in the Soviet classic *Chapaev* by Dmitrii Furmanov, to be discussed in Chapter 11, and in the Nobel Prize-winning *The Quiet Don* by Mikhail Sholokhov. The latter, to which Chapter 10 is devoted, chronicles the Cossack hero's deterioration and death in direct contrast to the growth of the Bolshevik hero. Both these novels are precursors to the socialist realist historical narrative, requiring the so-called realistic depiction of society in its revolutionary development. In socialist realism, only topics that support the establishment of socialism are acceptable. The contortions required to fit any historical character, and the Cossacks most of all, within the dictates of the official doctrine help explain the eventual disappearance of the heroes. Rarely was the historical Cossack a Bolshevik. In most cases he was not even a revolutionary. And although the hero of the Cossack myth is freedom-loving, freedom is defined apolitically and ahistorically.

Twentieth-century treatments of both types of Cossacks show a much greater interest in Sten'ka Razin than did those of the previous century. Although Pushkin had written imitations of Razin songs, the brigand-rebel had largely remained in the province of folk poetry, away from belles lettres. By the end of the nineteenth century he appears fairly frequently in cheap popular chapbook-like publications, or *lubki,* aimed at the newly literate lower classes. But the fact that these publications showed much greater interest in Ermak, a hero who never really moved into more sophisticated literature, suggests that they had little influence on more highbrow literature.[14] Razin's movement into the poetry and prose of educated Russians in the twentieth century seems to have another, perhaps more political explanation.

Russian cultural life in the first two decades of this century was dominated by an ever-growing sense of the inevitability of revolution. The belated establishment of a parliament after the Revolution of 1905 and the crisis of World War I provided temporary respites, but did not redirect the growing revolutionary fervor. In their search for appropriate representations of the revolutionary spirit that they sensed, writers and poets turned to the Cossacks and to their flashiest of historical leaders, Sten'ka Razin.

Razin's revolts were seen as uprisings of the downtrodden *narod,* as was, ideologically at least, the Russian revolutionary movement in this century. The title of a narrative poem about Razin by the Futurist poet Vasilii Kamenskii, *Native Heart—Sten'ka Razin,* suggests this association. In it, the "native" Razin fights

> For the people—for the poorly clad peasants and the poor
> And for my brave Rus'—
> (Za narod—za sermiazhnyi da bednyi
> Da za Rus' udaluiu svoiu—)[15]

This motif is obviously a continuation of the topos of Cossack as Russian soul, especially with this passage's reference to ancient Rus'. Adaptation is apparent, however, in the use of the topos within the work as a whole. The Cossack is no longer a simple expression of the Russian essence. He is a call to arms. *Sten'ka Razin,* Kamenskii's later poem based on *Native Heart,* ends on a typical rallying cry from Razin's day:

> Rabble to the bow!
> For Stepan Razin!
> (Saryn' na kichku!
> Za Stepana Razina!)[16]

And informs us:

We will start to remember
The Sun-Sten'ka: We are cut from Sten'ka's mold.
(Stanem pomnit'
Solntse-Sten'ku: My—ot kosti Sten'ki kost'.)[17]

We are all Sten'ka Razins, and must all take up the rebellious cause, claims the poet. The cause for Kamenskii and poets like him was not necessarily political revolt (although it could be), but more often artistic and cultural. Russian language, society, and consciousness all needed to be shaken up, as Razin had done to the tsarist regime. On the one hand the Cossack-rebel as symbol reflected the violent times, and on the other he represented the vanguard of that violence necessary for change.

Kamenskii's prerevolutionary poetry does not equate the rebelliousness of Razin specifically with the Bolsheviks, but later works, his and others', most assuredly do. Although Pugachev, Razin, and their fellow Cossacks most often saw their revolt as one against the landowners and boyars, not against the institution of monarchy per se, their own nonaristocratic origins and the grass-roots nature of their support allowed them to slip easily into the role of Bolshevik prototype. From rebel to revolutionary is only a small rhetorical leap. Characteristically, postrevolutionary literature played down the Cossack origins of these historic rebels and emphasized their peasant roots. Some texts, particularly from the more established Soviet years, omitted the term "Cossack" altogether. The former heroes, for whom the label "Cossack" had tremendous rhetorical strength, gradually became simple military leaders of the peasant masses.

Razin, therefore, comes into his own in the twentieth century as an organizer of peasant uprisings. In actuality more like anarchic brigandage, his rebellion could be made to look like protorevolution. The effort to remake the Cossack hero Pugachev into a proto-Bolshevik is equally pronounced in early Soviet literature. Books and essays published in the twenties attempt to prove that Pugachev was not at all the anarchist, bloodthirsty villain-hero of previous histories, including Pushkin's, but a well-organized, rational leader of the unjustly exploited peasants. And since a Marxist revolution technically rests on support of the urban workers, researchers rediscovered Pugachev's apparent role in the fomenting of dissent among the somewhat anachronistic proletariat.[18] Again, his Cossack origins are downplayed, his connection to the masses trumpeted. As an editor of the newly opened Pugachev archives wrote in the twenties:

When considering the movement [of the Iaik Cossacks and the nationals] as revolutionary, we speak out against the overevaluation of the leading role of Cossackdom. It is worthwhile remembering that Cossacks, like the miners, comprised a part of the same peasantry.[19]

The author of these lines further suggests that contemporary reporters used the term "Cossack" in simple opposition to a "soldier" of Catherine's army, and did not refer to any organized group. A Cossack became any armed peasant who objected to class and/or tsarist domination.

Returning to Razin, we can suggest a more literary explanation as well as a political one for twentieth-century interest in his character: a renewed fascination with folk poetry. The interest in folk forms accompanied a sense of growing nationalism, with its focus on the *narod,* now partially urbanized. This tendency is particularly evident among the Futurist poets, who sought to revitalize both the Russian language and the available pool of poetic images by turning to old Slavic word roots and to peasant folk literature. This use of folk poetry is both like and unlike the love affair of the romantics with the *narod* one hundred years earlier. Turning to Cossack songs and tales for inspiration, writers of the early nineteenth century unconsciously blurred the boundaries between fiction and history, assuming they were reporting the truth about the people. In the recapturing of folk tradition by early-twentieth-century writers, however, there was little unconsciousness about the crossing of generic boundaries. By mixing forms, the Futurists set out not to report, and not simply to reevoke the soul of the *narod,* but to create a new and perhaps more vital connection of the Russian people to its own present, past, and future.

Twentieth-century writers had the advantage of even more material than their romantic predecessors and, more important, were able to blend with the folk poetry and their own invention references to the "high" literature of Gogol, Pushkin, and Tolstoi. The Sech à la *Taras Bul'ba* merges with the brigand boats of the folk hero.

Razin was recaptured by this neoromantic interest in the *narod,* for songs about him and his exploits were especially widespread. Texts with Razin as hero tend to replace some of the imagery inherited from *Taras Bul'ba* and other works set in Ukrainian locales with imagery specifically associated with Razin's career. In particular, the Volga stands in the place of the steppe. All the attributes of the steppe—its role as mother, its expansiveness, its nurturing of life—transfer unambiguously onto the new location: the endless, eternal, and native Volga.

The Razin story, unlike tales of other Cossacks, includes and even centers on a male-female liaison. According to tradition, Razin brings home a Persian girl from his famous expedition across the Caspian Sea. When his men complain that their ataman has been led astray by his passion, he drowns her in the Volga, his feelings for Cossackdom apparently exceeding any love for the girl. Some stories claim that it was also a woman, in fact a wife, who betrayed Razin because of jealousy and caused his capture by the Russian authorities.[20] Thus the topos of woman as threat still dominates, for contact

105

with one female threatens to turn the Cossack into a *baba* and must result in her death, while contact with the other leads to Razin's own execution.

As with the Cossack stories of the nineteenth century, Razin refers repeatedly to the land as the Cossacks' mother and fiancée.[21] Razin himself is called "father" by his fellow Cossacks. Here again a Cossack abandons his earthly female companion and weds instead the limitless outdoors, often in the guise of the steppe, but in the case of Razin, the Volga River.

A final difference between nineteenth- and twentieth-century uses of the Cossack hero is the proliferation of genres in which he appears. In the past century, the Cossack myth was established to some extent in lyrics, but mostly in histories, narrative poems, and novels. In this century he waves his sword in short story cycles, sketches, plays, film scenarios, and poems. The explosion of genres in part results from the freedom of experiment heralded by modern art as a whole. It is also an important stage in the development of the myth, for the image of the Cossack had grown so solid by the end of the eighteen hundreds that writers no longer had to embed him in a strongly narrative context. The story did not have to be retold each time, for the hero himself carried all the associations of the myth.

The return of the Cossack to the lengthy historical novel in the Soviet period may be seen as a throwback to the nineteenth-century narrative tradition. These Soviet classics of the Stalinist period replay the lives of Razin and Pugachev without the added interest of stylistic experimentation. That the novels grew into trilogies, and each trilogy filled huge volumes, is an ironic manifestation of a myth gone wild. But epic length does not substitute for mythic grandeur, or for the energy of creative ambivalence.

The twentieth century adopted the Cossack in all his resplendent glory. Although the hero loses his mythic aura by the forties and fifties, earlier in the century he appears as the attractive representative of Russia's own inner energy. For many early-twentieth-century writers he still stood for the soul of Russia, the true, spontaneous spirit of the Russian male. Petr Struve argued in 1909 that the Cossacks were the spiritual ancestors of the writers and cultural representatives of the intelligentsia: "After the Cossacks had failed in their role as a revolutionary factor, a new element in Russian life evolved. However unlike the Cossacks socially, it replaced them politically and became their historical successor. This element was the intelligentsia."[22]

The Cossack myth, as Roland Barthes might say, had become fully naturalized; the epithet *kazak* had come to connote the liminal energy of the Cossack of nineteenth- and early-twentieth-century literature, with destruction riding uneasily in the background.

EIGHT

Isaak Babel and His Red Cavalry Cossacks

IN HIS *A History of Russian Literature,* D. S. Mirsky praises *Taras Bul'ba* with an enthusiasm rare among students of Gogol. The novel is "heroic, frankly and openly heroic," he writes, and "its place in Russian literature is unique—it has had no imitators or followers (except, perhaps, Babel in his stories of the Red Army)."[1] Maksim Gor'kii also suggested the comparison of Gogol and Isaak Babel (1894–41), but with little elaboration. He defended Babel, who had recently been attacked in the press, by claiming that Babel's Cossacks were bolder even than Gogol's.[2]

A critical tradition similarly links Babel with Tolstoi. "Like Tolstoi," writes Steven Marcus, "he [Babel] saw in the Cossacks a conjunction of beauty and fierceness, in which their athleticism gave grace to their aggressiveness."[3] In this reading, Babel's *Red Cavalry* is firmly planted within the Cossack tradition, but the myth is reduced to a unidimensional manifestation of the noble savage.

Babel's own approach was more complex. When asked in 1937 to name his favorite author, Babel expressed his increasing preference for the writings of Tolstoi, and particularly the epic story "Khadzhi Murat."[4] Babel explained his attraction to Tolstoi's work:

A current flows unobstructed from the earth, directly through his hands, straight to the paper, and completely and mercilessly tears down all veils with the sense of truth. Moreover, as this truth makes its appearance, it clothes itself in transparent and beautiful dress.[5]

In Babel's praise of Tolstoi, we cannot help but remember Gogol's aesthetic statements in "About Little Russian Songs" and "Sculpture, Painting, Music" from *Arabesques.* The art described is spontaneous, like the Cossack songs, and violent like the Cossacks themselves and like music, which Gogol considered the highest form of art. In the same interview, Babel cited Sho-lokhov, author of *The Quiet Don,* as his favorite contemporary writer, and praised him for writing "heatedly" *(goriacho),* the term Gogol applied to his own work on the Cossacks.

Babel's debt to Gogol, specifically to his early Cossack works, is made explicit in only one story, "Odessa":[6] "It seems to me that there must come—and soon—the productive and life-creating influence of the Russian South." He continues: "Do you remember the fecund sun of Gogol, a writer from the Ukraine? But if such descriptions existed, they were only an episode. That episode was overtaken by 'The Nose,' 'The Portrait,' and 'Notes of a Mad-man.'"[7] Babel calls for a writer who can recreate the spirit of Gogol's early Ukrainian stories, a spirit absent in the later northern tales, and implicitly issues his challenge as contender for the title of successor to Gogol's "fecund sun."

There can be no question that in creating his own Cossacks, Babel bor-rowed much of the baggage of Gogol's myth. The heroes of *Red Cavalry* resemble Taras Bul'ba and his Cossack comrades much more closely than they do General Budennyi and the real Cossack cavalry of Babel's own expe-rience in the Red Army. Babel enlisted in the army in 1917 and served on the Romanian front before contracting malaria.[8] He subsequently worked in various capacities for the new government during the early years of the Civil War, including propagandist for the newspaper the *Red Cavalryman.* During the war with Poland in 1920, Babel was assigned to Budennyi's First Cavalry, and spent several months living closely with Budennyi's Cossacks under the assumed name Kiril Vasilevich Liutov, the name he would give to the prin-cipal narrator in *Red Cavalry.*[9] He wrote articles for the division's propa-ganda sheet, as well as drafts of stories (lost during the campaign), and a diary soon transformed into *Red Cavalry.* Claiming instructions from Gor'kii, Babel joined the army in an effort to "go to the people," and to gather material for his craft.[10] The names, places, and situations in which his Cos-sack characters interact indeed grew from this material, but realism was far from Babel's preferred mode. As Mirsky asserts, his Cossacks are as mythi-cally heroic as Gogol's.

The biographies of Gogol and Babel are strikingly similar. Both writers were born and spent their youth outside Russia proper, in the southwestern region of the empire. Both were exposed to religious tradition and to liter-ature at an early age, impressions that were to shape their future art, and both moved to Petersburg as young men, to integrate into the cultural, Euro-peanized capital of the Russian state. Neither achieved immediate success as a writer, but both were lucky enough to receive encouragement from the most established writers of the time, Pushkin and Gor'kii, respectively. Ultimately, their works were widely published and duly acclaimed, and they remain popular to this day.[11]

Neither writer produced a large body of work, partly because of their untimely deaths,[12] but more centrally because of their perfectionism. Both were compulsive rewriters. In a letter to his friend Pogodin, Gogol calls his difficulty in writing "mental constipation."[13] And Babel's often quoted line from the story "Guy de Maupassant" ("No iron can enter into the human heart as chillingly as a period accurately placed")[14] suggests the attention that he lavished on the execution of his stories. Konstantin Paustovskii recalls his friend's perfectionism in "A Few Words about Babel":

> He hardly ever said "I am writing," but rather, "I am composing." . . . He wrote slowly and always put off handing in his manuscripts. He lived in a constant panic at the thought of words that could no longer be altered, and he was always trying to gain time—just a few more days, or even hours—so that he could sit over his manuscript a little longer and go on polishing, with no one pressing him or getting in his way.[15]

Dvoedushie

The two writers share an even more salient trait, and one that most likely affected their choice of Cossack heroes. Both Babel and Gogol bore a dual national allegiance: Gogol to Ukraine and to Russia, Babel to Russia and the Jews. As a Ukrainian in Petersburg of the 1830s, Gogol rode the crest of Russia's romantic fascination with its neighbor. *Dvoedushie* (literally, two-souledness, but in some circles carrying the connotation of double-dealing) was extremely fashionable at the time, and Gogol could claim an exotic southern temperament while flaunting his northern sophistication. He asserted that the two sides of his heritage were fully integrated,[16] although we have seen that his choice of Cossack characters would suggest otherwise. The mythic heroes served to reconcile that which is in fact disparate and contradictory.

As was the case with Gogol, Babel's own efforts to reconcile opposing heritages created difficulties in his writing. Although as a child Babel had learned Hebrew and some Yiddish, his parents' mother tongue, he decided to write his first stories in French. The ultimate choice of Russian as his literary language may then have been an attempt, as Renato Poggioli believes, "not merely to escape from the ghetto, but to turn, through Russia, to Europe and the West."[17] But Babel's choice of Russian was as much a matter of tone as theme. At the time he began writing, Yiddish literature was still closely tied to folk sources on the one hand, and to the European realist tradition on the other. But Babel was attracted to modern experimental prose, both Western European and Russian. (Although a modernist school of Yiddish literature did flourish in Kiev in the twenties, Babel was the model for, not student of, those writers.)[18]

Odessa, Babel's hometown, produced a circle of talented writers, some of them Jewish like Babel, who were to form the core of the new Soviet literature when they, and the century, reached their twenties. This group included Babel's friend Konstantin Paustovskii, Valentin Kataev, Iurii Olesha, and I'lf and Petrov, the early Soviet satirists. For all of them, the idiom was Russian. Like Gogol before him, Babel adopted the dominant cultural idiom of his time not as an escape from his unique experience, but as a mediating gesture that broadened both his readership and his cultural base.[19] Very few of his stories fail to include Jewish references, transformed but not eliminated by his choice of style and language.

Babel never rejected his Jewishness, and the tension of his dual nationality permeates his fiction. Liutov in *Red Cavalry* constantly feels other than any group he confronts. He struggles with the awareness of his Jewishness in the eyes of the Cossacks, and Russianness in the eyes of the Polish Jews and Catholics he meets.[20] As did Gogol, Babel set as a major problem the possible reconciliation of these opposing characteristics, as synecdoche for all alienating oppositions. The Cossack works of both men express a synthetic ideal that contrasts sharply to the fragmented world around them, and the intensity of these two writers thus draws from the centrality of the mythic process in their works.

And yet Babel and his literary predecessor differed in a major way. Although certainly not unique, the Ukrainian Gogol was nonetheless an oddity in Petersburg, where he consciously exploited his otherness as an aesthetic category. Babel, however, was far from unusual. Many members of the revolutionary leadership and the new Soviet intelligentsia were Jews, among them Averbakh, Kamenev, and Zinov'ev. These political leaders were Bolsheviks first, Russians second, and Jews a distant third. Many revolutionaries, among them Lev Davidovich Bronshtein (Trotskii), changed their obviously Jewish-sounding names, and rejected both their religious and their cultural heritage. To be pro-Bolshevik in the first years of the Revolution meant to be international, not parochial and ethnocentric. Later, when internationalism (or cosmopolitanism) became anathema, to be pro-Bolshevik came to mean insularly nationalistic, and largely Russian. It never meant being a Jew. Babel's Jewish heritage was thus far from exotic on the one hand, and allegedly discarded by the Revolution on the other. Yet his stories and letters indicate that he could not escape the contradictions of dual allegiance, and he suffered them in his life as well as his art.

Babel's *dvoedushie,* oscillating between Russian culture and Jewish background, did not encompass any claim to Cossack inheritance. Gogol's family myth included descent from a well-known Cossack, and his Ukrainian affiliation indirectly linked him to the glorious Cossack past. Babel, on the other hand, was a member of an ethnic group persecuted by the historical Cossacks, and ridiculed or condemned in the Cossack fiction that Gogol made famous. His glorification of the Cossack heroes in *Red Cavalry* clearly derives from the tradition of *Taras Bul'ba;* but Babel's Cossacks occupy a much different dimension because of his own cultural and historical situation. Babel went beyond the role of mythologizer, one who naturally accepts and promotes the reconciliation offered by myth, to that of mythologist, or myth analyst. He examined the myth from his Jewish distance, not necessarily rejecting it, but putting it to the test of contemporary reality.

Babel's distanced stance led to adaptations of the myth. Not only did he place a greater emphasis on the relationship between Cossack and creative artist, he also tested the mythic topoi by extending them onto characters other than Cossacks. Gogol wrote of heroes at odds with the manifest aspects of our mundane world; Babel of a heroic world that infuses the otherwise mundane individual. Although he did not spare descriptions of the often grotesque and arbitrary nature of that world, he refused to condemn it. Reality may be cruel, but it is marvelous as well.

The Cossack Topoi Dispersed

The setting of *Red Cavalry* is a world turned upside down, a liminal realm where all characters, though immersed in destruction, can experience renewal. The tone is set by the first story, "Crossing the Zbruch." Nature itself exudes passion, largely marked by the multiplicity of colors: purple poppies (polia purpurnogo maka), yellowing rye (veter igraet v zhelteiushchei rzhi), pearly fog (zhemchuzhnyi tuman), flowery slopes (tsvetistye prigorki), orange sun (oranzhevoe solntse), blackening Zbruch (pochernevshii Zbruch). The vivid visual description gives way to an aural one, with a large number of musical references, the art form previously associated with Cossack vivacity: the sonorous torrents (zvuchnye potoki), someone's ringing defamation (Kto-to tonet i zvonko porochit bogoroditsu), the river full of humming, whistling, and song (Reka useiana chernymi kvadratami teleg, ona polna gula, svista i pesen, gremiashchikh poverkh lunnykh zmei i siiaiushchikh iam) (23).

The first page of the story describes the vibrant landscape at all stages of the day, but the introduction of a temporal element recalls Gogol's technique that destroys instead of establishes historicity. The story begins like a dispassionate military dispatch:

> The commander of Division Six reported that Novograd-Volynsk was taken today at dawn. The staff left Krapivno and our transport stretched out like a noisy rearguard along the highway running from Brest to Warsaw, built on peasant bones by Nicholas the First. (23)

The first line identifies the division in question and the place of its maneuvers, information that also locates the action in time, for Novograd-Volynsk was a major arena in the Russo-Polish war of 1920. The reference to Nicholas the First widens the historical perspective. The present invasion becomes only one in a repetitive cycle that began even before Nicholas, for the reference to peasant bones also recalls Peter the Great's sacrifice of native labor to the establishment of his westward-looking capital of Sankt Peterburg. This string of associations backward into history forces the reader to lose his grounding in a particular historical moment.

The second paragraph refers in sequence to dawn, noon, evening, and night, setting up for the reader a progression through the day. Yet Babel negates movement through the repetitive ornateness of the paragraph, and the final sense is one of stasis.[21] The atmosphere of Babel's stories has often been compared to the paintings of Chagall:

> The space of both artists is color without a boundary, none even between heaven and earth. In this continuum of color there float images—some beautiful, some sordid; some delicately ethereal, some coarsely naturalistic; images of the peasants and Jews of Red Russia, their little towns, their huts, their horses and their cattle; and the moon in the most incredible, yet so real shades of color.[22]

As Victor Terras observes in this quotation, Babel creates a world that knows no barriers, a type of permanent liminality. Things and people trangress the restrictions normally imposed by gravity, the march of time, or the distinctions between discrete objects. Heaven is juxtaposed with earth, beautiful with sordid, incredible with real, and thus Babel creates a picture of a mythical realm.

Babel frustrates the readers' expectations of temporal progression in "Crossing the Zbruch" in order to indicate that the crossing referred to in the title is not from place to place, and certainly not simply from Russia into Poland as sometimes suggested (the title has been incorrectly translated as "Crossing into Poland"), but into a new realm altogether. The transgression of the spatial boundary represented by the river is the first of many in the cycle. That the actual crossing takes place at sunset, as does the action in so many of the stories,[23] suggests as well the temporal threshold between clear day and obscure night. On the other side, we find ourselves abandoned by normal referents, in a place where characters differ from our mundane world, and where all share in liminal aspects before associated only with the Cossacks.[24] The myth of the Cossacks, with its boundlessness, wholeness, and vitality, extends throughout the world of *Red Cavalry*.

Provoked by mention of the Jewish holiday of Passover in the story ("shards of secret pottery used by Jews once a year, on the Passover," 24), one critic suggests we compare the Zbruch to the biblical Red Sea: "The Zbruch is a symbolic boundary which relates the crossing to the Exodus from Egypt, with all the overtones of redemption in the Passover story."[25] Although he does not draw the parallel, in light of the myth we must recall the Cossacks of *Taras Bul'ba* who cross the Dnestr, like the Red Sea, and exit out of history into myth.

At Passover, Jews remember the historical Exodus from Egypt, but relate the story as if it were in the present. The Passover narrative is told largely in the first person; each year the participants in the seder recite: "In every generation one must look upon himself as if he personally had come out of Egypt, as the Bible says: 'And thou shalt tell thy son on that day, saying, it is because of that which the Eternal did to *me* when *I* went forth from Egypt.'"[26] Passover offers ritual renewal, when historical events are placed in an atemporal light. To have the Cossacks' transgression of their first boundary in *Red Cavalry* take place during this mythic time raises them as well to the level of myth. They cross over into a realm in which we confront reminders of at least ritual messianic reunion.[27]

"Crossing the Zbruch" ends with a Jewish girl's rhetorical cry, spoken "with terrible strength" (24). We would expect both the rhetoric and the potency from a Cossack, not a Jew. Yet Cossack heroism in this particular story appears only in a dream, albeit one that contains a reference to the heroes of *The Iliad* in the eyes that fall out of the head of the warrior, a common epic wound: "I dream about the commander of the sixth division. He is chasing the brigade commander on a heavy stallion and plunges two bullets between his eyes. The bullets pierce the brigade commander's head and both eyes fall out onto the earth" (24). But the Cossacks all appear puppetlike in this story, including the narrator, whom ironically we assume at this point to be a Cossack like his fellow cavalrymen. He is fidgety and negative, and frightened by his own nightmare.

By conferring a heroic stance on the girl instead of on the Cossack, Babel blurs the boundaries between the characters. On the one hand each character seems chosen from a stock repertory, almost like eighteenth-century puppet plays in which Cossacks play a clearly defined brave and exotic

113

role.[28] The Jews "jump about in silence like monkeys or Japanese at the circus" (24); the Cossack Savitskii pursues an enemy on a heavy stallion and "plunges two bullets into his eyes" (24). Yet already here in the first story Babel merges traits from one group onto another, a form of barrier crossing but one that could confuse the mythic image rather than clarify it. The girl is the one who embodies rebirth in the midst of destruction, for she carries a child in her womb as she cares for the corpse of her father. She is the one who calls out the challenge for heroism.

Babel's mythic motifs in *Red Cavalry* are wandering motifs. All the elements are present but they do not relate always to the Cossacks alone, as though his world as a whole is boundless and confers majesty on the heroes instead of the heroes on the world. In the second story, Babel presents us with a Polish Catholic who shares Cossack qualities: he moves "fiercely" *(iarostno);* his size is like a giant *(ispolin);* he acts "without pity" *(bez sozhaleniia);* he drinks and wears a "costume." (The wearing of strange clothing in *Red Cavalry* is generally associated with the Cossacks.)[29] The narrator in this story is first called *pan* as though he were Polish, then *tovarishch* as though he were Bolshevik. And we still do not know in this story that he is not a Cossack and, as we will discover, in many ways is the antithesis of the Cossack heroes. Yet here he calls himself a "violent intruder" and goes off, ironically into a church, to rejoin his comrades.

We can best discover the diffusion of topoi into non-Cossack characters in a cycle of stories—"Gedali," "The Rebbe," "The Rebbe's Son"—that is embedded within *Red Cavalry*. These three stories present the Jews of Poland, ugly and pathetic, but inexplicably attractive to Liutov, and made so to the readers as well. Critics often claim that Babel uses the Jewish characters to demonstrate his true allegiance to the values of his own past. Or, conversely, they assert that the portrayal of dying Jewish culture proves Babel's effort to embrace the new secular world of the Revolution. On more careful examination, we find that Gedali and his friends share many traits with the Cossacks, including their essential spirit of life. They are not contrasted to but compared with the mythic Cossacks. Babel makes the connection between Jew and Cossack explicit elsewhere, for certainly the Jews of Babel's Odessa stories, written at about the same time as *Red Cavalry*, differ from the Cossacks in name only. Benia Krik, the Jewish gangster of "The King" and "How It Was Done in Odessa," "was passionate, and passion rules the universe" (162).

The three stories of the minicycle describe the Hasidim of Eastern Europe. The title character of the central story is himself a Hasidic rebbe. A rebbe *(rabbi,* not *ravvin* or *ravvi,* in Russian) is the charismatic leader of a Hasidic community, not a traditional Jewish rabbi, as usually translated.[30] He represents the Hasidic movement that swept through Ukraine and Poland in the eighteenth century, still the heyday of Cossackdom, with its message of renewal and of the access of all human beings to the divine life-force. Hasidic Jews retained the practices of traditional observance, but claimed to reinfuse them with life, music, and joy. They rebelled against the ossified old order, as did the latter-day revolutionaries to whom they are here compared.

Liutov's attraction to these particular Jews stems from his general desire to participate in the paradoxical intensity of their world, just as he yearns to join the Cossacks in their immediate experience of life. "I roam around Zhitomir," says the narrator in "Gedali," "in search of the shy star [of Sabbath devotion]. Jews with beards like the prophets, with passionate rags (s borodami prorokov, so strastnymi lokhmot'iami) on their sunken chests sell chalk, blueing, and wicks by the yellow and indifferent walls of the ancient synagogue" (46). Here Liutov meets Gedali, the old Jew who proclaims a revolution that will be integrated with the Sabbath. As one critic notices, Babel finds a vital connection between the Cossacks of *Red Cavalry* and "elements of the Jewish tradition he could accept, elements of prophetic fervor and revolutionary awareness."[31]

Like the Cossacks, the Hasidic Jews of *Red Cavalry* form an all-male community. Both Gedali and the rebbe's son refer to "Mother," but only as an abstraction, a compelling force much like the fiancée-steppe of the Cossacks. Women play little role in the public or communal aspects of traditional Judaism. Babel stresses the Hasidic male's self-sufficiency when he presents a scenario in which life itself passes from male to male, as Il'ia Bratislavskii, the rebbe's son, dies practically in the arms of Liutov. In the process, however, the latter breathes in the breath of the former, adding strength to the "storm of imagination" already bursting out of his ancient body (147). The dying Jew reinvigorates Liutov; "I received the last breath of my brother" (147).

Adoption or Adaptation of the Cossack Topoi?

To understand why Babel may have chosen Cossack characters only to disperse their traditional heroic topoi over the rest of his fictional world, and more important, to clarify the effects of the mythic dispersal, we need to take a closer look at *Red Cavalry* specifically in light of the Cossack myth.

Babel's diary from his summer with Budennyi's Cossacks reveals his distance from the exotic but nonetheless flesh-and-blood soldiers. Babel was disgusted by war, deadened by the dull and destructive campaigns, and stricken by the insensitivity of the Cossack warriors to their environment. That Babel's association with the Cossacks occasionally tormented him is evidenced by an entry from July 24 when he describes being billeted with the

Cossack Prishchepa in the home of some Polish Jews on the Sabbath. The Cossacks ordered their hosts to cook a meal, an activity forbidden to religious Jews on their day of rest. Babel writes that he was forced to remain silent for in that context he was a Russian like the Cossacks, not a Jew like his hosts. The following day would be Tisha b'Av, a holy fast day in the Jewish calendar commemorating the destruction of the First and Second Temples. Babel notes here the parallel between the Polish campaign and, as he writes, the "frightful words of the prophet—they eat manure, the girls are raped, the men slain, Israel destroyed, angry, wailing words. The lamp smokes, the old woman howls, outside is Demidovka, Cossacks, everything like the time when the Temple fell. . . ."[32]

Babel modeled his heroes on men whom he actually knew in the early 1920s, and who participated in historical events well known to his reading public. We might be led to believe we are reading a war report. Reality and artifice, however, are inextricably tangled, as Babel uses the facts to create the impression of historicity only then to destroy it. He confuses chronology, as Gogol did, so we can no longer follow the march of the army as we might in his nonmythic diary.

Babel begins apparently objectively, but immediately introduces surreal descriptions into his war report.[33] And like Gogol, Babel makes veiled reference to the epics of Homer and *The Lay of Igor's Campaign,* as in the "standards of sunset" that "blow above our heads" in "Crossing the Zbruch."[34] The struggle in *Red Cavalry* becomes a mock-epic battle, as the Russo-Polish war definitely was not.

Babel's frequent references to song in general and bards in particular further associate his cycle with epic. The Cossacks' song "hums like a stream running dry" ("Berestechko" 87), and an epic songster joins the Cossacks as they ride past Cossack burial mounds from the time of Khmel'nitskii. The reference to the famous Cossack leader reminds the reader of history, and the bard then transforms that history into myth. He plays a bandura and sings of ancient Cossack glory *(slava/kleos).*

Yet *Red Cavalry* is no more a true epic than *Taras Bul'ba.* Homer created literature as we know it by writing down a linear narrative told in time and existing throughout time, but the mythic consciousness from which it had evolved saw the world spatially, not temporally.[35] Myth knew only space; postmythic thought learned both time and space. According to Joseph Frank, modern literature has the distinction of recapturing that mythic imagination for which historical time does not exist.[36] The relationship of Babel's *Red Cavalry* to myth becomes much clearer in this light, for the destruction of time associated with epic in the stories grows directly from and leads directly back into myth.

Many critics have pointed to the spatial quality of Babel's stories. Victor

Terras speaks of static space, filled with vivid, sensuous images. In this connection he compares Babel and Chagall. Patricia Carden remarks on Babel's interest in art as well as on the spatial aspect of his stories in Joseph Frank's special sense: "the Babel story is a carefully limited space, a canvas into which he paints the significant world-objects before our eyes."[37] We must apprehend that space in an instant, not through time. Like Gogol's work, Babel's cycle uses epic elements to point beyond epic, to mythic consciousness.

The very form of a fragmented cycle emphasizes its timelessness. Babel first published many of the stories separately, destroying their development as a temporal narrative. They are infinitely reorderable. And Babel specifically broke up the two minicycles within the larger cycle: "Gedali"—"The Rebbe"—"The Rebbe's Son" and "Story of a Horse"—"Continuation of Story of a Horse." In the cycle as a whole there is no progression, development, or maturity on the part of any of the characters. *Red Cavalry* does not take the reader through a narrative in which event follows event. Rather it forces the reader into a reading act that, in total, suspends linear time and causal expectations. The narrator himself must continuously refight his battle to be accepted by the Cossacks, only to lose the security of community he might have gained in the very next story. Only in "Argamak," the last story as now published, are we, and the narrator, allowed the satisfaction born of progress for any length of time. Babel added this story, however, long after he had completed the rest of the cycle. It functions as a demythologizing force and did not grow from the same artistic impulse as the rest of *Red Cavalry*.

Babel put date and place markers at the end of many of his stories in the space one would expect to find the date of composition. Instead, the markers refer to the month in which the action of the story supposedly occurred.[38] This practice in itself mythologizes by destroying the distance between event and literary recreation. To this day, many scholars confuse the sequence of writing and publication of Babel's stories. Babel creates the illusion that the "true" stories were written down as they were actually experienced, producing the "juxtaposition of past and present" that makes "history become unhistorical."[39]

Babel no doubt learned from Gogol one of the important techniques for crossing temporal barriers: the establishment of fluctuating distances between the narrator, reader, and heroes. The rapid alternation of narrative styles (lyrical, bureaucratic, dramatic, terse, florid, *skaz*) works in a similar fashion to Gogol's narrative technique in *Evenings*. Eventually we lose our bearings and do not know whom to take as an authority.

The stories told in first person, presumably from the mouths (or pens) of Cossacks themselves, particularly cause us to question our position, moral as well as temporal. We are uncertain, for example, how to evaluate a character like Matvei Pavlichenko ("The Life Story of Pavlichenko, Matvei Rodionych"), who returns to his home to seek vengeance on Nikitinskii, the man who has stolen his wife. He tells his story with such ardor and conviction that we are drawn to him. Yet how can we condone murder, and particularly a murder so personal, so physical, and so graphic as that of his former landlord? The devoted husband and revolutionary Cossack stomps another human being into a pulverized mass. The narrator, with whom we can usually associate quite easily, yearns desperately for just this ability to destroy.

We do not know how to feel about war in general. Babel associates it often with the bright sun, as though its raw violence is itself the fecund power he sought in "Odessa." The lyrical tone he uses to describe horrible acts of destruction disarms us of an immediate negative and moralistic response. Ultimately we must recognize that the world of *Red Cavalry* is mythic, and thus beyond the limits of our moral judgment. The characters play by different rules, rules which attract and repulse at the same time.

Most readers notice a lack of resolution in *Red Cavalry*. They feel ill at ease over Babel's apparent failure to choose between two opposing life-styles, whether "Cossack ethos versus Jewish ethos," "way of violence versus way of peace," "sun versus moon," or "outdoor world versus indoor world."[40] Many critics make the choice for Babel, despite his ambivalent messages, claiming that the author favored nostalgia for his Jewish roots over the future-oriented revolutionary fervor of the Cossacks, or vice versa.

Some critics do recognize the continued ambiguity of Babel's portrayal by allowing for conflict not simply between two groups, Cossack and Jew, but within each group itself.[41] The conflict between Jews is most apparent. Liutov, the Russian Jew, wanders through remnants of the dying Polish culture and yearns for the life of Odessa. Yet the Hasidim who confront him in the person of Gedali exude the life he associates only with the Jews of his youth. It is not necessary to determine which side of any opposition the author ultimately supports if we recognize that the combination of opposites itself is an aspect of the myth he evokes.

Even more significant for his adaptation of the myth, Babel adopts many of the elements involving regeneration through violence. The Cossacks of "Crossing the Zbruch" not only traverse the river but actually submerge themselves in it. The horses march in up to their backs, and one Cossack sinks. The submersion suggests baptism, further supporting the view already discussed of the crossing as a transgression of barriers between two metaphysical or in this case even religious realms. On the other side the narrator confronts a pregnant woman, the first figure described in Novograd. Despite the death around her, including that of her own father, she represents new life. The remnants of Passover dishes, although broken, also suggest new life through the symbol of the spring celebration of liberation and hope.

The human feces included in the list of debris in "Crossing the Zburch" foreshadows the manure into which Liutov grinds the head of the goose in "My First Goose." In this latter story his act of violence and murder, no matter how debased or ridiculous, marks a transition into a new state, into Cossackdom, if only temporarily. The juxtaposition of death (in the goose) and life (in the manure that provides fodder for new growth out of refuse) metaphorically parallels Liutov's rebirth as a member of the Cossack band.[42]

The stomping to death of the goose in turn suggests the death of Nikitinskii by the hand, or literally the feet, of Matvei Rodionovych Pavlichenko in the story already cited. In this case also the physical destruction leads to a form of rebirth, for the Cossack experiences the essence of life through his act of murder: "But ya know, I don't pity myself. So, ya know, I stomp on my enemy for an hour or so. I want to know life, to know it as it really is" (76).

In the second story of the cycle, "The Catholic Church at Novograd," the narrator dashes into the crypt of the church after having been frightened by two skulls. His action obviously deepens the morbid mood instead of annulling it. Once below, however, he notices a staircase leading up to the altar, and sees lights "running in the heights, in the very dome" (26). The lights, we learn, belong to candles held by the narrator's fellow Cossacks. The Cossacks then serve as metaphoric guides from darkness to light, from underground to high above ground, from death to new life.

Babel's portrayal of women in *Red Cavalry*, like the rebirth imagery, also derives from the Cossack myth. In his diary Babel expressed sympathetic interest in the women who traveled with the Cossack division.[43] In the stories, however, the question of sex and the Cossacks takes a different turn. Many critics have noted the strong sexuality of Babel's Cossacks. Like their violence, it lends intensity and urgency. The sexual tension attached specifically to women characters, however, always carries a sense of sickness or perversion, not life-giving force. Venereal disease is a recurrent motif ("The Ivans," "Sashka the Christ," "Continuation of Story of a Horse"), and any heterosexual union leads to grief. Irina's relations with Vasilii in "Evening" breathe corruption; in a scene of Gogolian fragmentation, we are told how her fat-heeled feet and his black crooked nail stick out from the kitchen door while the two make love. As cook, Vasilii deals with "the meat of dead animals and the greed of living ones" (95)—neither appetizing, much less life-engendering, images. Neither women's sexuality nor their particular nurturing aspects have any place in the real Cossack world.[44]

The Cossacks' sexuality, and the intensity derived from it, thus do not come from their association with women. Even the goose murdered by Liutov in "My First Goose" as a substitute for "spoiling a dame" (50) is actually a gander. In the Cossack myth, it is a male-male union that characterizes the true Cossacks; men are their own source of life and nurture.

The very male Cossack hero Savitskii in "My First Goose" has "long legs like girls sheathed to the neck in shining riding boots," and here we are not so far from *Taras Bul'ba* and the potent celibacy of the Cossack "monk." The Cossack army invades a virginal field in the very first story, and repeatedly unites with and is embraced by nature. As an added twist, Matvei calls the Revolution "sweetheart," suggesting a sexual union with the epic history of the cycle, and not only with its environment.

Much of the Cossacks' vitality in *Red Cavalry* takes the form of an immediate understanding of life itself. Matvei understands it through his involvement with death. On the other hand, the Cossack Afon'ka Bida condemns Liutov, the Jewish intellectual, for his misunderstanding of it ("The Death of Dolgushov"); Liutov cannot kill. Paradoxically, as in all of the Cossack myth, violence is a productive act.

The Violence of Creation

By stressing the sexual and regenerating topoi of the Cossack myth, Babel further adapts the Cossack hero. The historical Cossacks were enemies of his people, and by the twentieth century had come to represent repression for all citizens, not only Jews. The small percentage of Cossacks who joined the Red Army did not change this reputation, for they excelled in anarchic behavior and merciless retribution. Babel turned to the traditional hero despite, or in fact on account of, the disparity between the Cossacks he knew and his own sensibilities.

Babel operated, and attempted to reconcile the polar experiences of his life, in the world of literature, or creative art as a whole. Although Gogol was no stranger to this world, his primary concern was the "Russian soul," a category under which he subsumed vitality, productivity, and art itself. Babel's Cossacks are manifestations not so much of his Russianness as of his creative potential. They represent the energy necessary to write. That Babel believed energy is violent is suggested in the quote about Tolstoi's art cited at the beginning of this chapter, or in the famous simile from "Guy de Maupassant": the placement of a period is like a sword thrust. The harmony of violence and life in the Cossack myth provided a metaphor for Babel's own creative impulse.

Babel's most obvious artist character in *Red Cavalry* is Pan Apolek, the errant Pole who drew from the citizens of Novograd to create religious paintings labeled sacrilegious by the official Church. His renditions of holy persons resemble too naturalistically the profane models that inspired them. When he paints, Apolek ignores the boundary between human and divine, doing violence to the letter of the ecclesiastic law. That the painter's transgression in fact demonstrates the spiritual quality of our own world does not impress the Church authorities, but it is Babel's major preoccupation. The artist reconciles the spirit and the flesh; he makes the physical holy and the holy physical.

Here is yet another character who unexpectedly resembles the Cossack hero; a violent creator, he too must be understood in light of the Cossack myth. Speaking of Pan Apolek, a Polish character exclaims: "O, this man! This man'll never die in his bed" (40). One would expect such words only in praise of a Cossack warrior like Taras Bul'ba. But the artist Pan Apolek shares the energy and contradictory destructive creativity of the Cossacks. His name itself suggests both Apollo, god of sun and order, and Apol'lyon, demon of destruction and the bottomless pit.[45] The name also recalls Apollinarius and the Church controversy that attempted to determine the relationship of the two opposing natures in the person of Christ, human and divine.[46]

Yet, the difference between Gogol's creative destroyers and Babel's violent artist is one we have already seen. Gogol's Cossacks embody the ideal essence of the Russian soul that is hidden by mundane reality. Babel's characters, in that they all—Cossack, Jew, artist—resemble one another, show the ideal essence uncovered in the world around us.

To follow Apolek's example, as he vows to do at the beginning of the story, the narrator plays the role of his own bard. He is a wanderer, moving from Cossack to Cossack or hero to hero, collecting stories, like "Pan Apolek" itself, and eternalizing the glory of the events. His craft—storytelling—is his own creative act, juxtaposed with the physical violence of the Cossacks, the spiritual creativity of the Hasids, and Pan Apolek's heretical painting.

Babel must assume that the creative image of his mythic Cossacks is strong enough to prevent any confusion resulting from its presence among his other characters. He is mostly correct, for the non-Cossacks rise to the level of myth. The diffusion of topoi is, however, a profound adaptation of the myth. No longer are the Cossack heroes contrasted to mere mortals. Instead the world as a whole joins them in timeless grandeur.

Babel risks loss of clarity and, in turn, the disintegration of the myth. By this point, however, the Cossacks have a fixed identity. By spilling over their characteristics onto other heroes, Babel need not fear for their integrity. Rather, he points to a profound identity vacuum in the rest of the world. Like the metaphysical emptiness of Gogol's Poles, the weakness in a character such as Liutov makes him vulnerable to attack. He might not survive the incursion of the Cossacks, or he might manage to imbibe their spirit.

Although he does not become a Cossack (or a Hasid or a religious painter), he does befriend all, and ultimately expresses himself through a violently creative act—the stories he tells through the pen of Babel.

It would be misleading, however, to conclude on such an unambiguous note. A sense of distance, which some interpret as simple nostalgia but is more likely complex irony, pervades *Red Cavalry*. The reticence of the cycle as a whole to take a positive stand about its portrait of the ideal may well point back to Tolstoi more than Gogol. *Red Cavalry,* as does *The Cossacks,* balances precariously between mythic affirmation and ironic malaise, so that some readers are led to see Liutov's desire to join the Cossacks as not only vain but pathetic. Liutov says one thing, but Babel "means" the other.

The irony, as has been noted, however, is "double-edged";[47] it is "a battle in which both sides win and lose."[48] In a sense, all the characters in *Red Cavalry* are both unappealing and extremely attractive. Wavering between parody and myth, Babel suggests the possible affinity of destruction and progress, war and wonder. He adopts the Cossack myth not so much to glorify the heroes themselves as to emphasize the applicability to his own chaotic world of the creative power he recognizes they wield.[49]

Conclusion: Story of a Horse

Babel's adaptations attest to the continued power of the Cossack myth, but they reorder its priorities, placing an increased emphasis on the topoi of regeneration as it relates to the creative artist. Babel's understatement of the Cossacks' role as Russian national symbol is not necessarily typical of his contemporaries, but he does share with the poets to be discussed in the following chapter his association of Cossack and artist.

An analysis of the two-part story within *Red Cavalry,* "Story of a Horse" and "Continuation of Story of a Horse," can best recapitulate the differences and common ground between Gogol's and Babel's Cossacks. The story presents Savitskii—the same Cossack who shoots out his adversary's eyes in the opening story and sends Liutov to his Cossack tormentors in "My First Goose"—in the role of renegade Cossack. Abusing his authority as division chief, he appropriates a white stallion from Khlebnikov, commander of the First Squadron. The horse in question "had a magnificent yet untamed form" (perhaps a little heavy, from the narrator's non-Cossack point of view) (80). Khlebnikov received in exchange "a smooth-gaited dark mare from a not-so-bad line," that is, a domesticated, dull female for the brilliant male. Considering the emphasis placed on the horse as an extension of the Cossack in *Red Cavalry* and in all of the Cossack myth, it is clear that Khlebnikov felt deprived of that which symbolized his own masculine, Cossack essence.

122

Khlebnikov thirsts for revenge. He writes to the Army Staff for just retribution and receives back an order, written in dry official language, for the return of his horse. Meanwhile Savitskii has been replaced and sent to the reserves. He now lives in a Polish town with the horse and a Cossack woman previously found with a Jew. By this time he owns twenty other thoroughbreds, looked on as his own property. The former division chief lives alone, separated from the other Cossacks. In fact, Savitskii seems to have abandoned Cossackdom altogether. By settling in Poland he defies the Cossacks' traditional rejection of fixed home and their antagonism toward the Polish enemy; his association with a woman—and one already defiled by a Jew—ignores the Cossack bachelor tradition in which the warriors take the "virgin field and the good steed" for their tenderness and the sabre for their mother.[50] His possession of an entire stable ridicules the Cossack disregard for material wealth; as Gogol has shown, a real Cossack will drink away any gold in his pockets or carelessly forget the spot in which he buried his booty. Babel spares no details. Savitskii's residence is a "ragged slut," a "maimed little town," thus both defiled and miniature in contrast to the vast virginal steppe. "Drenched in perfume and resembling Peter the Great [the historical character associated earlier with the bridling of southern, Cossack freedom], he lived in disgrace" (80).

The whole environment suggests anti-Cossack domesticity: foals greedily suck the teats of their mothers, and Savitskii's Cossack woman lazily cares for her physical appearance and walks "carrying her breasts on high heels, breasts that wriggled about like an animal in a sack" (81). Savitskii calls not for *gorelka,* the traditional Cossack vodka, and not even for a samovar, but for a "little samovar," a diminutive that renders his request precious.

Savitskii turns a "deadened face" toward Khlebnikov when the latter comes to retrieve his horse, and utters a line of rhetoric that, albeit still Cossacklike, can only strike us as ironic given the description of his visage. "'I still live,' he said, embracing his woman. 'Yet can my legs march, yet can my steeds gallop, yet can my arms reach you and does this cannon of mine burn near my body . . .'" (81). He reaches for the gun that lies across his naked stomach, a feeble effort to prove his male potency, but enough to frighten Khlebnikov.

The remainder of the first episode of the story concerns Khlebnikov's reaction to Savitskii's refusal to honor the order of the letter from Army Staff, and the narrator's reaction to Khlebnikov. Like other "creative" Cossacks in the collection, Khlebnikov lays down his revolver and takes up his pen, becoming consumed in the writing of a letter voicing his grievances.

Khlebnikov's recourse to letter writing cannot help but recall the turn taken by the two antiheroes in Gogol's "The Tale of How Ivan Ivanovich Quarreled with Ivan Nikiforovich," discussed in the conclusion of Chapter

3. In "The Tale," the two Ivans, both descendents of Cossacks who renounced all heroic blood, argue over possession of a useless gun and the flinging of childish epithets. Babel's Khlebnikov chooses to solve his dispute through official channels rather than in battle with his fellow Cossack. Ivan Nikiforovich and Ivan Ivanovich similarly play out their quarrel with paper and pen instead of bullet and blood. And the outcome for each is equally unrewarding. Gogol informs us that the dispute stagnated in legal proceedings and stretched on interminably. Babel tells us that the chief of staff refused to listen to Khlebnikov's second plea since "your case has been decided. . . . Your stallion has been returned by me . . ." (81). Having fulfilled the letter of the law by writing the first order, the official feels that the matter is done. In both Gogol and Babel, action stops when writing begins.

"Continuation of Story of a Horse" is nothing more than a series of letters. Khlebnikov and Savitskii have apparently changed places, the former leaving the army, the latter returning. As in Gogol's story, the preliminary apparent difference between the two characters blurs as the story progresses.

Savitskii's letter that closes the episode ends on a curious note. The white stallion has died and the Cossack, too, will probably die soon in battle, he claims, but

> We will see each other, to give it to you straight, in the kingdom of heaven. But, as rumor has it, the old man in heaven doesn't have a kingdom, but a regular brothel. . . . There's gonorrhea enough as it is on earth, so maybe we won't see each other. With that, comrade Khlebnikov, I'll take my leave. (121).

Savitskii's discussion of divine venereal disease raises the suggestion that death may be nothing more than a continuation of life on earth. Thus, if Gogol ended "The Tale" with the narrator's declaration that "It is boring in this world, gentlemen" (Skuchno na etom svete, gospoda), Babel could have his narrator retort, "And in *that* one, too, I'm afraid." "Story of a Horse" can be read as an amplification of Gogol's travesty of the Cossack myth: two Cossacks exhibit non-Cossack behavior; one desires an object, a symbol of masculine Cossack power, that belongs to the other; they turn to documents instead of weapons to resolve their differences; and the dispute remains unresolved. Boredom reigns. This minicycle in *Red Cavalry* seems, on the surface, to deny the vibrancy of the Cossack myth. To be reborn means nothing, for life has no spirit anywhere, and no mythic world is possible.

Yet Babel's version may be read in another way as well. Gogol's story, which ends the *Mirgorod* collection of his southern stories and points to his "northern" fiction, is an inversion of the Cossack myth. *Red Cavalry,* as we have seen, represents rather a dispersion. The cycle does not end on "Continuation of Story of a Horse." Instead, the reader is sent back into the Cossacks' strange and wondrous world in the next story.

And Babel does *not* bring in his narrator for an ironic comment at the end of "Continuation of Story of a Horse," although this device is not unknown in *Red Cavalry*. In Gogol's story, the narrator's comment reinforces a clear ironic distance between the readers and the two Ivans, closing the door forever on our erstwhile relationship to the inhabitants of *Mirgorod*. Babel will not allow even this reassurance about the disjunction of fiction and reality. Babel originally published the story as "Timashenko and Mel'nikov," apparently having based it on an event he witnessed between those two members of the Sixth Division of the cavalry. Mel'nikov complained that the story misrepresented his case. Babel apologized in a letter to the editor of the journal *October,* and simply changed the names.[51] That this story is grounded in experience—and that contemporaries often reacted as though Babel's works were meant as documentary evidence—seems only too appropriate. Babel gives us a clear proof that truth is stranger than fiction. Or myth is truer than reality.

So, parody is not ruled out, but neither is the possibility that the wonder of the Cossacks and their fellow characters in *Red Cavalry* is an antidote to the metaphysical boredom of the two Ivans. Such mythic energy is not found in particular characters, however, who could repudiate it as does Savitskii, but is rather diffused in the world around them. Pan Apolek recognizes this fact and needs no other inspiration for his representations of a higher reality than the motley Poles and Jews that he meets in towns and villages of his own homeland.

The energy of a mythic realm can therefore be exploited by those who enter it. The distance or nostalgia perceived by readers of *Red Cavalry* is but a product of the difficulty of Liutov's continued search for a door into what is, in fact, the very world around him.

NINE

Modern Poets and
Their Cossack Rebels

By FOREGROUNDING the topos of violence as regeneration, however ambiguously, Babel in fact suggested the Cossack as metaphor for the modern poet. Like Pan Apolek, the twentieth-century poet is a lawbreaker; like the Cossacks, a rebel.

Cossack heroes were especially attractive to Futurist poets, a rebellious group that rejected "Europeanized" tradition in order to develop their own poetics based on native sources, both linguistic and thematic. Although the Futurists in fact owe a great debt to other early-twentieth-century poets, especially the symbolists whom they claimed to repudiate, their glorification of Cossack rebels points more directly to the nineteenth-century prose tradition exemplified by Gogol. The monumentality of Futurist poetry, especially in its pan-Slavic variety, found common ground with the Cossack myth.

The Futurists flourished in the early teens, although individual writers continued to be popular through the twenties, when the group, organized around Vladimir Maiakovskii, became self-proclaimed spokesmen for the Revolution. Maiakovskii himself did not adopt the Cossack, but his fellow Futurists Velimir Khlebnikov and Vasilii Kamenskii both embraced the violent hero as a metaphor for their rebellious poetry.

The turbulent prerevolutionary years, the return to patriotism brought about by the war with Germany, and the rebellion and hardships of the Civil War following the Revolution of 1917 are all refracted through these poets' vision of the early Cossack rebels. As Kamenskii wrote about his choice of Razin:

Possessed by enthusiasm, I dreamt of a bridge from the village to Futurism, as from Stepan Timofeevich Razin to modernity. And when world war broke out that summer, when all of Russian life suddenly stirred, when minds and hearts

126

surged with elemental force, any surety about work on Razin I might have had was increased twofold, as on a wave of majestic premonitions.[1]

Razin Lives: Velimir Khlebnikov

Velimir Khlebnikov (né Viktor Vladimirovich Khlebnikov, 1885–1922) was born in Astrakhan province, where the Volga River flows into the Caspian Sea and European Russia opens out onto the Central Asian steppe.[2] He attended school further up the Volga, in Kazan', where, as in Astrakhan, Eastern Asiatic elements are particularly palpable. By titling a major poem "Khadzhi-Tarkhan," the ancient Tatar name for Astrakhan, Khlebnikov suggests the importance of Asiatic and borderland motifs in his aesthetics.[3] His poem "The Trumpet of Gul'-mulla," written after Khlebnikov's first real visit to Asia only a year before his death, summarizes the poet's fascination with Orientalism, an attraction that fed his almost obsessive interest in the theme of the union of East and West, Asia and Europe. The meeting point, and the place that successfully combined aspects of both, was Russia as a whole, and the Volga River in particular, the locale, as Khlebnikov repeatedly stressed in his poetry, of Sten'ka Razin's brigandage.

In "Svoiasi," a prose piece intended as preface for a proposed 1919 collection of his works, Khlebnikov calls the Volga "the river of Indo-Russes."[4] The term "Russes" recalls two other of Khlebnikov's favorite obsessions: pan-Slavism and the glorification of Kievan Rus'.[5] Many of Khlebnikov's writings, including his abstract linguistic experiments and mathematical theories, grew from a desire to reveal and propagate the essential nature of the uncorrupted past, the past of Rus'. As the poem "Volga! Volga!" laments: "Volga, again be the Volga."[6]

Given the importance of the themes of reconciliation of East and West and the validation of the past, it is not difficult to fit Khlebnikov's oeuvre within the framework of the Cossack tradition. Several early prose works of Khlebnikov in fact make direct reference to Gogol's Zaporozhian Cossacks in *Taras Bul'ba*.[7] For both authors, the Zaporozhian Cossacks represent a life allied to old Rus' and to supposedly purer, Slavic roots. The use of Ukrainianisms in the work "The Great Day" ("Velik-Den'," the Ukrainian term for Easter) is particularly reminiscent of Gogol's early works, and the original subtitle for the piece was in fact "An Imitation of Gogol" ("Podrazhanie Gogoliu").[8] "The Death of Palivoda" ("Smert' Palivody") is set in the Zaporozhian Sech and contains numerous references to Gogol, not least among them being a strong emphasis on the special, even holy qualities of the Cossacks and their relationship to "Holy Russia."[9]

127

An incomplete early poem of 1911 called "A Song to Me"[10] mentions Razin for the first time. Here, the twenty-six-year-old poet evokes old Rus', and asserts his own role in resurrecting it. In this poem Khlebnikov understands Rus' as a mixture of opposites—science and romance, East and West, south and north, pagan, Muslim, and Christian—and he calls for brother to love brother, for there to be a true "mixing of blood." This mythic reconciliation is to come about through the rebellion of poetry. "We will be Huns," the poet claims, announcing the unrelenting force and perhaps even cruelty necessary for the task.[11]

At the end of "A Song to Me," Khlebnikov boldly states, "I come to you as the shade of Razin" (Ia prikhozhu k vam ten'iu Razina). The Cossack rebel becomes the prototype of the advocate of old Rus', and of the reunion of opposites it represents. And it is the poet who continues the task of the Cossack after the latter's death.

The very late poem "A Dinner,"[12] probably written in 1922, also concludes with the image of the shade of Razin:

Into the capital cities
The place of bullets' revelry, of doves' freeness, of freedom's firing,
To step out as the shade of Razin.
(V stolitsy,
Gde pul' gul'ba, gul' vol'ba, Vol' pal'ba,[13]
Shagnut' ten'iu Razina.)

Again the poet declares himself the recipient of the Cossack legacy.

Between the brackets of Khlebnikov's poetic output that these two poems represent we can find numerous references to Razin as well as to other Cossacks, especially Pugachev and Ermak. "Khadzhi-Tarkhan" (written 1911–12, published 1913)[14] evokes Razin, and again in connection both to Rus' and to the poet himself. Here Khlebnikov describes the area around Astrakhan as a corner of the world where "Russia looks like Africa" (Gde smotrit Afrikoi Rossiia) and where "Assyria breathes in the towers" (Gde dyshit v bashniakh Assiriia). Russia is primitive and vital, East as well as West, south as well as north.

Khlebnikov continues:

How dear to us is Pugachevshchina,
The Cossack with his earring and dark ear,
Known to us by rumor.
When, warlike, his knives
Fought with the German and the flap-eared cap.
(Mila, mila nam Pugachevshchina,

Kazak s ser'goi i temnym ukhom,
Ona znakoma nam po slukham.
Togda voinstvenno nozhovshchina
Borolas' s nemtsem i treukhom.)

The "German" refers to Catherine the Great. In Khlebnikov's mythology, the "dear" Pugachev fought the foreign Catherine to insure the integrity of Russia, so that here Pugachev/Russia is pure, Catherine/Germany—corrupt.

The next stanza introduces Razin, linked to red calico *(kumach)*, a signal for Razin in several other of Khlebnikov's poems as well.[15] But Razin himself is no longer present, and the Volga has "lost the practice of carrying the rebels' boats." The Cossacks' "holy cry" of "Rabble to the bow" is heard no more.[16]

Razin survives nonetheless. First of all, his story, specifically the drowning of his Persian mistress, is told in the present tense, and, we are informed, will be remembered (future tense) by the chronicler. Razin survives also morphemically in the line "V *nizov'*iakh mchashchegosia *Ra*" (In the lower reaches of the rushing Ra; my emphasis). Ra is the ancient name for the Volga,[17] and Khlebnikov thus equates Razin with the still-existing and ever-powerful river. It is the river, the "Volgan will" *(Volzhskaia volia),* that now rises up for the honor of Rus'. Again, we are told, the East, here as the Volga, symbolic of Razin, defends the purity of Rus' from the West.

Razin is further linked with the violence of the past, but a violence to be employed in the future.[18] And here, as we see in all Khlebnikov's poems with the Cossack hero, Razin and his task become equated with the poet and his. Razin represents not only the pure yet paradoxical union of opposites and the strength of Rus', but also the mission and strength of the poet, and the Futurist poet in particular. Ronald Vroon recognizes the similarity between the following lines and the Futurists' program:

We raise youth as a banner to the storm,
With a fiery hand we draw laughter.
(Kak znamia my molodost' v buriu vosvysim,
Rukoi ognevoiu nachertim my smekh.)
(11. 171–72)

The laughter recollects Khlebnikov's own "Incantation to Laughter" that first brought the poet fame.[19] Vroon further cites several lines from Khlebnikov's work "Zangezi" that again link laughter and Razinlike behavior:

I am laughter, I am a lightning conductor,
Where thunder curses like fire. ———

I am the brigand of the stormy word,
My words are a bludgeon on the Volga!
(Ia smekh, ia gromootvod,
Gde grom rugaetsia ognem, ———
Ia slova burnogo razboinik,
Moi slova—kisten' na Volge!)[20]

The brigand of the Volga is reincarnated in Khlebnikov, and the bludgeon of the former transmogrifies into the poetry of the latter.[21] We find, therefore, the typical Razin in Khlebnikov's works: the Cossack figure as both the preserver or resurrector of Rus', and as the Futurist poet. Ultimately, Razin symbolically links the poet with that resurrection. We see here the peculiar but powerful topos of violence as a regenerating force. The poet must be violent—destructive like the Cossack—in order to create. This kinship of violence and creation has roots in classical mythology as well as in romantic poetics, and many of Khlebnikov's contemporaries, notably Aleksandr Blok, Boris Pil'niak, and Evgenii Zamiatin, also made the connection explicit. What is new with Khlebnikov is the almost literal connection between a historical rebel, some would say murderer, and himself. His poetry is meant to destroy.

Khlebnikov suggests an even more complex relationship in "The Trumpet of Gul'-mulla."[22] Here the poet claims:

And in the celestial hunt
I am a celestial racer [jumper],
I am Razin in reverse,
I am Razin inside-out.
(I v zvezdnoi okhote
Ia zvezdnyi skakun,
Ia Razin naprotiv,
Ia Razin navyvorot.)

The reversal of Razin is not entirely clear. As will be shown, however, Khlebnikov probably refers here to biographical details, not moral qualities, for both characters engage in the same illicit but creative activity. Razin and Khlebnikov are not so much opposites as mirror images, identical in all ways, but reversed.[23]

The poem "Razin"[24] helps explain the contradiction. It is one of Khlebnikov's last works, and an ambitious experiment in palindrome; every line reads identically both backward and forward. We have Razin, in other words, coming and going. It is the Cossack and the poet who meet and unite in the middle. Khlebnikov concludes his poem with the line: "My, nizari [a palindrome of *i Razin*] leteli Razinym," or "We and Razin flew like Razin." The poet is both the Cossack's partner and his inverse.

Several lines earlier the poet states: "Razin na kobylu, ulybok nanizar'" (Razin [jumps] on the mare, [casts a look] of smiles at the *nizar'*). The word *nizar'* here, as above, refers to an inhabitant of the lower reaches of the Volga, and thus Khlebnikov calls himself.[25]

Khlebnikov intermingles phonemes from his own name with Razin's in these almost untranslatable verses from "Razin":

Колом о молоко,	Kolom o moloko,	[ko, l
Оперив свирепо.	Operiv svirepo.	o, v
Хама мах	Khama makh	kh, kh
Или	Ili	i, i
Махал плахам.	Makhal plakham.	kh, l, l, kh
Или	Ili	i, i
Сокол около кос!	Sokol okolo kos!	ko, ko, ko
Ищи!	Ishchi!	i, i
Иди!	Idi!	i, i
Мани раб, баринам!	Mani rab. barinam!	ni, r, b, b, r, i
Ин вора жаровни,	In vora zharovni,	in, v, ra,zh[z],r
И лалы пылали,	I laly pylali.	i, l, i
заре раз.	Zare raz.	zar, raz][26]

The poet bursts apart syllables, doing violence to sense, and moves in this section from himself, Khlebnikov (*Kolom o moloko/Kh*ama ma*kh*) to Razin (*Zare raz*). The transforming syllable is *i*: the conjunction *and* in Russian.

Behind the screen of its technical virtuosity and neologisms, the poem basically recapitulates the narrative of the Razin story, from brigandage and war to torture and death. Yet the poem evokes liminal space and time much more than any specific historical events. The word *Razin* is repeatedly associated with *zaria* and *zarevo,* meaning the transition period between both night and day and day and night. And Khlebnikov begins with the longest palindrome in the poem, covering two lines:

I am Razin with the banner of Lobachevskii of the broad gullies.
In the heads there is a candle, pain; an attraction to change, fall asleep dawn [or dusk].[27]
(Ia Razin so znamenem Lobachevskogo logov.
Vo golovakh svecha, bol'; mene man, zasni zaria.)

The non-Euclidean geometrist Lobachevskii represented for Khlebnikov the breakdown of the traditional confines of space, and thus a revolution in our perception of the world. In this poem the poet, as Razin, carries on the message of Lobachevskian unbounded space.[28]

In "Razin's Boat,"[29] a companion to "Razin" in subject matter but not experimental style, Khlebnikov refers to the Volga as howling and jumping (or galloping/racing) "without face and without end" (Volga voet, Volga skachet / Bez litsa i bez kontsa). Both time and space, associated with the Cossack and with the Volga, are without end. Khlebnikov further uses the verb *skakat'* to associate the Volga with himself, for in the poem "The Trumpet of Gul'-mulla" he called himself a "celestial racer (or jumper): "Ia zvezdnyi skakun" (I am a celestial racer).

The prose piece "Razin: Two Trinities"[30] further complicates the Razin motif. Written in the last six months of his life, it sums up much of the poet's biography and outlook.[31] The two trinities refer to two incidents in Khlebnikov's life (Trinity Day being the Orthodox equivalent of Pentacost) that the poet compares to Razin's. He begins with an announcement that he will sail "along the soul of Razin, on the wide waves, as on a wide river, . . . against the current . . . , having given to life another current, the opposite one in relation to the stars overhead, cutting across time in defiance of the current from the Kalmyk steppe to Zhiguli [i.e., upstream on the Volga], sailing across the noisy flow of his ego." The current of Razin's soul is here compared to the current of the Volga, *against* which the poet will travel.

On the simplest level, the reversal is in time and refers to the structure of the biography of Razin that follows this declaration, a biography that Khlebnikov traces backward from death to birth, from execution to childhood. He claims: "To swim from the end to youth" (Ot konchiny plyt' k molodosti).

The trip against the current also has a spatial meaning and refers to Khlebnikov's autobiography. The poet relates, in reverse chronology, Razin's movement from the north (when the young Cossack allegedly made a pilgrimage to a monastery on the White Sea) to his adult brigandage in the south. For his own biography, Khlebnikov suggests the reverse: his youth in the south and adulthood in the north. Razin went north again, to Moscow, for the last days of his life, and Khlebnikov went south to Persia, for the second Trinity in 1921, prophetically only one year before his own death.[32]

Khlebnikov's declaration of himself as "Razin's double," "Razin inside out," or the "shade of Razin" puts him in the context of so many Russian writers who sought to discover Cossack blood, real or metaphoric, in their own veins. Khlebnikov saw the poet in general and himself in particular engaged in a Cossack task: violent, aggressive, and monumental rebellion. In a letter to Kamenskii in 1914, Khlebnikov asks: "On the whole, isn't it time we threw ourselves onto Razin's boats? Everything is ready. We will form the Government of the Presidents of the Terrestrial Globe. Prepare a list and send it."[33] By calling the formation of his society "throwing ourselves onto Razin's boats," Khlebnikov associates his own social and linguistic revolutionary program with the Cossack rebel's activity. He tells Kamenskii that they must and will act like Cossacks, as he earlier claimed that they would be Huns. Khlebnikov's imagination came to rest on a more native expression of the same violence.

The poem beginning with the words "Who is he, Voronikhin of the centuries?"[34] most clearly sums up the Cossacks' mythic role in Khlebnikov's work as literary and linguistic rebellion. The poem sets up a contrast between space and time, the former shown to have enslaved the latter. Space is bounded and binding, while time means endless freedom. Razin frees time from its bondage, and causes the eventual disappearance of space, as, the poet says, the letter *ius* disappeared from the Russian language. The linguistic simile is no accident, for Razin and his rebellion are directly linked in the poem to Khlebnikov's poetic/linguistic program and to the "Slap in the Face of Public Taste" *(Poshchechina obshchestvennomu vkusu)*, a Futurist manifesto. Further he states:

> We gave the crowd a slap in the face,
> For the fact that the crowd beat Razin,
> Ourselves unaware of the reasons for the attack
> Of our courage.
> (My dali tolpe opleukhu,
> Za to, chto tolpa bila Razina,
> Sami ne znaia prichiny udara
> Nashei otvagi.)

The reader, however, is well aware of the reasons for the attack. Khlebnikov and Razin are one. The creativity of the Futurists and the rebellion of the Cossacks are the same. When Razin was executed, the poet stepped into the rebel's shoes, rejuvenated by his destructive/creative poetry.[35]

Marina Tsvetaeva's Male/Cossack Persona

The poet Marina Ivanovna Tsvetaeva (1892–1941) was not a Futurist, although we can find in her work many of the issues that preoccupied Khlebnikov and that caused him to turn to Cossack heroes: a love of Rus' and the desire to resurrect its purity over against the corruption of modern Russia and the West; an interest in history in general, and in its transformation into epic; a fascination with primitive forms—which Khlebnikov found in common Slavic morphemic roots and Eastern vocabulary, and Tsvetaeva in

133

Slavic, or sometimes German, folk poetry; and, mostly, an understanding of the poet's task as rebellion.

As personalities, however, the two poets differed greatly. Khlebnikov, though an iconoclast, belonged to a group whose cohesion was based to a large extent precisely on the unusualness of all its members. Despite their quarrels, the Futurists presented a formidable united front on the battlefield of immediately pre- and postrevolutionary Russian literature. Tsvetaeva, on the other hand, was always a loner. Although able to boast powerful supporters at various stages in her career, she was often ostracized by fellow writers from all points along the political and literary spectrum. As outspoken as Khlebnikov, she did not hesitate to cross poetic boundaries, invent new rules, and infuse her work with highly politicized stances. She was firmly against the Bolshevik takeover, and boldly wrote poem after poem glorifying the exploits of the White Army. (Her husband, Sergei Efron, fought on the side of the Whites until his emigration in 1921.) Curiously, some of her poems continued to be published in the Soviet Union even after her own emigration. An editor of her collected works in the authoritative *Biblioteka poeta* series minimizes Tsvetaeva's political opposition at the same time as he praises the Soviet Union's tolerance:

> The Soviet authorities magnanimously ignored this put-on frondism. They doled out to Tsvetaeva from their meager stores, printed her books in the Government press *(Versty, Tsar'-Devitsa)*, and, in May of 1922, permitted her and her daughter to go abroad—to join her husband who had been a White officer, who survived the utter defeat of [the White generals] Denikin and Vrangel, and at that time had become a student in Prague.[36]

Tsvetaeva, who was first welcomed by the emigré community in Europe, found herself increasingly isolated, especially after her husband and daughter returned to the Soviet Union, the former allegedly in complicity with the Soviet Secret Police. She herself returned in 1939 to find only closed doors, both personally and professionally. She suffered severely from both this ostracism and the poverty that resulted from it, culminating in her suicide on August 31, 1941. No former friends or fellow poets attended her funeral.[37]

Like Khlebnikov's, Tsvetaeva's involvement with the Cossack hero spanned the course of her career, and encompassed both prose and poetry. Tsvetaeva claimed a highly personal interest in one Cossack in particular, Pugachev, from the age of seven. In "My Pushkin" ("Moi Pushkin," 1936),[38] she relates how she discovered a collection of Pushkin in her sister's bookcase and devoured it secretly and fanatically.

Tsvetaeva recalls her precocious childhood enthusiasm for *The Captain's Daughter* in her essay "Pushkin and Pugachev" ("Pushkin i Pugachev," 1937),[39] where she claims that, for her, *The Captain's Daughter* has only one character: Pugachev. "The whole thing comes to life at the sound of his bell" (*IP* II:293). Furthermore, the poet acutely observes:

> It is curious that all, absolutely all figures in *The Captain's Daughter*—each in his own way—are counterfigures of Pugachev: the good brigand Pugachev/the low scoundrel Shvabrin; Pugachev who rebels against the tsaritsa/the commandant who dies for that tsaritsa; the wild wolf Pugachev/the devoted hound Savel'ich; the fiery Pugachev and the bland German general,—right up to the physical contrast of the physically charming Pugachev and his frightful crowd (the torn nostrils of Khlopusha). And finally, Pugachev and Catherine. (*IP* II:292)

"In my *Captain's Daughter*," writes Tsvetaeva, "there was no captain's daughter. She didn't exist to such an extent that even now I utter the title mechanically, as if it were one word, without any captain and without any daughter. I say: *The Captain's Daughter,* but I think: *Pugachev*" (*IP* II:282).

Pugachev attracted Tsvetaeva because of qualities imputed to him not only by Pushkin but even more by the entire history of the nineteenth-century myth. One of the most important qualities in this case is the paradoxical combination of opposites. Tsvetaeva stresses particularly Pugachev's moral ambiguity:

> Pugachev promised no one to be good. In fact, the reverse is true; not having promised, having promised the opposite, he turned out to be good. This was my first meeting with evil, and it turned out to be—good. (*IP* II:283)

Tsvetaeva sees the contradictory elements of Pugachev to reside first of all in Pushkin himself. She writes: "But Pugachev is a villain by reason of Pushkin's love, an enemy by Pushkin's love, despite everything and everyone not his enemy at all, but his non-enemy, his friend and almost his passion" (*IP* II:290). Pushkin himself has a contradictory heart that is "mortal, immortal, African, boyar, human, divine, poor, and already doomed" (*IP* II:290). Here Tsvetaeva ultimately explains her own affinity to the Cossack through what she sees as Pushkin's affinity. She is strongly attracted by the mythic nature of Pushkin's soul as she sees it reflected in the paradoxical character of Pugachev.

Pushkin loves Pugachev, and Tsvetaeva loves Pugachev, despite the fact that she knew him to be a "villain," to be "black" (*IP* II:282). Everyone *must* love him, she declares, perhaps best exemplified by Grinev's relationship to Pugachev, who loves his mysterious benefactor and political enemy "at first thanks to but then already in spite of [his own gentlemanly honor]." He loves, "with all the opposition of his birth, his upbringing, his milieu, his fate, his path, his stars, his essence. . . . Through all the villainy and arbitrary behavior, through everything and regardless of everything—he loved" (*IP* II:286). At the end of the essay, Tsvetaeva explicitly equates the reader's relationship with the contradictory Cossack, the "good brigand" (*IP* II:300), to Grinev's, thus confirming the hero's role as a metaphor for ourselves. "We do not want to, but we see. We do not want to, but we love," she exclaims (*IP* II:294). We cannot avoid our own attraction to and relationship with this contradictory hero.

Tsvetaeva attempts to explain the paradoxical attraction in several ways. She claims that Pugachev has a certain compelling energy: Pugachev was "power, no, more—violence, no more—life and death" (*IP* II:282). He is all-consuming. The power is not rational, however. It is a spell *(chara)*, and "Pushkin is enchanted by Pugachev" (*IP* II:287).

According to Tsvetaeva, poets in particular must succumb to Pugachev's spell:

> But there is yet something else, besides the charm, the physical charm of Pugachev over Pushkin: there is the passion of every poet for rebellion, for a rebellion personified by one individual. For the rebellion of one head with two eyes. For a one-headed, two-eyed rebellion. For one against all—and without all. For he who transgresses.
> . . . Without passion for the transgressor—there is no poet. (*IP* II:290)

With this statement Tsvetaeva betrays her debt to the Cossack myth on yet another level; her image of Pugachev contains the vital topos of regenerative violence. And, confesses Tsvetaeva, "I am obligated to Pushkin for my own passion for rebels—no matter how they are named or how they are dressed" (*IP* II:291). As with Babel and Khlebnikov, the foregrounding of the creative topos alters the balance of the Cossack legacy, transforming it from a national to an aesthetic myth. Tsvetaeva essentially dismisses Pugachev's villainy, his blackness, by taking it outside the realm of cultural morality or politics entirely and placing it in the realm of creativity. He is not good or bad; he is not a traitor or a patriot. He is charm and rebellion, he is poetry.

In the final pages of "Pushkin and Pugachev," in the course of a comparison of *The Captain's Daughter* and *The History of Pugachev*, Tsvetaeva lays bare the mythmaking process itself. She observes that no reader of Pushkin's history could feel love for Pugachev, for the author spares no details in his grim picture of the arbitrary, anarchic, and power-happy Cossack. Basing his statements on historical materials to which he had access, Pushkin shows Pugachev in *The History of Pugachev* to have reveled in grotesque murders, to be cowardly, to grovel before his own lust, to betray friends, to betray at last his faith itself, to be, in fact, totally devoid of the enchantment he has in *The Captain's Daughter*. Yet, Tsvetaeva reminds us, Pushkin wrote the history two years *before* the novel. It would be natural to assume that the author simply discovered revolting details after he had written the romantic tale that glorified Pugachev. But the reverse is true. Pushkin already knew the details, but still created the contradictory yet ultimately attractive hero of *The Captain's Daughter*. As Tsvetaeva explains, instead of "imagining" and then "knowing," Pushkin "knew" and then "imagined," or actually, as she points out, not imagined *(voobrazil)* but transfigured *(preobrazil)* (*IP* II:298). The poet takes the historical figure and recreates him into myth:

> He forgot the *truth* about the villain, that is that part of the truth that is incompatible with love: his pettiness.
>   . . . And having preserved the whole truth about him, but having taken from that truth only Pugachev's pettiness, he gave us another Pugachev, his own Pugachev, a native Pugachev, whom we *can* love, whom we cannot *not* love. (*IP* II:299)

Tsvetaeva mentions the Pugachev archives that were opened during the nineteen-twenties and that show the Cossack rebel in a better light than had been believed in Pushkin's time. But even then Pushkin knew the truth, she claims. In any case, Tsvetaeva concludes, "the issue for us is not in Pugachev, and what kind of a person he was or was not, but in Pushkin, and the person that *he* was" (*IP* II:302). Tsvetaeva is interested not in Pugachev as a historical phenomenon, but in him as myth, and in what that myth, that "transfiguration" of truth, tells us about Pushkin, about herself, and about all who embrace the myth in its creative potential.

Tsvetaeva compares Pugachev to the Cossack Sten'ka Razin in "Pushkin and Pugachev" in a passage that sends us back to a diary entry she wrote almost twenty years earlier, published under the title "Free Passage" ("Vol'nyi proezd," 1918, *IP* I:29–49). The diary entry describes Tsvetaeva's journey into the countryside in September of 1918 to barter for food. She reports various conversations along the way with her train companions and the peasants with whom she engages in usually unsuccessful trade. (Tsvetaeva was notoriously unable to cope with the details of everyday life.) One brief acquaintance turns out to be a young Red soldier in whom she believes she recognizes Sten'ka Razin. Her heart cries out and she exclaims, "*My* fairhaired Razin of song" (*IP* I:39, italics in original). She feels a personal relationship with this boy, who for her is the mythic Cossack.

> Pugachev is black, Razin is white. Why the word itself: Stepan! Hay, straw, steppe [Seno, soloma, step']. Could there possibly be black Stepans? And: Ra-

zin! Sunrise [*zaria*], the rush of water [*razliv*],—strike [*razi*], Razin! Where it is
expansive, it is not black. Black is a thicket.
Razin—still beardless, but already with thousands of Persian girls. . . .

Familiar already from Khlebnikov, this root play and the associations
with Razin—brightness, expansiveness, the combination of youth and experience—all point to a mythic rather than historical representation of the
Cossack hero. Curiously, the two speakers discuss mythmaking between
themselves, specifically the development of the myth of Karl Marx. It is easy
to make a hero, the boy says, out of a foreigner or a man long dead, someone
exotic and far away, someone who is only "other." Then, "it's no trick being
great" (*IP* I:41). But the boy goes on to mythologize his own father who
foresaw the collapse of tsardom. And the boy himself is a myth propagator, a
fact confirmed in the next few pages.

Tsvetaeva recites to him from her just completed cycle of Razin poems,
although she supports the boy's erroneous assumption that they were written
by "some man." She thus distances herself from the act of creation, transferring the process onto a generic, unknown, and male creator. Staring "Razin"
directly in the eyes, Tsvetaeva forms a bond between herself and the boy. She
as the "male" poet, and he as the young myth-propagating soldier, both have
a link to Razin. This leads her to call herself "not Russian, Razin, I am pre-
Russian, pre-Mongol,—I am from pretemporal Rus', and I come to meet
you" (*IP* I:42).

In return for the Razin poems, the boy offers to tell Tsvetaeva a mythic
story: the tale of a city that rings its bells to save itself from the Mongol
invasion, and ends by sinking into the sea. The drowning motif recalls the
fate of the Persian princess in the Razin tale. But the city drowns not in the
water but "in its own ringing," in the intensity of its own striving. The bell
therefore reminds us of the third poem from Tsvetaeva's Razin cycle, "Razin's
Dream," that relates the story of the drowned princess, whose bracelets
continue to ring from the bottom of the river.[40] The poem suggests that
Razin has drowned not so much the girl as "Stepan's happiness." The ringing
of both the city of Kitezh and the Persian princess thus represent ardor and
love in the midst of death and destruction. The bells signal resurrection, a
motif intimately connected with Tsvetaeva's Razin.

A diary entry from the previous year, "October in the Train" ("Oktiabr' v
vagone," 1917, *IP* I:21–28), discusses a meeting with a man in whom Tsvetaeva
recognizes not Razin but Pugachev. The poet is again traveling, this time to
return to her husband in Moscow, when a factoryhand addresses her, ex-
pressing surprise that she has eaten nothing during the long ride. The poet
sees her companion as black, like Pugachev: "black eyes, like coal, a black
beard, something from the tender Pugachev. A little sinister and pleasant" (*IP*

I:22). Significant here is her ascription of opposing characteristics to the Pugachev character. The man speaks of the Bolshevik takeover as the appearance of the Antichrist, but Tsvetaeva believes that "he himself is from the devil's host" (*IP* I:23). Continuing the paradox of his sinister but pleasant nature, she believes that he, as her enemy, and precisely because he is her enemy, will save her. He rides with her, occupying the final seemingly endless hours before her reunion with her husband; he will see her off the train in Moscow; and then disappear, like a fairy-tale character, in a puff of smoke (rassypetsia v prakh). Tsvetaeva feels for *this* Pugachev, this devilish savior, the same paradoxical attraction she felt for the "good brigand" of Pushkin's *The Captain's Daughter*. She recreates her reading experience in life, naturalizing and herself entering into the myth.

The same year as the above entry, Tsvetaeva wrote the series of three poems titled *Sten'ka Razin* referred to above, most likely inspired by Pushkin's three *Songs of Sten'ka Razin,* but united as well to her association of the revolutionary atmosphere with the Cossack myth. Unlike Pushkin, who experimented with folk rhythms and terminology but was apparently unconcerned with Razin's psychology, Tsvetaeva concerns herself solely with Razin's murder of the Persian princess, and his reaction to it.[41] The Cossack confirms his masculine bond to the collective by drowning his alien lover, but, in the third poem, mourns her death and hears in his sleep the continual ringing of her bracelets:

(Razin's Dream)	(СОН РАЗИНА)
And Razin dreams—a dream:	И снится Разину—сон:
As though a marsh heron cries.	Словно плачется болотная цапля.
And Razin dreams—a ring:	И снится Разину—звон:
Like silver droplets dripping.	Ровно капельки серебряные каплют
And Razin dreams the river bottom:	И снится Разину дно:
Dazzling—like a printed scarf.	Цветами—что плат ковровый.
And he dreams a single face—	И снится лицо одно—
Forgotten and black-browed.	Забытое, чернобровое.
She sits, like the Mother of God.	Сидит, ровно Божья мать,
Stringing pearls on a thread.	Да жемчуг на нитку нижет.
And he wants to tell her something,	И хочет он ей сказать,
But only moves his lips . . .	Да только губами движет...
A breath escapes—like	Сдавило дыханье—аж
A glass splinter in his chest.	Стеклянный, в груди, осколок.
And he walks, like a sleepy watchman,	И ходит, как сонный страж,
Between them—a glass curtain.	Стеклянный—меж ними—полог.
. . . .	. . . .

The helmsman steered by the dawn	Рулевой зарею правил
Downstream on the Volga River.	вниз по Волге-реке.
Why did you leave me	Ты зачем меня оставил
Over a single slipper?	Об одном башмачке?
Who will want a beauty	Кто красавицу захочет
With only one slipper?	В башмачке одном?
I will come to you, my little friend,	Я приду к тебе, дружочек,
For the slipper for the other foot.	За другим башмачком!
And ring-ring, ring-ring the	И звенят-звенят, звенят-звенят
bracelets:	запястья:
—You have been drowned, Stepan's	—Затонуло ты, Степаново
happiness![42]	счастье!

Tsvetaeva's focus on the woman instead of the warrior perhaps reflects her own female perspective, but is more likely an effort to humanize and thus demythologize the abductor Razin, only to remythologize him as poetry itself, and his dream as a poem. As she says about Pushkin and Pugachev, "without passion for the transgressor—there is no poet."

"Tsar and God! Forgive the small—,"[43] a poem written on the one-year anniversary of the October Revolution and included in her "White" collection, *Swan's Encampment (Lebedinyi stan),* again refers to Razin, but this time to his delivery to Moscow and subsequent execution:

Tsar and God! Forgive the small—	Царь и Бог! Простите малым—
The weak—the stupid—sinful—	Слабым—глупым—грешным—
mad.	шалым,
Sucked down a frightful funnel,	В страшную воронку втянутым,
Seduced and betrayed,—	Обольщенным и обманутым,—
Tsar and God! With a punishment	Царь и Бог! Жестокой казнию
so cruel,	Не казните Стеньку Разина!
Do not punish Sten'ka Razin!	
Tsar! The Lord will repay you!	Царь! Господь тебе отплатит!
Enough of orphans' wails for us!	С нас сиротских воплей—хватит!
Enough, enough deceased for us!	Хватит, хватит с нас покойников!
Royal Son,—forgive the Brigand!	Царский Сын,—прости Разбойнику!
To my Father's house—there are many	В отчий дом—дороги разные.
paths.	Пощадите Стеньку Разина!
Spare Sten'ka Razin!	
Razin! Razin! Your tale is told!	Разин! Разин! Сказ твой сказан!
The red beast is tamed and bound.	Красный зверь смирён и связан.

The frightful fangs are broken,	Зубья страшные поломаны,
But for his life, his dark life,	Но за жизнь его за темную,
And for his foolish daring—	Да за удаль несуразную—
Unbind Sten'ka Razin!	Развяжите Стеньку Разина!
Motherland! Source and issue!	Родина! Исток и устье!
Joy! Again it smells like Rus'!	Радость! Снова пахнет Русью!
Shine forth, dim eyes!	Просияйте, очи тусклые!
Make merry, Russian heart!	Веселися, сердце русское!
Tsar and God! In honor of this joyous day—	Царь и Бог! Для ради празднику—
Release Sten'ka Razin!	Отпустите Стеньку Разина!

Москва, 1-ая годовщина Октября.

Here, the Cossack is equated to the Red Army, which Tsvetaeva assumes will soon be vanquished by the Whites. She calls on "Tsar and God" to forgive the rebel, for her motherland again "smells like Rus'," and the "Russian heart" must again rejoice. As a variation on the myth, it is here not Razin himself associated with Rus' and the Russian essence, but the forgiving of Razin, or by extension, the reinclusion of Razin into the life of the motherland.

In the narrative poem *Perekop*,[44] Tsvetaeva's own husband Sergei is the Cossack:

As Ostap—with the face of Andrei,
As Andrei—with the soul of a warrior.
If this were a fairy tale—I would call him George,
As it is fact, I call him Sergei.

The reference is clearly to Ostap and Andrii, the two sons of Taras Bul'ba. If in Gogol's work Ostap represents the warrior and Andrii the sensitive, almost feminine boy (cf. Tsvetaeva's reference to his face), then the officer in *Perekop* unites both attributes. He is a true combination of opposites.

Shorter references to Cossacks occur sporadically throughout her oeuvre, including "red calico" (Razin) and "sheepskin coat" (Pugachev) in the conclusion to the *poema, The Tsar-maiden*.[45] What is most significant in all the references is the identity that Tsvetaeva recognizes between the Cossack spirit and herself. She is attracted, and sees in the romantic brigands something of her own "masculine," rebellious, and paradoxical self. The bitter fact that she, as a woman, would have been victimized by historical Cossacks has no more bearing on her attraction to the myth than did the fact of Babel's

Jewishness. For these writers, the Cossack loses his national and chauvinist aura in favor of his role as violent-creative poet.[46]

Kamenskii and the Cossack Transformed

In the years immediately preceding and following the Revolution, Cossack adulation in all the arts was at a peak. Sergei Esenin portrayed Pugachev in an extremely popular play by that title. Konstantin Trenev also wrote a play called *Pugachevshchina,* as well as short stories, and Tsvetaeva's friend Maksimilian Voloshin wrote a lyric titled "Sten'ka's Judgment" ("Sten'kin sud"). Several poems about Cossacks were published by Khlebnikov's friend and memoirist, Dmitrii Petrovskii, as was a narrative poem *Sten'ka Razin* by A. Glazunov. Even Gor'kii wrote a screenplay based on the legendary life of Stepan Razin. And on May 1, 1919, Lenin himself dedicated a statue to Sten'ka Razin in Red Square.[47]

During this time, the official attitude toward the Cossack past was taking a turn, and history was being rewritten with the help of the arts. A trilogy of narrative poems by the Futurist poet Vasilii Kamenskii, written over sixteen years, demonstrates this changing depiction of the Cossack hero through the twenties and thirties.

Vasilii Vasil'evich Kamenskii (1884–1961), together with his friend and supporter Velimir Khlebnikov, David Burliuk, and Elena Guro, organized the literary group of "Cubo-futurists" in 1910. Kamenskii was also one of the first Russian pilots, and although much of his early poetry called for a return to the quiet of nature, he had little trouble accepting the rapid changes brought about by the Revolution. He followed, as he entitled his biography in 1931, *The Way of the Enthusiast.*

It is difficult to say whether Khlebnikov influenced Kamenskii in the use of the Razin motif or vice versa,[48] since the latter claimed to have had an interest in Razin since childhood, when he bought a cheap popular publication about the folk hero and "went berserk with rapture."[49] Kamenskii replayed his enthusiasm about Razin in various genres. The novel *Sten'ka Razin* of 1915 (1916 on the cover) was rewritten and published under the title *Stepan Razin* in 1918, at which time Kamenskii also published a *poema, Native Heart—Sten'ka Razin,* already cited in Chapter 7. From this grew a play, *Sten'ka Razin,* subtitled a "Collective Presentation in Nine Pictures," published in 1919 (republished in 1923) and reworked into an "Epic Fairy Tale [*bylinnyi skaz*] in 5 Acts, 8 Pictures," published in 1925. Meanwhile, Kamenskii substantially rewrote the original *poema* and published it under the title *Stepan Razin,* dated 1912–20. This *poema* became the first section of his Cossack trilogy that also includes the long narrative poems *Emel'ian Pugachev* and *Ivan Bolotnikov.*[50]

In his third-person autobiography *His-My Biography of a Great Futurist,* Kamenskii discusses his reasons for turning to Razin:

> He [Kamenskii] was ignited by the flame of a great idea—to render the whole essence of the Russian soul, its whole high-yielding talent, its whole violent will, its whole folk wisdom—in the single figure of Sten'ka Razin, whose singular image has lived in us for centuries, in us, with our boundless love of a free life. He [Kamenskii] unfurled all of his creative powers from a sincere heart and without exception, becoming breathless from the onrush of songs and from its scope.[51]

Kamenskii thus turned to the Cossack as a symbol of "the whole essence of the Russian soul," of native Russian creativity, violence, willfulness, folk wisdom, and a boundless love of freedom. Kamenskii also mentions his own, as it were, Cossack energy, fed by fire, song, and expansiveness *(razmakh).* That Razin is an appropriate figure to express these qualities pays homage to the richness of the Cossack myth.

Kamenskii's play *Sten'ka Razin* begins with Razin's departure from his wife, Alena. He claims he must leave to fight

> for the people's happiness, no matter what the consequences—for the crowning will—for the land and sacred toil—for the mountains—the seas—the forests—towns—meadows—rivers. For the clear sky. For the wide openness. For love and all-inclusive truth. For true brotherhood—for the friendship of all men and for eternity.[52]

Razin obviously understands his mission in a broad, mythic sense. He is responsible for all of space (the wide openness) and all of time (eternity). He is the protector of the "concerns of the people," which, as Alena recognizes, "call out more heatedly" than his private domestic affairs. Inevitably, the Cossack abandons his wife in favor of his participation in the sacred brotherhood, as he claims, of the Russian *narod.*

Razin ends his final conversation with Alena on an explanation of the "Russian heart." It is as flowing, expansive, and deep as the Volga, he claims. "And it is as proud to reflect the heavenly calm of eternity and is as freely wise [*vol'nomudroe*] in storms." In other words, the "concerns of the people" that he is fated to protect exhibit all the boundlessness of the Cossack myth. Alena adds that the Russian heart is like song, again a connection between the "soul of Russia" and the traditional Cossack image. Furthermore,

143

And the heart is always a miracle—a suddenly changeable, suddenly revealing miracle—suddenly creating, suddenly fluttering its wings. Always fiery—loving—always a brave life, a young life. And the free blood burns like strong wine.[53]

In this passage, as hackneyed in the original as in translation, Kamenskii not only links Razin and the Russian heart, but attributes to that heart all of the Cossack characteristics: their youth, drink, creativity, spontaneity, and bravery.

As is the case so often with writers who adopt Cossack heroes, Kamenskii himself is repeatedly called a Cossack. Kornei Chukovskii writes: "His poem *Sten'ka Razin* shows that indeed the howling and cries of massacres live in this bright-eyed child, that the curved knife suits his hand, that Sten'ka Razin is no stranger to him."[54] Stepanov, the editor of Kamenskii's poetry in the *Biblioteka poeta* series, claims that the subject of most of the poet's work was himself, and that in the Razin work too, the Cossack is "a *gusli* player, a singer, very reminiscent of the personality of the author himself" (*Stikh* 17, 24).

Kamenskii began his mythic Razin works in the teens and continued to work on them during the early, experimental years after the Revolution. Not until 1931, however, did he write a companion piece to *Stepan Razin,* having turned to another Cossack character, Pugachev. The long narrative poem *Emel'ian Pugachev* (*Stikh* 181–267) reflects the reassessment of the historical Pugachev that was carried out in the twenties, already referred to in the Introduction to the second part of this study. In this poem, the mythic qualities of the Cossack begin to lose their impact. Pugachev has changed from a violent anarchist to a well-planned revolutionary, and comes to resemble more and more a miraculously prescient early precursor of Lenin and the Bolsheviks.

A play, *Emel'ian Pugachev* (1925), preceded the *poema* by a number of years. (Kamenskii's experimentation with a particular theme through various genres was already noted in the case of Razin.) Responding to this play, a revisionist critic in 1926 praises Kamenskii's work in contrast to similar plays by Esenin and Trenev: "Almost all of our history, and following it our fictional writing, is imprisoned by the old aristocratic, class-based representation of Pugachev and his rebellion," he claims. But Kamenskii gives us "a historically accurate *living* Pugachev, the sober politician and realist, and most of all, an exceptional organizer."[55] The spontaneous nature of the Cossacks' revolt for "Rus'" and the freedom it symbolically represents give way to a well-planned class uprising. No longer the romantic figure of a "peasant tsar," Pugachev becomes an organizer with acute political wisdom who rallies the workers even more ardently than he does the ideologically less savvy peasantry.

Kamenskii's *poema* that grew from the play in the early thirties further emphasizes Pugachev as revolutionary prototype. Many of the motifs are still borrowed from the Cossack myth:

> The steppe is our mother,
> Our father is Pugachev
> (Step'—nasha mat',
> Otets—Pugachev.)
> (*Stikh* 215)

> The steppe is mighty wide.
>   Beyond the steppe—wider than canyons.
> (Stepi shibko shiroki.
>   Za stepiami—shire iar'.)
> (*Stikh* 219)

Pugachev's men are compared to birds: "We are all free birds" (Vse my— vol'nye ptitsy, *Stikh* 196). Pugachev himself is compared to Razin: "Just like Razin— / A knight of the steppe" (Vrode kak Razin— / Stepnoi bogatyr', *Stikh* 197).

Nonetheless, a new view of the Cossack emerges. Pugachev still concerns himself with Rus', but now the noun is repeatedly modified to imply that the Rus' he defends belongs only to the poor class. Thus, Rus' is called "barefoot," "louse-ridden," and specifically "the peasant Rus'" (Rus' muzhitskaia, krepostnaia Rus', *Stikh* 184, 188, 190, 196). Workers converge from various areas of the empire, emphasizing the all "union" support behind the rebellion as well as the proletarian nature of it (*Stikh* 247). Kamenskii's Cossack has come a long way from Pushkin's strong-willed Pugachev and Gogol's Taras Bul'ba.

Kamenskii's poem *Ivan Bolotnikov* (1934) moves the Cossack hero even further in the direction of the revolutionary proletariat. Bolotnikov was a serf sold into slavery and finally freed. He incited a mass rebellion of Cossacks and peasants in support of the second False Dmitrii in the early years of the seventeenth century, and succeeded in advancing to the edge of Moscow. When the pretender to the throne failed to appear, however, dissension grew among Bolotnikov's followers, and the rebel leader was eventually imprisoned, blinded, and drowned.

The trilogy of narrative poems about Cossack heroes, published as a whole in 1935, reveals a striking progression from myth to revisionist history. Stepanov claims *Stepan Razan* was written passionately, *Emel'ian Puga-*

chev with more of an eye to historical and social causes, and *Ivan Bolotnikov* as a biography and episodes from the peasant revolt.[56] It is significant that the commentary to the poems in the *Biblioteka poeta* series nowhere refers to the three heroes as Cossacks, but only as peasant rebels.

Although Kamenskii's third *poema* of the trilogy does stray occasionally from a strict historical account and includes details of Bolotnikov's life unknown in the documentary evidence about the rebellion, it nonetheless portrays the Cossack in a much more historical, time-bound manner than we would expect from previous appearances of the mythic Cossack hero. When *Stepan Razin* was accused of not being historically correct, Kamenskii asserted that his work was not intended to be historical but free (*privol'noe*).[57] By the time Kamenskii wrote *Ivan Bolotnikov,* sixteen years after the Revolution, his priorities had changed.

This third *poema* is by far the longest of the three, almost five times the length of *Stepan Razin.* It contains more emphasis on detail and description of nontraditional Cossack locales, including Turkey and Venice, the latter complete with gondolas and palaces:

> All the horror
>> In countless bodies
>>> Is reflected around
> In all Venice
>> The palazzos, islands
>>> (More than one hundred of them)
> Canals everywhere,
>> Two hundred squares,
>>> Four hundred bridges.
> (Vsia zhut'
>> V beschislennykh telakh
>>> Otrazhena vokrug
> Na vsiu Venetsiiu
>> Palatstso, ostrovov
>>> (ikh bolee chem sto),
> Sploshnykh kanalov,
>> Dvukh soten ploshchadei,
>>> Chetyresta mostov.)
> (*Stikh* 309)

In Venice, Bolotnikov marries Mariia, with whom he returns to Russia. On the way home through Poland he has an audience with Molchanov, a Polish nobleman who has decided to enlist the Cossack (again, nowhere referred to as such) in an effort to usurp the Russian throne in Moscow. But the self-serving pretender is a power-hungry conniver who plans to steal Bolotnikov's wife and discard the Cossack after he has claimed Moscow:

146

```
       I would sit
          Behind the tsar's table
   With the love
       of Mariia Kolomba,
          as my own,
              And as for him [Bolotnikov], onto the
                 threshing floor with him.
       ("Za tsarskim stolom by
          Sidet' mne
   S liubov'iu
       Marii-Kolomby,
          Mne,
              A emu na gumne."
   (Stikh 336)
```

Molchanov's protestations about the necessity of freeing poor Rus' are delivered hypocritically against this background. Yet, in the largest departure from the Cossack myth, Bolotnikov is easily duped. He is not the all-knowing, fatherly Taras Bul'ba, or even the clever and independent Razin of Kamenskii's own early verse. Instead, after a very short speech during which Molchanov pleads for his favors, Bolotnikov responds:

```
   Tsar Dimitrii!
       I have heard
          Many rebels,
   But I have not heard,
       Nor seen kings
          or tsars.
   And I thought,
       That a tsar
          Is the executioner of the people.
   Yet here,
       With you,
          You cry about the people.
   And I give my word—
       For the great honor
          I will carry over the earth
              the good news:
   Tsar Dimitrii—
       Our tsar,
          Is the true tsar!
   (Stikh, p. 337)
```

For the peasant rebel to confess disillusionment with tsardom is anachronistic at the least ("I thought that a tsar is the executioner of the people").

147

And for him to join the campaign of a non-Cossack so quickly, although claiming to have no experience with tsars in order to judge the veracity of this one, is perhaps required by the historical account, but most certainly not the mythic tradition. Ignorant and easily manipulated, Bolotnikov becomes pathetic rather than tragic at his eventual capture.

Most important for a change in the twentieth-century Cossack tradition, no more do we find parallels between the violence of the Cossack and the creativity of the poet. There is no evidence that Bolotnikov in any way represents Kamenskii, or that his rebellion relates to the poetic process. No longer does the Cossack preserve much less resurrect boundless, eternal Rus'—the origins and essence of the author—through the medium of poetry. He is not "self" and "other," not paradoxically destructive creation, but simply one of many historic precursors of the Leninist revolutionary.

Socialist realism, the doctrine of art officially accepted by the Soviet Writers Union in 1934, the year Kamenskii wrote *Ivan Bolotnikov,* had no room for violent creativity. The artist's job was to further the development of socialism, not express ambivalent attractions to politically suspect characters. Poetry in fact became just that: a job, not a revolution.

Speculations on why writers of the Stalinist period found it difficult to continue to embrace the boundless aspects of the Cossacks will be made later in this study, after an analysis of Sholokhov's treatment of the myth, which parallels Kamenskii's development. What is abundantly clear is that Soviet nationalism no longer had room for anarchic, independent symbols of freedom like the Cossacks of old. As always, the Cossack is both attractive *and* threatening. For political purposes, the threat now required taming.

TEN

Mikhail Sholokhov and Transfer of the Staff of Power

Mikhail sholokhov (1905–84), like Babel and the Futurist poets, embraced the Cossack tradition with perspicacity and ardor. Nonetheless, a study of his major novel, *The Quiet Don* (*Tikhii Don,* 1928–40), reveals the deathblows Sholokhov actually dealt to his supposedly beloved heroes. Although Cossacks appear sporadically in the work of later Soviet writers, they no longer exude the mythic force of their literary ancestors.

Sholokhov's early stories, all of which concern the Don Cossack region of southern Russia, fit into one small volume of *Don Stories* (*Donskie rasskazy,* 1926). They contain a number of stock lyrical descriptions of the steppe and the Don, but will not concern us in the following pages. Instead, this chapter will focus exclusively on the novel that led to Sholokhov's Nobel Prize, a work he began in the mid-twenties but did not complete for an entire decade.

Like Tolstoi and Babel, Sholokhov personally knew Cossacks on whom he could draw for his characters. Born illegitimately to a maid who was quickly married off to an elderly Cossack, the future author had legal if not natural Cossack status until the age of seven, when his widowed mother married his actual father, a Russian merchant. Except for two years spent in school in Moscow, even his participation in the Revolution and Civil War as an adolescent did not take Sholokhov far from the Don Cossack region of his birth. Only at the age of seventeen did he leave to seek his adult fortune in Moscow. Eventually Sholokhov penetrated the literary circles of the young Soviet Union and became a major apologist for socialist realism until his death in 1984.[1] Sholokhov considered himself a spokesman for Cossack rights in the Soviet Union, and many look to his novel for information on Cossack history and cultural life.

The Cossack Legacy

Countless pages have been written on Sholokhov's realistic depiction of the Don Cossacks, and too few on the relationship of that depiction to literary myth.[2] *The Quiet Don* clearly claims its place among other Cossack works by use of the mythic topoi identified in Part 1. Yet at the same time we can detect a self-conscious distancing in Sholokhov's portrayal of his heroes, bordering occasionally on parody. Thus Sholokhov begins to demythologize even as he glorifies.

That Sholokhov adopts the Cossack myth is obvious from easily identifiable quotations from other famous Cossack works. Though the action of major sections of *The Quiet Don* transpires in the area around the town of Veshenskaia where Sholokhov himself was born, references occur throughout the novel to works that depict Cossacks from other areas and other times, establishing the book's heroes as descendants of literary, not actual, Cossacks. At one point, the narrator lapses into speech patterns familiar to us from Gogol:

> O native steppe! Bitter is the wind settling on the manes of the mares and stallions, and on a horse's dry snout, salty from the wind. And the horse, breathing in the bitter salty smell, chews its silky lips and neighs, sensing on them the aftertaste of wind and sun. O native steppe beneath the low Don sky! The twisting paths of the gullies and the dry valleys, of the red-clayed ravines, the expanse of feather grass with its overgrown nestlike trace of a horse's hoof, the mounds, guarding the buried Cossack glory in wise silence. . . . I bow low and like a son I kiss your fresh earth, o Don steppe, soaked with unrusting Cossack blood![3]

The apostrophe to the land, the claim of kinship, the poetic style and repeated use of exclamation points, and the sudden switch to first-person, present-tense narration all remind the reader of *Taras Bul'ba* and the lyrical relationship of its narrator to the steppe and the Dnepr. The passage from *The Quiet Don* takes the reader unawares, however, as it contrasts strongly to the less personal narration that surrounds it. Sholokhov uses this literary quotation to remind readers of the Cossack tradition on the one hand, and to denaturalize the myth on the other. By consciously pointing to it, he diminishes its power.

References to Tolstoi's *The Cossacks* serve the same purpose.[4] Sholokhov repeats almost word for word Eroshka's famous philosophical statement about the grass that grows over our graves when we die, indicating the majesty and wholeness of life compared with the insignificance of individual moments within it.[5] Sholokhov writes: "The graves will grow over with grass—the pain will grow over with time" (III:192). Later in the novel he alters the quotation somewhat, though not enough to obscure the reference to Tolstoi:

> Only the grass grows on the earth, indifferently accepting the sun and bad weather, feeding on the earth's life-giving juices, submissively bowing under the fatal breath of the storms. And then, tossing its seed to the wind, it just as indifferently dies, with the rustle of its dying blades it greets the autumn sun, illuminating death. (IV:278)

Sholokhov thus self-consciously associates his Cossacks with those of Gogol through a similar stylistic digression, and with those of Tolstoi through a similar enunciation of philosophy. He may also refer to "The Death of Dolgushov," Babel's story from *Red Cavalry*, by an identical narrative event: a wounded Cossack lies with his insides hanging out of his body, and begs his comrades to shoot him (II:371). Again, the repetition assumes literary competence on the part of the readers, and thus distances them from un-mediated involvement in myth.

The only direct reference to a specific literary work about Cossacks most certainly parodies the myth. The hero, Grigorii Melekhov, receives a letter in which he is chastised for treating enemy prisoners too harshly: "You go around with your squadron like Taras Bul'ba from the historical novel by the writer Pushkin. You give everything over to fire and sword and upset the Cossacks" (IV:222–23).

By citing the novel but confusing the author, the letter writer does more than demonstrate the low level of his literacy. He also indicates how the particular qualities Gogol gives to Taras have become a general model. The writer may never have read Gogol's novel, or any novel at all, but he still feels confident of the reality of the image of a Cossack he preserves in his imagina-tion. He feels so confident, in fact, that he can compare what seems real (but is in fact only a character in a book) to an actual Cossack of his experience (who is, of course, only a character in *our* book).

Cossack characters themselves, in fact, are most strongly captivated by the power of the Cossack myth in *The Quiet Don*, and thus Sholokhov lightly parodies his heroes, disallowing full identification by the supposedly more sophisticated reader. Chubatyi,[6] a particularly violent Cossack nationalist, teaches Grigorii to slice a man in two and proclaims, as though reciting some Cossack creed, "To kill an enemy in battle is a holy deed" (II:323). A Cos-sack named Chikamasov later has an argument with Bunchuk, a major rep-resentative of the socialist movement in the novel, during which the former asserts that the freedom fighter Lenin must be, in fact, a Cossack. Chika-masov asks:

"Lenin, what nationality is he? I mean, where was he born and where did he grow up?"

"Lenin? He's a Russian."

"Whah?!"

"Really, a Russian."

"No, my brother. It's obvious you don't know much about him. . . . You know what kind of blood he has? Ours. He's a Don Cossack, born in the Sal'skii region, in the village of Velikokniazheskaia. You get it? He served as an artilleryman, so they say. And he looks exactly like a Cossack from the lower region. He has those strong cheekbones and those same eyes."

"Where did you hear that?"

"The Cossacks talked it over themselves, so I got to hear."

"No Chikamasov! He is Russian, a native of Simbirsk province."

"No, I don't believe you. And it's simple to see why. Wasn't Pugach [Pugachev] a Cossack? And Stepan Razin? And Ermak Timofeevich? That's how it is! Everyone who raised the poor folk against the tsar, they all were Cossacks. And you say he's from Simbirsk province. Why, it's shameful to hear you say such things . . ."

Smiling, Bunchuk asked:

"So they say he's—a Cossack?"

"And he *is* a Cossack, only he won't say so yet. The minute I set eyes on him, I'll know for sure." (III:158–59)

Another Cossack speaks in language as flowery as that of Gogol's narrator in *Taras Bul'ba,* suggesting that his attraction to the Cossack land is based much more on the romanticism of myth than on the reality of experience. He rhapsodizes:

I love the Don insanely—all that old Cossack way of life, laid down over centuries. I love my Cossacks and the Cossack women—I love them all! The smell of steppe wormwood makes me want to cry. . . . And what's more I love so deeply and painfully the smell of sunflower blooms and vineyards moistened by the rain wafting over the Don. . . . (III:112)

Despite elements of parody, however, the reader is not always able to distance him or herself from "naturalized" expectations of the Cossack heroes, just as the characters cannot. Sholokhov carefully draws on mythic topoi to establish Grigorii Melekhov as a Cossack of tradition, only to undermine the myth as the novel progresses.

The Quiet Don begins with a history of the Melekhov family. The laconic descriptions of primal events lend an almost biblical tone to the opening. Such a tone helps the reader understand the first few pages as an iconic history of all of Cossackdom, and sets up the Melekhovs as archetypal Cossacks.

The Melekhovs' farm is located at the very edge of the village *(na samom kraiu)*, like the Cossacks themselves on the border of the empire, surrounded only by the free Don River and the open steppe. Prokofii, the primogenitor of the Melekhov family, has returned to the village from Turkey and brought back typical Cossack booty: a Turkish woman who soon produces a son. The latter grows up to marry a Cossack girl: "And from that time on, Turkish blood intermingled with the Cossack" (II:12). Thus Sholokhov informs us that the Melekhov family grew from a mixture of opposites—Turkish and Cossack, East and West.

Prokofii lives isolated with his wife, "in his own hut, on the outskirts of town by the Don, as a lone wolf" (II:10). The dialect word Sholokhov chooses for "hut," *kuren'*, is also the term for a Zaporozhian Cossack military unit. The Melekhovs are Don, not Zaporozhian, Cossacks, but Sholokhov implies a connection between the two with this homonym. They are the true Cossacks who set themselves apart from the other village dwellers, the "non-Cossacks" of this iconic tale. Although the neighbors would of course be Cossacks if this were history, not myth, here Sholokhov stresses their separation from the Melekhov family in order to establish the essential Cossack nature of the central characters.[7]

Rumors fly around the town that the Turkish wife is a witch, a common topos of the Cossack myth. The townspeople eventually attack the alienated couple, killing the wife and causing the premature birth of the son mentioned above. The baby is born from violence, an auspicious beginning for a Cossack, as for any mythic hero. Little Pantalei, named after his grandfather and cared for by his grandmother, details which stress the continuity of the Cossack line, is described as "somewhat Turklike." Pantalei in turn fathers Grigorii, the main hero of the novel, and passes on to his son the mixture of olive skin and Cossack blood.

Although Sholokhov grounds the action of his novel in the Revolution and Civil War years, he also destroys historicity by associating his Cossacks with the limitless steppe and liminal space and time. He uses descriptions of the steppe and the Don River almost interchangeably to evoke a sense of expanse and of abundant, enduring life. A song sung by two Cossacks in book 3 of *The Quiet Don* announces that "our Don, the quiet Don" is "our father" *(nash batiushka)* and the Don steppe "our mother" *(nasha matushka)* (III:111). The Cossacks respond to each on equally personal and exalted terms. The narrator names the steppe "the virgin, never plowed, inviolable steppe" (IV:30) and calls it, as had Gogol, "a green, limitless expanse" (IV:33). At one point the narrator tells us that "the eastern wind acts Cossacklike [*kazakuet*] along the native steppe" (IV:144). Not only do the Cossacks take on the free characteristics of their environment, but the environment correspondingly draws from them.

Sholokhov's use of epic references—tales, song, and the typical comparisons of the heroes to birds of flight—further associates his Cossacks with those of the literary tradition through the destruction of historical verisimilitude.[8] In the very beginning we meet Grandpa Grishaka who tells tales of the past to an assembled crowd (II:19). Sholokhov sets up Grishaka as a bard figure who remembers and transmits the past for the benefit of a changing present. In many ways he is a comic figure, like Tolstoi's Eroshka, who preserves the Cossack heritage at the expense of respect from the modern world. It is interesting that Grishaka becomes a prophet of doom in the novel (IV:293–94), for to prophesy is to tell tales of the future, just as to sing like a bard is to tell tales of the past. Thus the character of Grishaka connects past, present, and future as he watches the world decay around him. The coincidence of his name and Grigorii's, especially when the latter is called by the endearing nickname "Grishka," passes the suggestion of endurance onto the Melekhov household.

Several pages after the introduction of Grandpa Grishaka, we are told that Grigorii possesses a good singing voice (*zvuchii golos,* II:30). His loss of that voice at one point in the novel signals the distance he temporarily feels from the life and joy of his Cossack spirit. Grigorii's heart constricts as he thinks that "I played long ago as a boy, but now my voice has dried up and life has cut off the songs" (II:391). Songs return, however, and although the new ones are "decorated with a black joylessness" (III:21), the urgent, invigorating words of the ancient Cossack song "still burst through" (III:22).

Not only Grigorii's voice but he himself is thought to die and be reborn. After his family has already mourned his fall in battle, Grigorii sends a letter informing his brother that he is, in fact, alive. Several pages after the description of the family's reaction to Grigorii's rebirth, and to his new medal of valor, Sholokhov provides us with a retelling of the events in which Grigorii's fellow soldiers also think him dead. When he reappears among them, one exclaims, "Where have you turned up from?" and Grigorii answers, "From the other world" (s togo sveta, II:368). The sarcasm of this response pushes the traditional topos of rebirth toward parody; irony continues to reverberate with heroic overtones.

The motif of rebirth is parodically reinforced when Stepan, Grigorii's neighbor and the husband of his lover, undergoes a similar experience. Rumors circulate that he has been killed, and when he returns he too is asked: "So where have you turned up from?" (IV:66). The repetition draws attention to the iconic, not realistic, nature of the event; Cossacks may die, but death is only a precursor to their returns. In Stepan's case, he returns from

154

prison in Germany smoking a cigar, sporting stylish clothes and a silver watch, and having cut off his traditional Cossack forelock. Grigorii's mother remarks: "You're not like a Cossack anymore" (IV:69). When he drinks, however, he loses his foreign accent, showing him to be still a true Cossack at heart. These episodes suggest that it takes more than war or prison to kill the Cossack heroic tradition. The end of mythic Cossackdom can come only through literary devices, in the way it first developed.

The women of *The Quiet Don* demonstrate again Sholokhov's conscious manipulation of traditional Cossack topoi, parodying as well as praising. The Turkish woman who founds the Melekhov family, who is rumored to be a witch, has questionable gender, and she usurps the male role, like Grigorii's sister-in-law, Dar'ia, by wearing pants. On the other hand, the matriarch of the family contemporaneous with the main events of the novel, Grigorii's mother Il'inichna, appears not as a seductress-devil, but more like the all-suffering, ever-patient mother in *Taras Bul'ba*. Mothers do not threaten because they are asexual. All the other major females, however, provide nothing but pain for the Cossacks, and almost always through the medium of their sexuality. Aksin'ia, of course, is the prime example, with her "evil will" and "black pride" (IV:76), labels that refer directly to her sensuality and consequent entanglement with Grigorii.

The character of Dar'ia develops the theme of female sexuality and corruption to an almost caricaturelike extreme. Her loose behavior spawns talk among the villagers and eventually leads to her own suicide, provoked by the knowledge that she has contracted a venereal disease. Described on numerous occasions as masculine (IV:148, IV:210, V:128, V:200), she can wield a gun and kill in cold blood. Thus she both flaunts her sexuality and refuses to remain in the prescribed and nonthreatening female role of mother of Cossacks, rejecting the model of Il'inichna and the wife of Taras. Interestingly enough, her marriage to Petro produces no Cossack sons. In fact, the only union that produces surviving children is the least sensual one, that between Grigorii and his legal wife, Natal'ia. In *The Quiet Don,* as in the Cossack myth in general, women whose presence is too sexually threatening lead only to grief.

The nonheroic characters in *The Quiet Don* further reinforce the novel's inheritance from and comment on the Cossack myth. Evgenyi Listnitskii is a Cossack whose family has long since given up its connection to Cossack life and become landed aristocracy in the Russian empire. His huge estate, Iagodnoe, is surrounded by a brick wall, an indication in its very first description that the home is utterly different from the unbounded, open space associated with the Cossacks. One building even sports a mosaic of tiles tracing the numerals 1910, connecting the family to a specific year in recent history, rather than the timelessness of Cossack myth. And the fact that Iagodnoe is located far from the Don is frequently repeated, stressing its alienation from the source of Cossack life.

While living at Iagodnoe with Aksin'ia, Grigorii confesses, "I miss the Don. You can't see the flowing water here. It's a tedious place" (II:213). The estate lies sunk in "wooden boredom, and, walling the estate off from the rest of the world, the days pass, each like the one before" (II:216). The reference to boredom recalls Gogol's two Ivans and points again to Sholokhov's inclusion of the inverted myth within his otherwise heroic tale. The inversion, like the parodic elements already referred to, begin to erode the foundations of the myth. Sholokhov does more than merely contrast the Cossacks to the non-Cossacks, as Gogol did with the Poles, or to Cossacks who have betrayed their fellows, as with Andrii. The heroic Cossack himself is infected.

The most poignant inversion of the Cossack world is the presence on the estate of birds that do not fly, including ducks, guinea fowl, and peacocks. The old Listnitskii, Evgenyi's father, keeps a wounded crane whose wing hangs lifelessly by its side and who is unable to join his fellow wild cranes in flight (II:216–17). Both the older and the younger Listnitskii enjoy shooting birds, a clear betrayal of the Cossacks who themselves are compared to birds of flight.

We first meet Listnitskii after he has proposed a horse race against Mit'ka Korshunov. Mit'ka, the underdog, wins the race and our sympathies as well at this point, but Sholokhov soon indicates that he, too, is not a true Cossack. His family, we are told, is richer than the other Cossack families in the village. Their wealth isolates them, although certainly not to the extent it does the Listnitskiis. Their house contains articles not found in other Cossack huts, including an oilcloth on the table with pictures of the tsar and tsarina and of the imperial princesses, a detail that connects the family to the Russian empire, not to the free Cossack land.

The name Korshunov derives from the Russian word for kite, a large bird similar to a hawk that soars over the steppe, preying on small animals. In the division of good and evil birds in the Cossack tradition, kites clearly fall in the latter category. Mit'ka Korshunov ends the novel as an executioner in the punitive detachment of the White Army, where he is famed for his cruelty. Cossacks of the myth are also cruel, but even other Cossacks condemn Mit'ka's actions. The Melekhovs claim he has turned out to be a "genuine Satan":

> Look at the type of service he has found for himself, not like the other Cossacks who serve in real areas. Why, he's joined the execution squad! And is that a Cossack's business—to be an executioner, to hang old women and chop up innocent babies with his sabre?! (V:108)

156

Early in the novel Mit'ka seduces the daughter of Mokhov, the richest merchant of the village. This liaison connects him yet again with a non-Cossack. It is also a perverse parody of the illicit affair between Grigorii and Aksin'ia. If the latter union between Cossack and female is condemned to grief and torment, so much more is the former condemned in light of the myth, for it transpires passionlessly. Liza Mokhova shows up once again in the novel, in the pages of a diary found by Grigorii on the body of a dead soldier. She has apparently gone on to lead other Cossacks astray.

Mokhov's name is derived from the Russian word for moss, and like moss his family quickly overgrew the Cossack village in which it settled. Mokhov traces his ancestry back to Peter the Great, under whose tutelage a Russian peasant by the name of Mokhov had come to the region as a secret agent. He is connected to the autocrat who suppressed Cossack freedom, as well as to illicit spying and peasantry. From that time, "they firmly sank into the Cossack land. They seeded and grew in the Cossack village like a tall weed that you cannot pull up no matter how hard you try" (II:112). Mokhov in the novel is a powerful symbol for all that stifles Cossack freedom: women, money, and official government. It is not external forces alone, however, which bring the destruction of the Cossacks in *The Quiet Don*.

The Cossacks Die Out

As early as the first volume, Sholokhov begins to cast doubt on the positive, life-engendering aspects of the myth. After Chubatyi associates Cossack military killing with holiness, as cited above, Grigorii notices with astonishment that horses do not like the violent Cossack and shy away when he approaches. "I have a hard heart in me, and they sense it," Chubatyi explains (II:324). The scene successfully severs any bond the reader may have formed with the violent Cossack, and induces questions about the values for which he stands. Grigorii is at first attracted to this Cossack and later disillusioned, his changing allegiance a mark of his own confusion. But his heart too grows hard as the novel progresses, even as he questions the Cossack way.[9]

Grigorii's ambivalence throughout the novel, the split allegiance, and his wavering between the White and Red camps or between the Cossack separatists and those who sought to join the Russians, parallels in microcosm the split among the Cossacks as a whole. The division among the Cossacks, often between the older and the younger Cossacks, was always part of the myth, usually as a way to suggest its historical aspects. Yet the infighting never led to the destruction of both sides, but rather to the reinvigoration of one, if not both. Taras Bul'ba becomes stronger as a result of his anger at Andrii and others who "went over to the Warsaw side." In Sholokhov's case, the emphasis falls decisively on increasing divisiveness, and never leads to reconciliation.

Book 3 of the novel begins with an authorial comment on the "great division" that occurred among the upper and lower Cossacks in 1918.[10] The narrator then steps back to make a general historical remark that focuses on the split evident among the Cossacks almost from their origins:

> History finally divided the upper from the lower Cossacks only in 1918. But the origin of the division took shape hundreds of years ago, when the less wealthy Cossacks of the northern districts, who had neither fertile lands around the Azov, nor vineyards, nor rich hunting and fishing grounds, broke away from Cherkassk [the Don Cossack capital]. They carried out voluntary raids on White Russian territories, and served as the most reliable strongholds for all the rebels, beginning with Razin and ending with Sekach.
>
> Even in later days, when the entire host was agitating mutely, crushed by the strong arm of autocracy, the upper Cossacks rose up openly and, led by the atamans, shook the tsarist foundations. (IV:9)

In this passage, Sholokhov reveals the undercurrent of dissension against which, he implies, the unified Cossack spirit will not hold out. A Cossack is a Cossack, the myth tells us, but by the end of *The Quiet Don* the Cossack brothers no longer recognize each other as all of one family.

The brothers Petro and Grigorii paradigmatically fight at times on opposites sides of the war, and less than halfway through the novel the narrator comments on what he calls the internecine strife *(semeinaia mezhdousobitsa)* rampant among the Cossacks, seen when the older men cannot get along with the young fighters returning from the front (III:194). Petro blames the army for dividing the Cossacks: "Look how they've split the people, the vermin! As though they had passed through with a plow, dividing us to opposite sides" (IV:25). But Grandpa Grishaka invokes a higher authority, deliriously citing Scripture to conclude: "And so it has come upon us that son rose against father and brother against brother" (IV:423). The whole Melekhov family loses its sense of unity and togetherness:

> The family fell apart before Pantalei Prokof'evich's eyes. He and his old woman were left alone. Kindred ties were destroyed unexpectedly and quickly, the warmth of mutual relations was lost, and more and more often notes of irritation and alienation crept into their conversations. They no longer sat around the communal table as a single and harmonious family, but rather as though they had accidentally gathered together. (V:120)

The family's dissolution parallels the breakup of the entire Cossack force.[11] The dissolution is complete when non-Cossack officers arrive to lead the troops (V:145). The Cossacks no longer rule themselves: "The Cossacks resent the officers, it seems. They've stuck us with such swine, there's no living with it. And they're almost all Russians, no Cossacks among them" (V:177).

The dissolution of the Cossack host is so complete that one character is forced to conclude: "All of a sudden we've become like the Jews—dispersed over the face of the earth" (V:293). The Wandering Jew of tradition is a pathetic model for the once powerful Cossacks. Like those with no home, the Cossacks no longer enjoy their former organic connection to the vast steppe. By the end of the novel, the narrative focus has narrowed from its former huge canvas to follow a small handful of Cossacks, as though they are all who remain. Those Cossacks have become bandits whose loyalties fluctuate and who group and regroup erratically, paying respect to no whole larger than their own individual selves.

Sholokhov reinforces the idea of the death of Cossackdom with the metaphor of aging in the members of the Cossack group. The soldiers grow gray as the war continues. Only the young sixteen- or seventeen-year-old "greenhorns" still approach the fighting with any excitement, and Sholokhov implies that they too will age. "The war is a novelty for them, something like a child's game" (IV:286). The more experienced soldiers look on the enthusiastic newcomers with contempt.

The Melekhov farm itself decays, in sympathy with the dying family. One by one the Melekhov household is depleted: Petro, Pantalei, Natal'ia, Dar'ia, and Grigorii's little daughter. The death of the matriarch, Il'inichna, summarizes the whole familial decline, for after her only an outsider, Koshevoi, is left to take charge. Unrelated old women prepare the body for burial, as though no family member concerns himself with the continuity of the line, and the Melekhov daughter, Dun'ia, must ask Aksin'ia to take Grigorii's children after their grandmother's death. This move out of the ancestral hut exemplifies the total break with the past and the dispersal of the family (V:324).

The Cossacks are not only dispersed but demoralized. When Grigorii reunites with his father at one point, the latter asks for news of the Cossack offensive: "I've heard some nonsense that the Cossacks don't want to go beyond the border. . . . Is it true?" he asks (IV:89). Grigorii answers evasively, for, in fact, the Cossacks have decided to stay within their former boundaries. "So, you're really planning to go no further than the borders?" repeats Pantalei (IV:90). One "sick and submissive" Cossack lazily justifies the Cossacks and expresses the general disillusionment at the same time: "Why go farther? I'm left with orphans here after my wife's gone. So why should I go and lose my life uselessly?" (IV:90).

No Cossack of myth would question death, but the Cossacks at the end of

The Quiet Don are worn out and worn down. By placing such an emphasis on the pathos of the exhausted community, Sholokhov profoundly alters the traditional Cossack attitude toward life as self-perpetuating and indeed extracorporeal. His Cossacks lose their "Cossackness" and thus their claim to immortality by accepting barriers instead of transcending them.

The general atmosphere at the end of the novel is one of boredom, as though Cossack life has become no better than the monarchist Listnitskii's estate. The narrator remarks, "The days dragged on and on, emasculated by boredom" (IV:94). Petro is reduced to pleading for his life (IV:215), the total opposite of Ostap Bul'ba's behavior at his execution, when he "endured the trials and tortures like a giant."[12] Even Grigorii feels his knees buckle at the sound of a shot by the end of the novel (V:459), and another Cossack finds himself unable to shoot at all. "Do you call this living?" Grigorii asks a fellow bandit at the end of the novel (V:485).

Grigorii Melekhov finally returns to a farm that is no longer his and embraces his abandoned son. "That was all that remained for him in life, all that for the time being linked him to the earth and to this whole huge world shining beneath the cold sun" (V:486). And the last Cossack prepares to die, just as the entirety of Cossackdom has already done.

A telling passage in the last volume captures the mood of despair surrounding the demise of the Cossacks. Grigorii finds himself in the middle of a retreating transport. As he lies huddled in his wagon he hears how "a steadfast and somewhat coarse voice flew out suddenly in the front, like a bird over the quieted steppe" (V:273). The voice begins an ancient Cossack song about the freedom of all the Cossacks—Don, Grebensk, and Iaik—and about the glorious steppe. Hundreds of Cossack voices join in the song, including that of Grigorii:

> It was as though something had snapped inside Grigorii. . . . A surging sob suddenly shook his body, a spasm clutched his throat. Swallowing tears, he waited avidly for the soloist to begin again and soundlessly whispered after him the words he had known since adolescence. (V:273)

But the Cossacks feel only pain as they immerse themselves in a melody which formerly belonged to them:

> A single ancient song that had survived the centuries now lived and ruled over the black steppe. In ingenuous and simple words it spoke of the free Cossack ancestors who had once thundered against the tsarist army, who had gone out thieving on the Don and the Volga in light boats, who had pillaged imperialist tsarist ships, probing merchants, boyars, and commanders, and taming distant Siberia. . . . And the descendants of those free Cossacks listened to the mighty

song in a morose silence as they shamefully retreated, having been beaten apart in the inglorious war against the Russian people. . . . (V:273)

The song survives, but the Cossacks do not. The spirit lives on only in incorporeal music. Even the steppe is dark corresponding to the beaten spirit of the heroes. As the song continues, the only response on the part of the Cossacks is a tense and gloomy silence. The mythic Cossacks themselves can no longer sing.

Passing of the Bunchuk

Thus Sholokhov chronicles the death of Cossackdom. Its unity is broken as brother fights brother, the youthful heroes grow old and decrepit, and the jubilant Cossack spirit itself declines into a miserable muteness.

The Quiet Don, however, does more than chronicle the end of the Cossack nation. It manipulates the myth, inherited from nineteenth-century literature, so that the traditional Cossack topoi are eventually transferred to the Bolsheviks. The new mythic hero to whom Sholokhov pays the most attention, Bunchuk, first appears in book 1 of *The Quiet Don.*[13] He is referred to as a "russified Cossack" who lived in Moscow and worked as a simple laborer before enlisting in the army (II:343). The fact that he was once a Cossack but is no longer one sets up a paradigm for the transfer of the Cossack topoi onto the new hero. When Bunchuk stands up to address a group of Cossacks, he fears he may have lost the ability to communicate with his former brothers: "He knew that one must speak with Cossacks using some other kind of words, and fearfully felt that, perhaps, he would not find a common language" (III:157).

Having mingled with the workers for so long, Bunchuk had learned their "language" and abandoned his own.

Yet the Cossack-turned-Bolshevik still retains his former characteristics. His hand is constantly described as "hairy,"[14] a curious detail until we realize that it is contrasted to the "white" hands of characters like Listnitskii who do *not* share Cossack characteristics. Even his name retains its Cossack connotations: a *bunchuk* is the traditional staff of a Cossack hetman. Bunchuk thus carries the mark of Cossack authority into the Bolshevik camp, and symbolizes the transfer of mythic power.

Like a mythic Cossack, Bunchuk even survives a metaphoric death: "a black emptiness, swollen with silence" closed over him (III:223). But Bunchuk's friend Anna acts as his mother, reviving him, feeding him, and bringing water to her totally dependent, childlike patient. She even reteaches him how to walk. "Why, you're just like a baby!" she exclaims when he whines for more milk (III:293).[15]

As a group, the Bolsheviks take up the Cossack proclivity for singing. As Sholokhov describes the Cossacks engaged in song less and less, he has the Red army soldiers sing more and more. And between songs, they act "like Cossacks," pillaging, raping, and murdering (III:322), so that rumors of their cruelty travel far (III:361).

The final link in the transfer of topoi from Cossack to Bolshevik occurs when Misha Koshevoi, one of the first Cossacks to join the socialists, marries Grigorii's sister and moves onto the Melekhov farm. The house and barn had fallen into total disrepair as the male Cossacks were forced away or died off. The place comes back to life, however, when Koshevoi moves in:

> From the day Koshevoi established himself in the Melekhov hut [again *kuren'*, the word for Cossack military unit used in the beginning of the novel], the entire farm took on a new look. In a short time he repaired the fence and brought steppe hay to be used on the threshing floor, and skillfully built a hayrick. To prepare for the grain harvest he redid the shelf and wings of the reaping machine, carefully cleared out the threshing floor, repaired the old winnowing fan, and cleaned up the horse's gear. . . . (V:317)

This passage ends with the statement that "the Melekhov hut grew, as it were, younger, looking out on the world with the bright-blue eyes of its windows."

The rejuvenation of the Cossacks' ancestral estate at the hands of the young socialist takes place literally in front of the dying Il'inichna and figuratively before all of disintegrating Cossackdom. The staff of power passes from the aged warrior survivors to the young couple, who help build the socialist future. Grigorii's return to the farm at the very end of the novel is only a pathetic whimper among the dying strains of the ancient Cossack song.

Sholokhov could not kill the Cossack myth—a myth is a cultural phenomenon larger than any one author—but he does profoundly alter it. By transferring onto the Bolsheviks many of the Cossack topoi, he perpetuates the heroes under a different name. The spirit, energy, life, and unity associated with the Cossack since the romantic period, that is, the very specialness of the Cossacks, now belong to another group entirely.

In her book *The Soviet Novel: History as Ritual,* Katerina Clark claims that the new socialist heroes of literature of the 1930s were *bogatyri,* or knights of folk literature, and linked to each other by their relationship to their horses.[16] The case of *The Quiet Don* suggests that the lineage of the new hero reaches back not to the medieval folk tale, as Clark suggests, but rather more directly to the Cossack of nineteenth- and early-twentieth-century literature. The horse mounted in the thirties was only recently abandoned by the Cossack hero.

The question remains why the heroes of the new Soviet literature after Sholokhov are referred to not directly as Cossacks but only as one aspect of the traditional hero, as *bogatyri*. Historians and writers of the twenties already removed Cossack references from Pugachev and Razin, disassociating the heroes from the anarchic Cossack tradition and narrowing their mythic scope. The label of *bogatyr'* similarly limits the hero. The Cossacks were frequently referred to as *bogatyri* in both folk literature and the stories of the nineteenth century, but the comparison points only to the exotic aspect of the heroes and ignores their role as representation of self. It was the interplay between self and other that made the Cossacks such ideal cultural models. The folk knights had superhuman powers, beyond the possibilities of the average public. But the Cossack hero bequeaths more than strength to the socialist realist one.

It is quite possible that the very ambivalence of the Cossack myth, that which makes it reverberate so well as part of Russia's cultural mythology, is also the aspect that rendered it dangerous when Soviet culture consciously attempted to develop its own definition under Stalin and socialist realism. The Cossacks' boundlessness leaves room for disloyalty. Just as the Cossack rebels fought the boyars and merchants but supported the tsarist model, the Soviet hero fights bureaucracy and bourgeois holdovers, but remains ever loyal to Stalin and the Party. Yet the distinction might have been too subtle in a society where potential Cossack freedom from establishment norms was no longer acceptable.

Ultimately, the *bogatyr'* is a fantastic hero, not a mythic one. Fantasy rests on the recognition of boundaries between realms. Myth, on the other hand, eliminates boundaries. The Soviet-Stalinist cultural definition would then logically exploit the fantastic over the mythic, for it consciously affirms limits, regardless of the rhetoric of "Ever higher" that Clark identifies.[17] Soviet heroes might stretch beyond the frontier—metaphorically or actually—but as a means not an end. Instead of reveling in the boundless realm they find beyond the former border, they stake out a further boundary. The new heroes conquer space in order to extend and defend their value system within it, rather than to be transformed themselves by the openness into which they have crossed. The standards of family, of patriotism, and of labor that the new heroes uphold require by definition the elimination of unrestricted Cossack liminality.

ELEVEN

Socialist Realism and Death to the Cossack Myth

THE EPILOGUE to *The Trial Begins* (*Sud idet,* 1960, written 1956), Abram Terts's literary attack on socialist realism, includes the following ironic assessment of the novel's hero, Vladimir Globov:

> How dearly I love this Emel'ian Pugachev who has turned into Aleksandr Suvorov, like the thunder of tanks along the cobblestones and the mad roar of loudspeakers, all the refined coarseness of our heroic epoch proudly marching across the land, clanking its medals and decorations.[1]

Somewhat earlier in the short novel, Globov is fascinated by a concert specifically because "the music did not flow on its own, but was controlled by the conductor."[2] His son Serezha, by contrast, is impressed by the same music as a chaotic, revolutionary flood that overwhelms; Globov by the flood that has been dammed. The apparent desire of the Soviet hero for order and structure explains the narrator's ironic comment above. Pugachev, the free and elemental Cossack, becomes Aleksandr Vasil'evich Suvorov, the eighteenth-century military tactician who delivered the defeated rebel to captivity. The metaphor shows Globov championing energy that has been tamed, enthusiasm that has been channeled to the good of the state. What remains of the Cossack is but the clank of medals and the thunder and roar of a self-proclaimed heroic age.

Terts's depiction of his socialist realist hero can stand as a model for the closing chapter of the story of the Cossack myth. Soviet literature parades before us a historical figure minus any inner paradoxes and contradictions, a warrior whose outer trumpery is all that remains of the once boundless hero.

"On Socialist Realism" (1959), the theoretical companion piece to *The Trial Begins,* includes a reference to Razin, and to his new role in Soviet literature. According to Terts, socialist realist novels are distinguishable by their adherence to an etiological view of history: all events lead toward the grand "Purpose" of the establishment of a communist state. As he realizes, however, "in more remote eras it is, alas, harder to find the movement toward Communism." Purpose, nonetheless, can be injected into works about historical characters:

> [Socialist realist writers] substitute and anticipate the as yet missing Purpose. And so the leaders of the past (Peter the Great, Ivan the Terrible, Pushkin, Sten'ka Razin), though they did not know the word "Communism," nonetheless know quite well that something bright awaits us in the future. They do not tire of speaking of this future from the pages of our historical works, constantly gladdening the readers with their astonishing perspicacity.[3]

The major forum for the Cossack hero after the end of the twenties became the "purposeful" historical novel. Yet as the books grew to epic length in the trilogies of the thirties, forties, and fifties, the Cossacks' stature shriveled. By granting Razin and Pugachev historical prescience, the authors took away their historical boundlessness. We are thrown back to the Cossack as one-dimensional allegory, as we could have found him in eighteenth-century puppet plays.

Terts's contribution to our understanding of the Cossack hero is thus twofold: like Sholokhov he suggests the transformation of the Cossack into a Soviet hero, but he also describes the binding of Cossack freedom and thus the elimination of the new hero's mythic stature. What we find instead is a superficial mythologizing based on only one facet of contradictory and ambiguous national symbols.

Chapaev: Ataman of the Steppe

Ironically, we can find the new Cossack/Communist hero in a novel written a number of years before the official establishment of the doctrine of socialist realism, about a commander fighting *against* Cossack forces in the Civil War. This book is *Chapaev* (1923) by Dmitrii Furmanov (1891–1926), which chronicles the career of Vasilii Ivanovich Chapaev, a valiant but anarchist military leader of the Twenty-fifth Division of the Red Army. In 1919, the forces under Chapaev's command helped counter the White offensive led by Kolchak.

The real hero of the novel is not Chapaev, but Fedor Klychkov, a thinly disguised depiction of Furmanov himself.[4] Through references to known events and actors in the Civil War, and by informing the reader that Klychkov/Furmanov kept a detailed diary of his experiences, Furmanov makes a claim to historical accuracy. Klychkov declares that out of his fragmented observations, "a history will come."[5] This assumption is neither more nor less verifiable than other such claims to historical truth in the texts discussed in this study. Likewise, Furmanov's Chapaev is as mythic as any Taras Bul'ba and, we shall see, mythic in a similar way. The novel stands as one of the first of any number of other attempts to recast the Revolution and its aftermath in an epic light. What is significant for us at this point is the unabashed use of Cossack topoi to bestow upon Chapaev his mythic aura. For Furmanov and his readers, "Cossack" had become firmly equivalent to "mythic hero." The skillful transfer of Cossack motifs onto Chapaev is all the more striking considering the fact that Cossacks themselves actually appear in the book. They are described, however, in negative terms, as vultures (i.e., "bad" birds of prey in the language of epic) and exploiters, or cowards who "always hit from behind" (61).

It is Chapaev and not a Cossack commander who is repeatedly called "ataman of the steppe." Although *ataman* may mean colloquially a leader of any type, its Cossack associations are unavoidable. In fact, Chapaev is explicitly compared to Cossack chiefs: "'He really is a native hero,' Fedor thought to himself. 'A hero from the camp of the freemen, like Emel'ka Pugachev, Sten'ka Razin, and Ermak Timofeevich'" (26).

The local regiments of Bolshevik workers and soldiers are called by the names of famous Cossacks; Chapaev's own is the Stepan Razin Regiment. Characteristically, as in most of the literature of the Soviet era, nowhere does Furmanov mention that Razin or Pugachev or Ermak is a Cossack. They are simply heroes, and as such Chapaev and his Red Army men have a heavy legacy: "For the Stepan Razin Regiment to retreat would have meant to disgrace its heroic name forever!" (165).

Chapaev, like the hero Taras Bul'ba before him, is particularly well known for his horsemanship. Klychkov notices immediately "how firmly and solidly Chapaev sat in the saddle, as though welded there" (59). And his men excel in singing. Chapaev is the best and most ardent singer among them. Song, of course, is not in the sole provinence of Cossacks, but the songs that Chapaev's warriors prefer glorify Cossack heroes:

In the evenings a choir would gather in the Sten'ka Razin Regiment. There were about twenty-five singers, and among them many with excellent voices. The problem was, they had no time to practice, what with all the battles and campaigns! But the desire to sing was so strong that at every stop, even if there was only a moment to rest, the singers would gather in a bunch around their beloved and respected director, each on his own without being called. . . . And the singing would begin. . . . They sang all kinds of songs, but the favorites were about Sten'ka Razin and Ermak Timofeevich. (206–7)

The Red Army men, we learn on the same page, also dance. "They sing and sing until they can no more—and then they start to dance." They continue to dance until they drop from exhaustion, and then take up song again. This passage cannot help but recall a similar description of the first sight that the Bul'ba sons catch of the Sech: a Cossack dancing away his last ounce of strength to the accompaniment of a crowd of musicians.

Again in a reference to *Taras Bul'ba,* we are told that Chapaev was not comfortable sitting idle. "The effort of the battle was Chapaev's element" (165). In Taras's case, "the idle life was not to his liking—he wanted real action,"[6] so he concocted the campaign against the Poles that precipitates the events of the book.

Chapaev further resembles the Cossack hero of *Taras Bul'ba* in his ability to use rhetoric to stir his fellow men on to action. And his figure on horseback, "in a black hat with red band, in his black cloak flapping in the wind like devil's wings" (77), reminds us of the dramatic, costumed Cossack of myth. Other borrowings from the Cossack myth in this text are extensive: the warriors are called eagles; the steppe is their mother; and Chapaev's regiment forms an indivisible but organic unit, a family with Chapaev, married to his sword, as father.

Perhaps most telling is the analysis within the text of the mythmaking process itself:

> For resounding glory [*slava*], resounding and glorious deeds are never enough. It is always necessary to have heralds, blindly dedicated people, who would believe your greatness, would be blinded by it, inspired, and would find their own joy in the singing of your glory. (166)

Furmanov here is describing epic bards, who sing stories of the epic glory of heroes. That his heralds are not blind, but blinded, does not alter the reference. Indeed, he immediately follows this passage with just such a "song," a laudatory letter from a soldier of Chapaev's regiment who is in fact blind.

Cossacks, of course, were not the only heroes upon which Furmanov may have drawn. An excellent case could be made comparing the Red Army men to warriors as far back as Homer's Achaians. But the specific references to Razin, Ermak, or Pugachev, combined with the various topoi clearly associated with Cossacks from nineteenth-century literature, suggest their closer, native Russian prototype. Furmanov transferred onto his Bolshevik hero the mythic tones of the earlier Cossack.

Chapaev does more, however, than duplicate Sholokhov's transfer of Cossack topoi onto Bunchuk when it suggests the harnessing of the new "Cossack" Bolshevik hero. The process that begins here ends in the socialist realist novels of the Stalinist period. There, the hero may still be called Razin or Pugachev, not simply "in the Razin regiment," but his mythic aura has been lost. He has been channeled into the Purpose of the State.

The harnessing of Chapaev, in fact, may be the main theme of the entire novel. Klychkov, the politically sophisticated Party spokesman, has been sent to the front specifically to bridle Chapaev, "the wild horse of the steppe" (97). In this striking metaphor, the "Cossack" hero moves from skilled horseman to domestic mount. References are made to the danger of anarchist activities, and a negative light is cast on spontaneous, uncontrolled energy in general. One of Klychkov's co-workers has the following response to what he calls "mob" actions: "'Devil take this anarchy!' Andreev muttered angrily. He fell silent a moment and then confidently and calmly proclaimed, 'We've broken worse than this—we'll get the best of all these, too'" (35). Andreev's desire to turn anarchy into order, and his belief in the inevitable success of his mission, set the tone for the whole novel. Klychkov himself realizes that he must gain the upper hand, must establish his own authority, and "then cross him, bridle him, direct him on the path of conscious struggle—not only of blind and instinctive struggle, no matter how colorful and heroic, no matter how resounding and glorious" (97). Only conscious, i.e., rational, structured, and Party-condoned, rebellion is viable for the new socialist realist hero.

It is telling that Klychkov masters Chapaev's horsemanship and bravery in battle more easily than Chapaev acquires Klychkov's political control. The message is obvious: although heroic spontaneity is all fine and good, the Soviet ideal requires order.[7] The friendship that Klychkov forges with Chapaev testifies to Lenin's call for the transformation of spontaneity into consciousness, and the union of heroic name and political savvy heralded the socialist realist hero of future historical novels. The new "Cossack" was not unbounded but rather carefully confined by Soviet strictures.

The Cossack in Historical Fiction

When Soviet historical fiction turned from the recent past to more distant events, it retained the values enunciated in *Chapaev*, including praise of channeled rebellion and support of and by the masses. Gor'kii reportedly told the writer Aleksei Chapygin (1870–1937), whom he urged to turn to the writing of history, and who followed the advice by publishing the multivolume *Razin Stepan* in 1925: "You must not shun history. Every historical subject depicted by an artist of the word following actual historical documents is equal to contemporaneity."[8] Historical subjects, and among them the Cossacks, would have a place in the new fiction for they could be shown to correspond to contemporary values. The "facts" of the historical Cossacks could be read now not through the filter of the nineteenth-century myth but through new Soviet glasses. And for this rereading, the genre of historical novel proved most appropriate.

The official preglasnost' Soviet view claimed that a socialist realist historical novel differs significantly from the traditional definition of the genre. In fact, the thirties in the Soviet Union presumably saw the birth of a new genre entirely: a historical narrative *(istoricheskoe povestvovanie)* as opposed to a novel *(roman).*[9] Walter Scott had always placed at the center of attention an imaginary hero whose fate is linked in some way to important historical figures, who in turn appear only on the periphery. Later historical novels supposedly turned to the depiction of real historical personages as the main heroes. But Soviet writers, the official view claimed, found even this inadequate. The Soviet historical novel instead reveals historical process through the presentation of the life of the people. Although major historical characters may share center stage, they do so only by right of their connection with the fate of the *narod.*[10]

Obviously, not every Soviet novel lives up to these precepts. In actuality, the injunction to feature the *narod* is a difficult one to fulfill. Not only must authors resort to the contortions perceived by Terts: the retrospective insertion into historical events of a class consciousness or purposefulness belonging to the Soviet era, and not necessarily to the period of the novel. Perhaps more difficult is the actual depiction of the masses as hero. When an author does choose a single hero, as in the numerous Stepan Razins or Pugachevs of the novels of the thirties, forties, and fifties, he must efface personal references, so that his Cossack becomes not only a generic Cossack but a generic member of the *narod* as well.

As in *Chapaev,* the historically documented rebellious aspects of the heroes must be downplayed, if not erased entirely. Or the rebellion must be channeled into politically acceptable forms. A certain tension is created in Soviet treatments of the Cossack in novels of the thirties and forties by an unbalanced equation of Cossack past to Stalinist present, mediated by the revolutionary Bolshevik. The Cossack operates as both rebel against tsarist control and upholder of a Soviet-style value system based on stability. In the first case he is an actor in the Marxist march of history toward socialism. In the latter he is a timeless bandit who submits to higher authority, a child in a family drama with the state as father. The problem revolves around control as negative in one historical period but positive in the other. The Cossack is good because he rebels against one form, good because he upholds another.

The contradiction is resolved not through the timeless juxtaposition of opposites as in the nineteenth-century tradition, but linearly and psychologically. In the course of the narrative, the Cossack leader repents of his early anarchic brigandage and, having seen the error of his ways, devotes himself instead to inciting the masses to carefully controlled revolt.

The so-called revolutionary "historical narrative" of socialist realism thus turns toward traditional bildungsroman. Over the course of the novel, the hero matures from rebellious adolescent to sophisticated ideologue. Such emphasis on psychological development necessarily belies mythical associations; maturation equals acceptance of the authoritative values of the state.

As socialist realist literature aimed at a larger and generally less sophisticated audience than the masterpieces of the nineteenth or early twentieth century, it was natural for it to draw some of its image of the Cossack hero from the lowbrow *lubok* literature of the turn of the century. There, too, individual brigandage is often condemned, the paternalistic social authority upheld. The Cossack was a particularly popular bandit-hero in these cheap novels and chapbooks. As in the higher literature, his freedom and energy were celebrated, but true to the moralistic quality of the popular fiction in general, his bachelor rebellion was shown to falter in the face of the more stable values of family and government.[11]

Like the *lubok* bandit, Razin and Pugachev also fail in Soviet historical novels, which almost always end with their execution. Yet they do not take off directly from the *lubok*, just as they do not from *Taras Bul'ba* and the Cossack tradition. They are captured and beheaded because of the superior strength of the tsarist forces which have not *yet* broken down (but inevitably will, we are led to believe, from their own internal corruption), aided by counterrevolutionary forces within the Cossack's own camp. The Cossack rebellion is nonetheless, or all the more, good, in so far as it is organized and represents the will of the people. The stability of the *narod*, not the government, is the value praised. As in the *lubok*, however, firmness and equilibrium, not boundlessness, dominate.

A good example can be found in Stepan Zlobin's (1903–65) monumental *Stepan Razin* (1951), a book so popular, and so orthodox in its socialist realism, that it was abridged and edited for schoolchildren. In the novel, Moscow has consolidated power over the Crimean Tatars and the Turks, and many Cossacks have turned away from war and instead bought land to farm. The destitute, however, still live poorly in Rus', a term repeated frequently as Razin's base of operations, implying that the downtrodden have inherited the true Russian soil.[12]

Razin's purpose, we are told, is not brigandage: "Stepan Timofeich Razin was not a brigand ataman. He was a Don Cossack, the son and grandson of Don Cossacks," who is even rumored to have relatives in the Zaporozh'e (13, 66). He has, in other words, a long and healthy Cossack pedigree. And he is by no means an anarchist, for he has a plan: "He went [to the Volga area] in order to transform Rus', now dependent and enslaved to the tsar and the boyars, along the lines of the new, Cossack order" (32).

Here we see how the Cossack of Soviet literature rejects tsardom, as well as exploitation by the rich landed gentry. No mention is made of the long association of Cossacks with pretenders to the throne. When Razin burns old papers after the taking of Astrakhan, "that old slavish life writhed into flames. . . . A new, just life arrived with Ataman Stepan Razin" (44).

True to form, however, Razin's actual Cossack ancestry cannot dominate. As he takes on leadership of the revolt, he is told: "Now you are not a Cossack ataman—you are ataman of the Russian peasants, you are a native leader" (45). And, although his lesser assistants worry about the particular fate of the Cossacks, Razin himself has thoughts only for the *narod* in general, the peasants and the poor (55). Vas'ka Us, a traditional companion of Razin and the one who grants him power in this version of the tale, himself denies being a Cossack: "Our truth is a peasant, not a Cossack, truth" (33). The terms of the myth have been inverted: Cossack truth is limited, peasant truth comprehensive.

It would seem odd to choose a Cossack hero only to deny his connection to the Cossack tradition. Zlobin is faced with the problem of how at once to praise and not praise the Cossack past. He can do so only by abandoning some of the more vital topoi, in particular the Cossacks' boundless and timeless nature. Again, the self-conscious creation of a new hero who represents Soviet values of order requires the abandonment of the ambiguity of myth, and Cossack as a term loses its resonance.

Razin is executed in the end of the story, but he lives on—"*zhiv Stepan!*"—through his son, who has been hidden away by a "grandad-bandura player," a traditional bard figure (76). (His wife drowned herself, a variation on the story of the drowning of the Persian princess.) This motif allows for the implication of descent through to the leaders of the twentieth century, so that Cossack-peasant revolt leads directly to Russian Revolution.

Dmitrii Petrov-Biriuk's (1900–1977) *Sons of the Don Steppes (Syny stepei donskikh)*, written in 1953, follows a similar model. This novel describes the defeat of Napoleon, thanks to the strength and patriotism of the Cossack regiments. Both Lord Byron and Sir Walter Scott have the opportunity in the book to praise the Cossacks as true, brave, and heroic Russians. Yet, despite the loyalty of these Cossacks to the tsar and his army, two Cossacks about to enter Paris anachronistically discuss the need for revolution. The author resolves the contradiction by allying the Cossack soldiers even more closely with the people. At one point we are told how the *narod* successfully demanded the replacement of the former commander with Kutuzov, not the tsar's choice, for "even the tsar cannot go against the will of the people."[13]

The Cossacks speak of the poverty of the Russian *narod* and of their dream to free the people from the yoke of oppression: "The *narod* will not bear it . . . It will revolt . . . Remember the uprisings of Stepan Razin, of Kondrat Bulavin, and of Emel'ian Pugachev."[14]

They will not succeed, of course, until the superior organization of the Party comes their way.

The Post-Stalinist Cossack

The flood of Cossacks in Russian literature diminished after Stalin's death, perhaps because writers, or more likely editors and censors, finally perceived the political volatility, if not artistic inconsistency, of a hero both loyal and rebellious. Or perhaps the final demise of the Cossacks as a social reality took them off the printed page as well. Many writers on Cossack themes had or claimed to have Cossack roots, and now even those roots were weeded out.

More likely, the Cossack simply lost his previous attraction. Overuse of his name in novels such as those just described caused the dispersal of any mythic energy still attached to his image. He turned into a trite allegorical tag. A novel of the seventies by the popular writer Semen Babaevskii, *The Cossack Village (Stanitsa)*, begins much like *The Quiet Don* with an elegiac family history, but turns away from any traditional Cossack subject matter and concentrates instead on the theme of the modernization of the village. The elimination of Cossack culture is so complete that when an old man asks what is happening to the *stanitsa*, he is told: "We shouldn't have to explain, to waste our time on empty conversations. We need to build. That's where our task lies."[15]

Sten'ka Razin does appear briefly in the sixties in a work of somewhat experimental form, if not content. Evgenii Evtushenko's (1933-) long poem *The Bratsk Hydro-Electric Station (Bratskaia GES)* includes a short section titled "The Execution of Sten'ka Razin" ("Kazn' Sten'ki Razina") that describes the reaction of the spectators to Razin's delivery into Moscow and his beheading.[16] Razin's figure, however, only confirms the reading of the Cossack in Soviet literature spelled out in this chapter.

The section begins with several unflattering portraits of negative characters, as defined by socialist realism: the tsar squeezes a pimple; a fat baby boyar gorges on candy; a merchant farts; and prostitutes feel sexually aroused at the thought of Razin's execution. Razin himself stands firm in his faith in rebellion despite the saliva spat upon him by the jeering crowd. The Cossack reproaches himself only for having failed to take his revolt far enough. He has correctly directed his anger against the boyars and merchants, but he realizes in his last moments that he should have turned his energy against the institution of tsardom as well. He thinks: "I thought of fighting / for a good tsar. / There are no good tsars, /Fool. . . ."[17]

What Evtushenko has done here should come as no surprise. As Terts would say, he bestowed upon his hero prescience about the coming Bolshevik Revolution, almost two hundred and fifty years hence. He has Razin realize that Communism dictates the collapse of monarchy before the victory of the proletariat over the capitalist. The poet thus remade the Cossack in his own ideal socialist image.

Evtushenko provided solace for his condemned hero by allowing him to read the revolution-to-come in the eyes of the crowd, a crowd that miraculously changes mood and refuses to celebrate after the death of its new revolutionary leader. The executioner's axe gleams like the Volga River, and in it Razin catches sight of "FACES / There was distance and the heights in the FACES" that reflect his own rebellion in embryonic form.[18] His decapitated head therefore speaks hoarsely: "Not in vain" has he lived.[19]

When Evtushenko returns to the main narrative of his poem, he equates Razin's words with those of other rebels through the ages: Spartacus, Jan Hus, Munzer, Marat, Bolotnikov, Pugachev, the Decembrists, and the sailors on the battleship *Potemkin*. The Cossack no longer has a unique place. By converting him into a rebel for the proletariat cause, and placing him indiscriminately alongside a French Jacobin, a Greek slave, or any other proto-Bolshevik, Soviet literature took away the Cossacks' special role in Russian cultural mythology. Evtushenko's depiction of the Cossack suggests that the Soviet Russian required a new mythology, one which borrowed from the heroic tradition, but shackled the horseman-warrior in assimilating him. Such a prisoner of the official system could no longer carry the name of the COSSACK.

TWELVE

Conclusion: Nabokov's Postmortem

Early in this study, works by Voltaire, Byron, and Hugo were suggested as foreign contributions to the Cossack myth. As is so often the case in Russia's literary history, stimuli from outside proved a catalyst for internal developments. In the case of the Cossacks, however, an even stronger impulse came from the search by Russian writers for native symbols in their own past. The Cossacks were transformed into epic heroes who could represent the desired spirit and freedom of the people.

Ironically, it is again a non-Russian work that can best close this study of the Cossack myth. Admittedly, its author was Russian, but the novel, *Pnin*, by Vladimir Nabokov (1899–1977), was written neither in Russian nor for a specifically Russian audience. Nabokov, his narrator, and his main character all speak as outsiders, removed from the Russian soil. And only a small paragraph, an offhand observation, concerns a Cossack. The passage, however, is a perfect parody of the Cossack myth and, as such, makes a fitting capstone to this book; it is a pathetic postmortem for the mythic Cossack topoi.

In the description of a summer that the protagonist spends at the country home of an acquaintance, Nabokov inserts the following passage:

> The household was looked after by Praskovia, a sturdy, sixty-year-old woman of the people with the vivacity of one a score of years younger. It was an exhilarating sight to watch her as she stood on the back porch surveying the chickens, knuckles on hips, dressed in baggy homemade shorts and a matronly blouse with rhinestones. She had nursed Alexandr and his brother when both were children in Harbin and now she was helped in her household duties by her husband, a gloomy and stolid old Cossack whose main passions in life were amateur bookbinding—a self-taught and almost pathological process that he was impelled to inflict upon any old catalogue or pulp magazine that came his way; the making of fruit liqueurs; and the killing of small forest animals.[1]

Nabokov introduces the "gloomy and stolid old Cossack" only after a detailed description of Praskovia, and merely to report that he assists his wife in her household duties, hardly Cossacklike behavior. Gogol told us that a Cossack is not intended to *"babit'sia s zhenoi"* (become womanly hanging around with his wife). Perhaps the passions of Nabokov's Cossack still keep him heroic, for the Cossacks of myth felt passionately about any number of things: their commitment to each other, the holy Russian Church, the fatherland, and the fight itself. But a passion for bookbinding is nothing less than a paradox by the terms of the myth. It is stasis instead of action, preservation of lifeless texts, not resurrection of heroic deed-doers, and totally at odds with the endeavor to learn through experience *(opyt)* of the Cossacks of *Taras Bul'ba*.[2]

The "gloomy and stolid old Cossack" does drink like a Cossack, it seems, but his passion leans toward dandified fruit liqueurs. Taras Bul'ba rather calls for "tons of *gorelka,* only not these fancies of *gorelka,* not with raisins and all sorts of whims, but pure, frothy *gorelka,* that should frolic and fizz as if it were mad." "We've no need for little fritters [*pampushki*]," he goes on, "for little honey and poppy cakes [*medovniki, makovniki*], or other sweets [*pundiki*]. Bring on a whole lamb, give us a goat, and forty-year old mead."[3]

Not even his passion for killing can reclaim for Nabokov's Cossack a place in the mythic tradition, for he is interested only in *small* animals who hide in the *forest.* The Cossacks of Gogol lived on the immense, wide open, and treeless steppe. The boundless Cossack would just as soon spend his time in a confining forest as he would invite his wife to ride behind him on a raid.

Nabokov's brief Cossack parody thus inverts the traditional Cossack topoi. Ultimately, it turns a mythic image of life and freedom into a pathetic recluse, torn from his native Russia and betraying the heroic name of his ancestors. Denied so much as an ever so doleful ride into the sunset, our hero of old drops his beloved sabre and chooses to sleep inside. Praskovia's domestic helper outlived his place in Russian cultural mythology, and the COSSACK rides no more.

Notes

Selected Bibliography

Index

Notes

Chapter One. Introduction: From History to Myth

1. George G. Grabowicz and George S. N. Luckyj have studied the Cossack in Polish and Ukrainian literature. See bibliography for specific titles.

2. Much of the vocabulary I will use to speak of myths and mythologies I have borrowed from "Myth Today," an early essay by Roland Barthes in *Mythologies,* essays selected and translated by Annette Lavers (London: Jonathan Cape, 1972). Here Barthes views myths as insidious weapons in the hands of the class in power—the bourgeoisie—and assumes his role as mythologist, or myth demystifier, with a revolutionary seriousness. My own view is less political than Barthes's, although I do recognize the ultimate power of cultural myths to control national consciousness. Although I am aware of the extensive recent bibliography on myth (and see bibliography for some works that have been provocative, if not always central to this study), I discovered that newer is not always better, and the early Barthes, depoliticized and rehistoricized, remains the clearest guide through the ambiguity of myth. Readers may also detect the influence of the historiographer Hayden White (see especially *Metahistory: The Historical Imagination in Nineteenth-Century Europe* [Baltimore and London: Johns Hopkins University Press, 1973] and *Tropics of Discourse. Essays in Cultural Criticism* [Baltimore and London: Johns Hopkins University Press, 1978]). Other illuminating studies of specifically Russian cultural myths may be found in *The Semiotics of Russian Cultural History,* edited by Alexander D. Nakhimovsky and Alice Stone Nakhimovsky (Ithaca: Cornell University Press, 1985).

3. A myth in the sense used here is a phenomenon obviously more, not less, real than ordinary life. Although myth in common parlance means a fiction, or made-up story, this study views myths as "The instruments by which we continually struggle to make our experience intelligible to ourselves. A myth is a large, controlling image that gives philosophical meaning to the facts of ordinary life; that is, which has an organizing value for experience." Mark Schorer, "The Necessity of Myth," *Daedalus* 88, no. 2(Spring 1959): 360, excerpted from *William Blake* (New York: Henry Holt, 1946).

4. Barthes, "Myth Today" 129.

5. Any history is itself a narrative, connected to myth by the cultural assumptions of its creator. The following historical account does not claim to report the whole truth about the Cossacks any more than Gogol or Tolstoi could in their own narratives. Hopefully, however, the elements that have been naturalized by myth can be again highlighted.

6. Albert Seaton, however, claims they "had little influence on the development of the latter-day Russian 'free' Cossack hosts," in *The Horsemen of the Steppes. The Story of the Cossacks* (London: Bodley Head, 1985), 31.

179

7. The perhaps unusual term "host" is desirable here, for it carries the connotation of multitude as well as an established army, and therefore suggests the sometimes ad hoc and popular formation of Cossack military organizations.

8. See Linda Gordon, *Cossack Rebellions: Social Turmoil in the Sixteenth-Century Ukraine* (Albany: State University of New York Press, 1983), 61–77.

9. Scholars of Ukrainian literature and history insist on the integrity of the Zaporozhian Cossacks and consider them a purely Ukrainian phenomenon. Without denying the vital role that the Zaporozh'e played in Ukrainian history and society, this study purposely views the Ukrainian Cossacks through the eyes of Russian literature, written in Russian for a Russian audience. The myth in Russian literature incorporates Ukrainian, Tatar, Caucasian, and Siberian Cossacks into its idealized hero.

10. Ermak Timofeevich (?–1584) organized a force funded by the powerful Stroganov family to penetrate into and conquer Siberia. He belonged to the Volga Cossacks, a group formed from Don Cossacks who had migrated eastward and settled on both sides of the Volga River. His band was dispersed by the tsar's forces in 1577 and its ataman was wanted as an outlaw. It is therefore a bandit who largely holds responsibility for bringing Siberia into the Russian empire. Ermak died defending the land he had occupied, never successfully establishing a settlement, but he demonstrated nonetheless the power a small, well-organized Cossack group could wield. Ermak became extremely popular in historical songs of the sixteenth century.

11. Bogdan Mikhailovich Khmel'nitskii (1595?–1657) was a Hetmanate Cossack who became influential in the movement to free the Ukrainian lands from Polish domination. During his time, Ukraine suffered under the control of Poland and the authority of the Polish Catholic Church. In order to avoid conflict with Polish authorities, many Russian Orthodox inhabitants of the Ukrainian lands accepted the Unions of Brest (1596) and Uzhgorod (1646) which established the Uniate Church, an amalgam of the ritual of Eastern Orthodoxy with an acknowledgment of the supremacy of the Roman Catholic pope. By its connection to the Western Church, it guaranteed Polish hegemony over the area, and many Ukrainians continued to rankle under the Polish and Catholic domination. In 1648, Khmel'nitskii, who had been a registered Cossack in Polish pay, raised a rebellion against the Poles and was elected hetman of the Zaporozhian Host. After six years of devastating war, he was forced in 1654 to turn to the Muscovite government for aid. The treaty he signed eventually transferred power over Ukraine from the Poles to the Russians. Although later Ukrainian nationalists came to rankle no less under Russian domination than Ukrainians had under Polish, Khmel'nitskii is still heralded as a national leader and a statue of him stands proudly in the center of Kiev.

Khmel'nitskii features more frequently in Polish and Ukrainian literature, but he does surface periodically in the history of the Cossack myth in Russian literature as well. His public profile does not stand so tall in Jewish circles, however. In the battles to free Ukraine, the Jew often served as scapegoat, and thousands of innocent people were slaughtered in this prototype of later pogroms. The name Khmel'nitskii became synonymous with anti-Semite.

(The Russian version of Ukrainian names will be used throughout this study, as the names would be found in the Russian literature under consideration.)

12. The war largely concerned rule over the Ukraine. See previous note on the Cossack Khmel'nitskii.

13. The changes included correction of the spelling of the name of Jesus, the number of Hallelujahs said at various points during the liturgy, and the fingers used to make the sign of the cross. The reforms were designed to "modernize" the Russian Orthodox Church by bringing it in line with contemporary Greek practice.

14. See Paul Avrich, *Russian Rebels: 1600–1800* (New York: Schocken Books, 1972), 76.

15. See Patricia Ann Krafcik, "Sten'ka Razin in Russian Historical Folksongs: A Robin Hood of the Volga," Ph.D. Diss., Columbia University, 1980.

16. Other important Cossack names occasionally appearing in Russian literature include Ivan Isaevich Bolotnikov (?–1608), an early Russian rebel; and Petr Sagaidachnyi (?–1622) and Stepan Ostranitsa (?–1638), two Ukrainian Cossacks.

17. Seaton, *Horsemen of the Steppes* 233–35.

18. Several good historical accounts of the Cossacks exist in English. The present study has made most extensive use of the following: W. E. D. Allen, *The Ukraine: A History* (Cambridge: University Press, 1940); Avrich, *Russian Rebels,* cited above; Gordon, *Cossack Rebellions,* cited above, and the dissertation from which that work grew, "Revolutionary Banditry: An Interpretation of the Social Roles of the Ukrainian Cossacks in Their First Rebellions, 1590–96," Ph.D. diss., Yale University, 1970; Philip Longworth, *The Cossacks* (New York: Holt, Rinehart and Winston, 1969); Ivan L. Rudnytsky, "A Study of Cossack History," review of Longworth's book in *Slavic Review* 31(Dec. 1972): 870–75; and Longworth's response to Rudnytsky's review and Rudnytsky's counterresponse in *Slavic Review* 33(June 1974), 411–16; and Seaton, *The Horsemen of the Steppes,* cited above.

19. The first argument can be found in V. G. Glazkov, *History of the Cossacks* (New York: R. Speller, 1972), 16–18, where the author, himself a Cossack, claims that the "spurious myth" that Cossacks are of fugitive Russian extraction dates from as late as 1834, and was used as an official justification to make serfs of and assimilate the Cossacks. The latter statement is argued in a pamphlet published in emigration by the Publication of the Organization of Cossack Nationalists, entitled "Cossacks, a Nation or a Russian Estate" ("Kazaki, narod ili russkoe soslovie"). See also the extensive argument in George V. Gubaroff, *Cossacks and Their Land: In Light of New Data,* translated by John Nelson Washburn (Providence, R. I.: Cossack American National Alliance, 1985).

20. Lev Tolstoi, *Polnoe sobranie sochinenii,* (Moscow-Leningrad: Gosudarstvennoe izdatel'stvo, 1952), 48:123. Also quoted in P. B. Bekedin, "Drevnerusskie motivy v *Tikhom Done* M. A. Sholokhova (k postanovke voprosa)," in *Russkaia literatura* 2(1980):96.

21. "Slovo o polku Igoreve" tells the story of Igor's unsuccessful campaign against the neighboring Polovtsy people during the Kievan period. As such, it glorifies the patriotism of a prince of Rus', not Russia, and cannot technically be called a "Russian" epic, if "Russian" refers to the Russian empire centered in Moscow. Russians, however, as we will see later in this study, often associate Rus' with their own political and cultural origins. When the manuscript of the tale was rediscovered in the eighteenth century, Russian writers accepted it as a story about their

own past. At present, both its genre and its authenticity are subjects for scholarly debate.

22. The idea that peoples create their history from these three processes is persuasively argued by Bernard Lewis in *History Remembered, Recovered, Invented* (Princeton: Princeton University Press, 1975).

23. This discussion of liminality is deeply indebted to the work of Victor Turner in *The Ritual Process: Structure and Anti-Structure* (Ithaca, New York: Cornell University Press, 1969).

24. N. V. Gogol', *Taras Bul'ba, Polnoe sobranie sochinenii* [henceforth *PSS*] (Moscow: Izdatel'stvo Akademii Nauk SSSR, 1937–52), 3:70–72.

25. Daniel Mordovtsev, *Sagaidachnyi, Polnoe sobranie istoricheskikh romanov, povestei i razskazov* [henceforth *PS*] (St. Petersburg: Izdatel'stvo P. P. Soikina, n.d.), 1:25–28.

26. Mikhail Bakhtin, *Rabelais and His World*, translated by Helene Iswolsky (Cambridge, Mass.: M.I.T. Press, 1968), 8.

27. I say "himself" here, since very few women writers embraced the Cossacks, no doubt because of the difficulty of identifying with the strongly male host. A curious exception, Marina Tsvetaeva, will be discussed in Part 2.

28. For an excellent discussion of other binary oppositions in pre-nineteenth-century Russian society, see Iurii M. Lotman and Boris A. Uspenskii, "Binary Models in the Dynamics of Russian Culture (to the End of the Eighteenth Century)," in *The Semiotics of Russian Cultural History* 30–66.

29. The Westernizers were those critics and writers, such as Vissarion Belinskii and Aleksandr Gertsen (Herzen), who looked to Western philosophy and social institutions for cures of Russia's ills. The Slavophiles, notably Ivan Kireevskii and Aleksei Khomiakov, similarly focused on Russia's backwardness, but believed the cure must come from within, from a reclamation of native Russia values. For brief discussions and some examples of essays, see *Russian Philosophy*, Vol. 1: *The Beginnings of Russian Philosophy. The Slavophiles. The Westernizers*, edited by James M. Edie, James P. Scanlan, and Mary-Barbara Zeldin, with the collaboration of George L. Kline (Knoxville: University of Tennessee Press, 1965, 1976). See also Andrzej Walicki, *The Slavophile Controversy: History of a Conservative Utopia in Nineteenth-Century Thought*, translated by Hilda Andrews-Rusiecka (Oxford: Clarendon Press, 1975).

30. Peter Chaadayev (Petr Chaadaev), "Philosophical Letters. Letter I," translated by Mary-Barbara Zeldin, in *Russian Philosophy* 1:109.

31. Ibid. 1:120. Chaadaev accused Russia of remaining complacently in her childhood.

32. Marina Tsvetaeva, *Izbrannaia proza v dvukh tomakh, 1917–1937* (New York: Russica Publishers, 1979), 2:294.

Chapter Two. Folk Poetry, Pushkin, and the Romantic Cossack Hero

1. Cossacks play primary roles in a few lyrics, a narrative poem or *poema*, a historical study, and a short novel by Pushkin. They also appear incidently in the

drama *Boris Godunov,* in the figure of Karela, leader of the Don Cossacks. The Pretender accepts the latter's services, relying on the Cossacks' (as well as the peasants' and nobles') dissatisfaction with the institution of serfdom. These Cossacks, however, are not principal characters in the play, and will not be discussed in this chapter. A booklength study would be necessary to analyze the full range of Pushkin's use of and ambivalent attitude toward the Cossack.

2. See Caryl Emerson, *Boris Godunov: Transpositions of a Russian Theme* (Bloomington: Indiana University Press, 1986), 3–11, for a definition of the "poetics of transposition." Emerson quotes Pushkin's response to Karamzin's work: "It was for us a new discovery. Ancient Russia, it seems, was discovered by Karamzin as America had been by Columbus" (31). From A. S. Pushkin, "[Iz avtobiograficheskikh zapisok]," Nov. 1824, *Polnoe sobranie sochinenii* (Moscow: Izdatel'stvo Akademii Nauk SSSR, 1948), 12:305 [henceforth *PSS*]. See also Margaret Ziolkowski, *Hagiography and Modern Russian Literature* (Princeton: Princeton University Press, 1988), 6–7, 37, where the author cites Karamzin's history as a crucial bridge between the past and modern Russian literature.

3. Excellent sources on Russian historical songs are B. N. Putilov, ed., *Istoricheskie pesni XVII veka* (Moscow-Leningrad: Nauka, 1966); A. D. Soimonov, ed., *Istoricheskie pesni XVIII veka* (Leningrad: Nauka, 1971); L. I. Emel'ianov, ed., *Russkaia istoricheskaia pesnia,* Biblioteka Poeta series (Leningrad: Sovetskii pisatel', 1987); and B. N. Putilov, ed., *Narodnye istoricheskie pesni,* Biblioteka Poeta series (Moscow-Leningrad: Sovetskii pisatel', 1962). See also the study of Razin songs in particular in Patricia Ann Krafcik, "Sten'ka Razin in Russian Historical Folksongs: A Robin Hood of the Volga"; and A. N. Lazanova, ed., *Pesni i skazaniia o Razine i Pugacheve* (Moscow-Leningrad: Akademiia, 1935).

4. "I vy porokhu ne teriaite i snariadov ne lomaite— / Menia pulechka ne tronet, menia iadryshko ne voz'met." From "Razin i voevoda," in Putilov, *Narodnye istoricheskie pesni* 180; or Emel'ianov, *Russkaia istoricheskaia pesnia* 159.

5. "The Tale of the Taking of Azov" has come down to us in several generic forms. See N. K. Gudzy, *History of Early Russian Literature,* translated by Susan Wilbur Jones from the second Russian edition (New York: Macmillan, 1949), 441–47. For Russian texts of this tale see V. P. Arianova-Perets, ed., *Voinskie povesti drevnoi Rusi* (Moscow: Izdatel'stvo Akademii Nauk SSSR, 1949).

6. Early collections include M. D. Chulkov, *Sobranie raznykh pesen, Sochineniia Mikhaila Dmitrievicha Chulkova, 1770–1773,* reprint (St. Petersburg: Otdelenie russkogo iazyka i slovesnosti Imperatorskoi Akademii Nauk, 1913); N. I. Novikov, ed., *Novoe i polnoe sobranie rossiiskikh pesen* (Moscow: Universitetskaia tipografiia, 1780–81); and I. P. Sakharov, ed., *Pesni russkogo naroda,* Part 4 (St. Petersburg, 1839).

7. The full text of the poems can be found in Pushkin, *PSS* 1:462–63. Compare the following by Mikhail Lermontov, excellent as poems but less successful as imitations: "Ataman" (1831) and "Kazach'ia kolybel'naia pesnia" (1840).

8. J. Thomas Shaw, ed., *The Letters of Alexander Pushkin* (Bloomington: Indiana University Press, 1963), 1:189. Pushkin seems to have used the term *kazak* in a slightly different sense when referring to Razin than he did in his works on Mazepa, as we will see later. According to the editors of the *Slovar' iazyka Pushkina,* "Cos-

sack" in the meaning of "a free man [*vol'nyi chelovek*] who has fled to the border of the land in order to escape serfdom or excessive governmental obligations" is used 32 times, designating Sten'ka Razin and the Cossacks in *Boris Godunov;* and 285 times in the second meaning: "From the 18th century, in several regions of Russia, a person from a particular class of landowners, obligated to carry out an extended military service in the cavalry in exchange for specific privileges." See the entry "Kazak (kozak)" in V. V. Vinogradov et al., eds., *Slovar' iazyka Pushkina* (Moscow: Gosudarstvennoe izdatel'stvo inostrannykh i natsional'nykh slovarei, 1957), 2:271.

9.   Razin does reappear in early-twentieth-century literature, as we will see in Part 2.

10.   For more on the fascination of late-eighteenth- and early-nineteenth-century intellectuals with the *narod,* and its relation to the development of Russian national consciousness, see the chapter "The Discovery of the Folk" in Hans Rogger, *National Consciousness in Eighteenth-Century Russia* (Cambridge: Harvard University Press, 1960), 126–85.

11.   For an understanding of the term at the turn of this century, see entry "Ukraina," F. A. Brokgauz and I. A. Efron, eds., *Entsiklopedicheskii slovar'* (St. Petersburg, 1897), 68:633–35. See also Maks Fasmer, *Etimologicheskii slovar' russkogo iazyka,* trans. and ed. O. N. Trubachev, 4 vols. (Moscow: Progress Press, 1964–83), 4:156–57. "Ukraina" remained the standard term for the eastern part of the country alone until 1918.

12.   See George Luckyj's discussion in *Panteleimon Kulish: A Sketch of His Life and Times* (Boulder, Colo.: East European Monographs, 1983), 26. Kulish was an important nineteenth-century Ukrainian writer, who published in Russian as well as in his native language, including a self-translation of his Cossack novel, *The Black Council (Chernaia rada),* histories of the Ukraine, and a biography of Gogol.

13.   For a definition of the names of Russia and Ukraine, see George W. Simpson, "The Names 'Rus',' 'Russia,' 'Ukraine,' and Their Historical Background," *Slavistica* 10 (1951):5–18.

14.   For further comment on the typical confusion of Ukrainian and Russian Cossacks, see Gordon, *Cossack Rebellions* 64. Also see the polemic between Professors Longworth and Rudnytsky in *Slavic Review* cited in the notes to the previous chapter. Longworth claims that "Cossackdom commonly fulfilled similar functions elsewhere [than only in Ukraine], particularly in the seventeenth and eighteenth centuries but to a lesser extent in other periods as well" (412).

15.   See George Luckyj's entry on "Duma" in *Handbook of Russian Literature,* edited by Victor Terras (New Haven and London: Yale University Press, 1985), 117–18, where this specialist on Ukrainian literature argues that Ryleev's *dumy* have nothing in common, structurally or thematically, with native Ukrainian songs, although the Decembrist "showed deep affection for the Ukraine and for Ukrainian strivings for independence in his later poems 'Nalivaiko' (1825) and 'Voinarovsky' (1825) which bear some resemblance to the Ukrainian *dumy.*"

16.   As Mikhail Maksimovich writes: "Russian songs are marked with deep dejection, despondent oblivion, a kind of expansiveness and wide range. Little Russian songs have less of these luxuries: being an expression of the struggle between the spirit and fate, they are characterized by gusts of passion, compact firmness and

strength of feeling and equally of natural expressiveness." "Predislovie," *Maloros-siiskiia pesni* (Moscow, 1827), XIII–XIV. Translated and cited in George S. N. Luckyj, *Between Gogol' and Ševčenko: Polarity in the Literary Ukraine, 1798–1847* (Munich: Wilhelm Fink Verlag, 1971), 31–32. Other early collections of Ukrainian folksongs include: Mikhail Maksimovich, *Ukrainskie narodnye pesni* (Moscow, 1834), and *Sbornik ukrainskikh pesen, izdavaemykh M. Maksimovichem* (Moscow, 1849); N. A. Tsertelev, *Opyt sobraniia starinnykh malorossiiskikh pesen* (Moscow, 1819); N. Markevych, *Ukrainskie melodii* (Moscow, 1831); Platon Lukashevich, *Malorossiiskie i Chervonorusskie narodnye dumy i pesni* (St. Petersburg, 1836); and I. I. Sreznevskii, *Zaporozhskaia starina* (Kharkov, 1833–1838). For the original Ukrainian variations see G. A. Nud'ga, ed., *Dumi*, Biblioteka Poeta series (Kiev: Radians'kii pis'mennik, 1969). For the influence of the romantic interest in folklore on the growth of Ukrainian nationalism see Luckyj, *Between Gogol' and Ševčenko* 25–37.

17. Native Ukrainian instruments also include the *kobza* and *lira*, but by the end of the eighteenth century, the *bandura* had far surpassed the *kobza* in popularity, and from that time the terms became synonymous. B. P. Kirdan, *Ukrainskie narodnye dumy* (Moscow: Nauka, 1972), 10.

18. It is generally acknowledged that, as in Europe, "nor was the identification of romanticism with the national past lacking in Russia. Both poets and novelists strove to glorify their country's antiquity and traditions, paying particular attention, as they had never done before, to local color and native traits and characters." E. J. Simmons, *English Literature and Culture in Russia, 1553–1840* (Cambridge: Harvard University Press, 1935), 238.

19. In fact, the boundaries between history, ethnography, literature, and myth itself were remarkably fluid. Poets wrote histories and historians wrote novels with no questions of disciplinary integrity. As Hans Rogger notes: "In the absence of a sharp separation between ethnography, geography, and history, almost all the materials descriptive of Russia's past and present contained information relating to folk customs, beliefs, rituals, and literature. Russia's remote areas, her outlying districts in time, in space, in social distance were all coming under observation, were described and brought to the attention of the country" (*National Consciousness* 164). Only in very recent historiographical theory has the interdependence of the disciplines again been recognized. See White, *Metahistory* x and 2. Claude Lévi-Strauss writes of the inherent relationship of history and myth in "Overture to *Le Cru et le cuit*," printed in *Structuralism,* ed. Jacques Ehrman (New York: Anchor Books, 1966), 48, and cited in White, *Tropics of Discourse* 56 and 91.

20. N. L. Rubinshtein, *Russkaia istoriografiia* (Moscow: Gospolitizdat, 1941), 197.

21. Pushkin wrote a review of the published manuscript in 1836.

22. Published in *Chteniia v imperatorskom obshchestve istorii i drevnostei rossiiskikh pri Moskovskom Universitete* nos. 1–3 (1846). For a discussion of the authorship, see Andriy Iakovliv, "Istoriya Rusov and Its Author," *Ukrainian Academy of Arts and Sciences in the U.S., Annals* 3, no. 2 (Fall–Winter 1953):620–69; and Oleksandr Ohloblyn, "Where Was Istoriya Rusov Written." *Ukrainian Academy of Arts and Sciences in the U.S., Annals* 3, no. 2 (Fall–Winter 1953):670–95.

23. "The work itself is in the province of fiction rather than history," claims Luckyj, *Between Gogol' and Ševčenko* 17.

24. "The average man's ideas on the rapport between the Ukrainians and Poles, the Orthodox and the Uniates, were formed by *Istoriia Rusov* seen through *Taras Bul'ba*." Elie Borschak, *La Légende historique de l'Ukraine 'Istorija Rusov'* (Paris: Institut d'Etudes Slaves, 1949), 168.

25. Ibid. 163.

26. "Istoriia Rusov," *Chteniia v imperatorskom obshchestve istorii i drevnostei rossiiskikh pri Moskovskom Universitete,* no. 1 (1846) Introduction, p. i.

27. Pavel Ivanovich Pestel', the main leader of the Southern Society, enunciated this policy in his "Russian Law," a draft constitution for Russia. A translation of selections is available in Marc Raeff's short study *The Decembrist Movement* (Englewood Cliffs, N.J.: Prentice-Hall, 1966), 124–56. Raeff provides an excellent analysis of the Decembrists, incorporating psychological, political, and historical factors, as well as providing a number of primary documents produced by the movement and the trial of its members after the failed uprising.

28. George G. Grabowicz includes a detailed analysis of this work in "The History and Myth of the Cossack Ukraine," Ph.D. diss., Harvard University, 1975, 377–80.

29. Kondratii Ryleev, *Polnoe sobranie stikhotvorenii,* Biblioteka Poeta series, 2d ed. (Leningrad: Sovetskii pisatel', 1971), 227.

30. Narezhnyi's generic experiments in fact contributed greatly to the development of the Russian novel, and his Ukrainian novels must be understood in this light. Ronald D. LeBlanc makes a strong case for the importance of this minor writer in *The Russification of Gil Blas: A Study in Literary Appropriation* (Columbus, Ohio: Slavica, 1986).

31. Western writers tended to spell Mazepa's name using two *p*'s. This study will follow the European spelling when citing titles, but will keep to its own transliteration system when translating from Russian sources or referring to the historical figure.

32. George Gordon, Lord Byron, *The Complete Poetical Works,* ed. Jerome J. McGann (Oxford: Clarendon Press, 1986), 4:177, ll. 119–25.

33. See Hubert Babinsky, *The Mazeppa Legend in European Romanticism* (New York and London: Columbia University Press, 1974), 21–46, for such an analysis of the poem.

34. Victor Hugo, "Mazeppa," *Oeuvres Complètes* (Paris: Club Français du livre, 1967), 3:591. For a very sympathetic analysis of the poem and its hero, see Babinsky, *Mazeppa Legend* 67–72.

35. Wallenrod was grand master of the Teutonic Knights, but his unpredictable leadership during an invasion of Lithuania forced a humiliating defeat for the order. Mickiewicz suggests that Wallenrod was actually a Lithuanian who joined the Knights in order to destroy it from within and thus save his beloved homeland. The parallel of the powerful Knights of the Cross to imperialist Russia, which attempted to suppress its weaker neighbor, is obvious. Mickiewicz wrote the poem while in exile in Russia on the charge of conspiracy with fellow Polish patriots. Scholarship on the relationship between Pushkin and Mickiewicz has been extensive, especially by Poles. See

Jozef Tretiak, *Mickiewicz i Puszkin: Studya i szkice* (Warsaw: Nakładem Ksiegarni E. Wende I Sp., 1906); and Wacław Lednicki, "Pouchkine et Mickiewicz," *Revue de littérature comparée* 17 (1937):129–44, or "Mickiewicz's Stay in Russia and His Friendship with Pushkin," in *Adam Mickiewicz in World Literature: A Symposium*, ed. Lednicki (Berkeley and Los Angeles: University of California Press, 1956), 13–104.

36. For the relationship of *Voinarovskii* and *Poltava*, and opposing views on Mazepa's patriotism, see John J. Pauls, "Two Treatments of Mazeppa: Ryleyev's and Pushkin's," *Etudes slaves et est-européennes* 8 (1963):109; and Frank Mocha, "Pushkin's 'Poltava' as a Reaction to the Revolutionary Politics and History of Mickiewicz's "Konrad Wallenrod' and Ryleev's 'Vojnarovskij,'" reproduced as a separate pamphlet from *Antemurale* 19 (1975).

37. John J. Pauls argues that Ryleev looks upon Mazepa as a hero who sincerely sought "to save Ukraine from her chains." "Two Treatments of Mazeppa: Ryleyev's and Pushkin's" 98–99.

38. Ryleev, *Polnoe sobranie stikhotvorenii*, 217.

39. Ryleev's poem actually repeats much of the Mazepa legend, substituting the nephew for the uncle. Voinarovskii has an exhausting ride on a horse and is nursed back to health by a Cossack girl who later becomes his wife. The girl is separated from Voinarovskii during the battle of Poltava, but eventually finds him in Siberia, where she dies, far from her beloved Ukraine.

40. Donald Fanger reminds us of a similar fictional duel involving Pushkin, Bulgarin, and Narezhnyi, concerning stories by the latter two about "Ivan Vyzhigin" or a "Russian Gil Blas." *The Creation of Nikolai Gogol* (Cambridge, Mass., and London: Belknap Press of Harvard University Press, 1979), 31. Pushkin's contribution was a lampoon: the announcement, including chapter breakdown, of the never-published "The Real Vyzhigin: A Historico-Didactic-Satiric Novel of the Nineteenth Century," "which will go to press or remain in manuscript, depending on circumstances." J. Thomas Shaw, "The Problem of the *Persona* in Journalism: Puškin's Feofilakt Košičkin," *American Contributions to the Fifth International Congress of Slavists, Sofia, 1963* (The Hague: Mouton, 1963), 319–21.

41. Bulgarin accused Pushkin of "borrowing" material without acknowledgment for the latter's *Evgenii Onegin*, when, in fact, as Pushkin himself noted, Bulgarin himself had plagiarized from *Boris Godonov* in his novel *Dmitrii samozvanets*. See Shaw, "The Problem of the *Persona* in Journalism: Puškin's Feofilakt Košičkin" 305–6.

42. An interesting example from the Polish perspective is the play *Mazeppa* by the Polish author Juliusz Słowacki.

43. Aleksandr Slonimskii argues that *Poltava* includes three intertwining "spheres of action," each narrated on its own linguistic level: "Ukrainian-social" and the language of song; "Ukrainian-political" in Western Russian; and "Russian-imperial," using the language of ode. See *Masterstvo Pushkina* (Moscow: Gosudarstvennoe izdatel'stvo khudozhestvennoi literatury, 1959), 276. Paul Debreczeny suggests that there are two narrative voices in *Poltava*: an "author-narrator" who shows Mazepa as attractive, and a "bard-author" who praises Peter and calls Mazepa base and deceit-

ful. The result is two perspectives on reality, neither absolutely valid. *The Other Pushkin: A Study of Alexander Pushkin's Prose Fiction* (Stanford: Stanford University Press, 1983), 35–36. Debreczeny presents an even more ambiguous narrative picture in "Narrative Voices in *Poltava*," *Russian Literature* 24 (1988), where he states that "life spoke through the poem in many different voices, none of which had absolute authority by itself," and "the most innovative feature of *Poltava* was that its overall message was not interpreted for the reader" (345–47).

44. Pushkin, *Poltava, PSS* 5:16 [henceforth in text].

45. Peter had committed the unpardonable offence of pulling the Cossack's moustache. See 5:39, ll. 135, 148.

46. Regarding *dumy* Luckyj writes: "In content they deal with the fate of the Cossacks in Turkish captivity, the exploits of various Cossack heroes, or the pain of parting from relatives. In form they are the finest tragic songs in the Ukrainian oral tradition. They have no stanzas, vary in length, and were transmitted orally. As a genre they are related to funeral laments and music plays an important part in their performance." "Dumy," *Handbook of Russian Literature* 117.

47. Debreczeny argues that *Poltava* was written in a period of Pushkin's life "when he had grown to see aesthetic appeal in strong passion even if it was evil." "Narrative Voices in 'Poltava'" 346. We could argue that Pushkin thus makes his hero appealing despite his own conscious attitude toward the historical figure.

48. V. M. Zhirmunskii, *Bairon i Pushkin* (Leningrad: Academia, 1924), 176.

49. For more information about Scott's publication and reception in Russia, see W. M. Parker, "Scott and Russian Literature," *Quarterly Review* 305 (April 1967): 172–78.

50. William Thomas Weeks, letter of Feb. 15, 1828, in the National Library of Scotland, MS. 885, cited in Parker, "Scott and Russian Literature" 173.

51. See "Istoricheskii roman," in *Biblioteka dlia chteniia,* Vol. 1(1834), 1–44, cited in Ernest J. Simmons, *English Literature and Culture in Russia, 1553–1840,* p. 263.

52. See Iurii Oksman, "Neosushchestvlennyi zamysel istorii Ukrainy," in *Literaturnoe nasledstvo* 58 (1952):211–221. In 1820, Pushkin also planned a Don Cossack history, "Zamechaniia o donskikh i chernomorskikh kazakakh." See "Zapisi Pushkina," in Lazanova, *Pesni i skazaniia o Razine i Pugacheve* 323.

53. The Pugachev of the novel draws from but still differs from the Pugachev of the history. For one thing, as John Henry Raleigh has pointed out, Pushkin ahistorically blended some anecdotes from Razin's life into his portrait of Pugachev. Cf. "Scott and Pushkin," in *From Smollett to James: Studies in the Novel and Other Essays Presented to Edgar Johnson,* edited by Samuel I. Mintz et al. (Charlottesville: University Press of Virginia, 1981), 79–81. In fact, Pushkin sketched initial plans for the novel *before* beginning work on the history. See N. N. Petrunina, *Proza Pushkina (Puti evoliutsii)* (Leningrad: Nauka, 1987), 241–86, for discussion of the plans for the novel.

54. Gerald E. Mikkelson, "Pushkin's *History of Pugachev:* The Litterateur as Historian," in *New Perspectives on Nineteenth-Century Prose,* edited by George J. Gutsche and Lauren G. Leighton (Columbus, Ohio: Slavica, 1981), 39.

55. Alexander Pushkin, *The History of Pugachev*, translated by Earl Sampson (Ann Arbor: Ardis, 1983), 65.

56. Ibid. 106.

57. "There is an element of admiration, however grudging, for Pugachev himself in Pushkin's work," writes Mikkelson of *The History of Pugachev*, "Pushkin's History of Pugachev" 35.

58. Pushkin, *Kapitanskaia dochka*, *PSS* 8-1:329. References to this edition will henceforth appear in the text.

59. Unresolved contradictions, in character as well as structure and theme, in fact mark Pushkin's style. As J. Thomas Shaw states: "He scorned didacticism. One of his striking qualities is the presentation of unreconciled contradictions—between a work and its introduction or epilogue, or between parts of a work. It is left to the reader to infer the unified version behind the entire work." "Alexander Pushkin," in *European Writers: The Romantic Century*, ed. Jacques Barzun (New York: Charles Scribner's Sons, 1985), 660.

60. A recent article by Michael Finke discusses the subtext of the Aesopic fable in this episode. "Puškin, Pugačev, and Aesop," *Slavic and East European Journal* 35, no. 2(1991):181–82.

61. The bibliography on the influence of Scott on Pushkin is extensive. See particularly Militsa Green, "Pushkin and Sir Walter Scott," *Forum for Modern Language Studies* 1(1965):207–15; D. P. Iakubovich, "*Kapitanskaia dochka* i roman V. Skotta," *Vremennik pushkinskoi komissii* 4–5(1939):165–97; B. V. Neiman, *Kapitanskaia dochka* Pushkina i romany V. Skotta," *Sbornik otdeleniia russkogo iazyka i slovesnosti AN SSSR* 101, no. 3 (1928):440–43; Raleigh, "Scott and Pushkin" 48–83 Simmons, *English Literature and Culture in Russia, 1553–1840;* and V. M. Zhirmunskii, "Pushkin i zapadnye literatury," *Vremennik pushkinskoi komissii* 3(1937): 66–103.

62. Debreczeny, *Other Pushkin* 271; Gerald F. Mikkelson, "The Mythopoetic Element in Pushkin's Historical Novel *The Captain's Daughter*," *Canadian-American Slavic Studies* 7(1973):309; Roger B. Anderson, "A Study of Petr Grinev as the Hero of Pushkin's *Kapitanskaia dochka*," *Canadian-American Slavic Studies* 5(1971):482. J. Thomas Shaw points out a parallel "mother substitute" in the relationship between the captain's daughter and Catherine the Great. See Shaw, "Alexander Pushkin" 689.

Chapter Three. Gogol's Cossacks and the "Russian Soul"

1. V. P. Arianova-Perets, ed., *Voinskie povesti drevnei Rusi* 65.

2. V. Antonovich and M. Dragomanov, eds., *Istoricheskie pesni malorusskago naroda* (Kiev, 1877), 1:95. For a discussion of these texts in light of the concept of "Holy Russia" see Michael Cherniavsky, "'Holy Russia': A Study in the History of an Idea," *American Historical Review* 63, no. 3 (April 1958):630–31.

3. Mordovtsev, *PS* 1:111.

4. P. V. Bykov, introduction to Mordovtsev, *PS* 1:xxxviii.

5. Iulian Oksman, "Pushkin v rabote nad *Kapitanskoi dochke*," *Literaturnoe nasledstvo* 58 (1952):233.

6. Mikkelson, "Pushkin's *History of Pugachev*" 35.

7. Nabokov writes in his book on Gogol: "There is nothing more dull and sickening to my taste than romantic folklore or rollicking yarns about Lumberjacks or Yorkshiremen or French villagers or Ukrainian good companions. It is for this reason that the two volumes of the *Evenings* as well as the two volumes of stories entitled *Mirgorod* (including *Vii, Taras Bulba, Old World Land Owners,* etc.) which followed in 1835 leave me completely indifferent. It was however this kind of stuff, the juvenilia of the false humorist Gogol, that teachers of Russian schools crammed down a fellow's throat. . . ." *Nikolai Gogol* (New York: New Directions, 1961), 31. Hugh McLean shares the opinion, though on a less impressionistic level, that *Taras Bul'ba* represents the fantasies of a young boy about mature masculine prowess and bravery. "Gogol's Retreat from Love: Towards an Interpretation of *Mirgorod*," in *American Contributions to the Fourth International Congress of Slavists* (The Hague: Mouton, 1958), 232.

8. For an overview of Gogol's contact with Cossack material, see in particular I. M. Kamanin, "Nauchnye i literaturnye proizvedeniia N. V. Gogolia po istorii Malorossii," in *Pamiati Gogolia. Nauchno-literaturnyi sbornik,* ed. N. P. Dashkevich (Kiev, 1902), 75–132. For broader biographies in English see Victor Erlich, *Gogol* (New Haven: Yale University Press, 1969); David Magarshack, *Gogol: A Life* (New York: Grove Press, 1957); Vsevolod M. Setchkarev, *Gogol: His Life and Works* (New York: New York University Press, 1965); Henri Troyat, *Divided Soul: The Life of Gogol,* trans. Nancy Amphoux (Garden City, N.Y.: Doubleday, 1973).

9. Some critics question not only the extent of any Cossack atmosphere in Gogol's household, but the actual authenticity of Gogol's Cossack lineage as well. Leon Stilman argues that the connection of the Gogol family to any Cossack heritage was a fabrication of Gogol's own grandfather. "Nikolaj Gogol' and Ostap Hohol," *Orbis Scriptus. Dmitrij Tschižewskij zum 70. Geburtstag* (Munich: Wilhelm Fink Verlag, 1966), 811–25.

10. A. de Jonge, "Gogol," in *Nineteenth-Century Russian Literature: Studies of Ten Russian Writers,* ed. John Fennell (Berkeley and Los Angeles: University of California Press, 1973), 74.

11. Gogol, *PSS* 8:91. Unless otherwise noted, all quotations from Gogol will be from this edition and indicated in the text.

12. Cited also in Kamanin, "Nauchnye i literaturnye proizvedeniia" 111. Gogol wrote to I. I. Sreznevskii: "I have grown cold toward our chroniclers, I have tried in vain to find in them that which I sought" (March 6, 1834, 10:298).

13. Here we should compare the statement of Gogol's contemporary, the critic Belinskii, in this case about Don, not Zaporozhian, Cossack songs: "The songs of the Don Cossacks deserve the label "historical" more than the native Russian songs that are actually called historical. In them we find the entire mode of life, all the history of that military community where Russian daring, valor, bravado, and revelry found itself a free and expansive nest. There is more historical reality in them, and the poetry is more energetic and bold." Cited in *Pesni Donskikh kazakov,* ed. B. P. Ekimov (Volgograd: Nizhne-Volzhskoe knizhnoe izdatel'stvo, 1982), 5.

14. This quote is originally taken from Pushkin's review of *The History of the Russes* called "Sobranie sochinenii Georgiia Koniskogo, Arkhiepiskopa Beloruss-

kogo, izd. protoiereem Ioannom Grigorovichem. SPb. 1835" and quoted in *Sochineniia N. V. Gogolia,* 10th ed., ed. Nikolai Tikhonravov (Moscow, 1889), 1:664. Tikhonravov remarks that Gogol totally ignores Pushkin's opinion about the unreliable nature of "Konisskii's" historiography and only expands on his praise. Which historical works Gogol actually used to create his Cossacks, particularly in *Taras Bul'ba,* has been a topic of scholarly debate. See *Sochineniia N. V. Gogolia,* 10th ed., 1:569–79, 655–56, 661–64; and *PSS* 2:717–725. A dissertation by Paul A. Karpuk, "N. V. Gogol's Unfinished Historical Novel 'The Hetman,'" University of California, Berkeley, 1987, takes a revisionist look at Gogol's use of his sources. See also Karpuk, "Gogol's Unfinished Historical Novel 'The Hetman,'" *Soviet and East European Journal* 35, no. 1(1991):36–55.

15. Gogol had evidently read some Walter Scott and other European historical novelists. See, however, Romana Bahrij-Pikulyk, "*Taras Bul'ba* and *The Black Council:* The Adherence to and Divergence from Walter Scott's Historical Novel Pattern," Diss., University of Toronto, 1978, where the author concludes that Gogol's story differs from more than it conforms to the Scottian model.

16. See Richard Peace, *The Enigma of Gogol: An Examination of the Writings of N. V. Gogol and Their Place in the Russian Literary Tradition* (Cambridge: Cambridge Univ. Press, 1981), 28, 29, 32, 33, 48, 54, 55, 75, 76, 81–85, for examples of how Gogol "quarried" material from Narezhnyi.

17. V. G. Belinskii, *Polnoe sobranie sochinenii V. G. Belinskogo,* 13 vols. (Moscow: Akademiia nauk SSSR, 1953–59), 1:293. The contemporary reaction to Gogol's "Ukrainian tales" concentrated primarily on the question of whether the stories accurately depicted historical and ethnographic "reality." See Paul Debreczeny, "Nikolay Gogol and His Contemporary Critics," *Transactions of the American Philosophical Society,* n.s. 56, Part 3 (April 1966) for a detailed discussion.

18. V. F. Pereverzev, *Tvorchestvo Gogolia,* 3d ed. (Ivanovo-Voznesensk: Osnova, 1928), 29.

19. Wasyl Sirskyj finds the transformation of Gogol's Cossacks into Russians much more apparent in the 1842 edition of *Taras Bul'ba* and concludes that this russification was caused by "practical reasons, mainly because of the pressure of his Russian friends and benefactors." See "Ideological Overtones in Gogol's *Taras Bulba,*" *Ukrainian Quarterly* 35(1979): 284. I disagree with this reduction of a literary decision to personal apologetics.

20. "It was impossible, apparently, to say *Sviataia* (holy) *Rossiia:* one could only speak of *Sviataia Rus'.* And it was equally impossible, apparently, to speak of *Russkaia Imperiia* (Russian Empire); one could speak only of *Rossiiskaia Imperiia,* where the adjectival "Russian" was formed from *Rossiia* and not *Rus'.*" Michael Cherniavsky, *Tsar and People: Studies in Russian Myths* (New Haven and London: Yale University Press, 1961), 119.

21. My claim for the significance of Gogol's Cossacks agrees with that of Jesse Zeldin: "What Gogol has done, of course, is to make the Cossacks and their struggle symbolic of (if not parallel to) Russia and its struggle, as Gogol perceived it, against the West. His continued interest in the Ukraine was not, thus, a fascination with the Ukraine for its own sake, but for the sake of his interpretation of it as a spiritual model. In this sense, the story is both nationalistic and religious, although, perhaps,

in a crude way." *Nikolai Gogol's Quest for Beauty: An Exploration into His Works* (Lawrence: Regents Press of Kansas, 1978), 25.

22. Note, however, that Gogol nonetheless contrasts the early Russians to the "spiderlike" Western Church: "Here we find the total antithesis of the West. There you find an autocratic pope with, as it were, invisible power, whose mighty word could halt or instigate battle. That was a place where the threat of terrible damnation bridled passions and the half-wild nations" (8:40–41). Apparently, even the chaos of early Rus' was preferable to what Gogol saw as the pope's monolithic control. At least the former prepared the way for a true and free society.

23. Chapter 4 will demonstrate that the ideal nature of the Cossacks exists not *in spite of* their violence but in fact *because of* it.

24. Although applied in a rather unorthodox manner, Gogol's depiction of the Cossacks' "multiplicity-in-unity" was no doubt influenced by the Orthodox ideal of *sobornost'*, a term coined by Gogol's friend Aleksei Khomiakov. In "The Church Is One," Khomiakov explains the concept of a whole composed of elements which are not fused but at the same time not divided. "The unity of the Church," he wrote, "is not imaginary or allegorical, but a true and substantial unity, such as is the unity of many members in a living body." The union is indivisible, just as an arm or an eye must live in symbiotic harmony with the whole human organism, yet each member is complete in and of itself. The term "Church" refers to both the "Church visible, or upon earth," which is a group of distinct local churches and believers, organically united in common love of God; and to the "whole body of the Church, of which Christ is the Head," which exists outside of time and space. The concept of *sobornost'*, therefore, pervades both the physical and the metaphysical structures of Russian Orthodoxy. Aleksei Stepanovich Khomiakov, "Tserkov' odna," *Polnoe sobranie sochinenii,* 8 vols. (Moscow: Universitetskaia tipografiia, 1900–1904), 2:1–26.

25. See Gogol's reference to *zemnost'* in a letter to G. I. Vysotskii of June 26, 1827, *PSS* 10:98. Donald Fanger reminds us that in Gogol's day *poshlost'* carried the sense of low in quality or simple, and was only beginning to signify "the obviously trashy" or "the falsely important, the falsely beautiful, the falsely clever, the falsely attractive," as Nabokov so aptly defines it. *Creation of Nikolai Gogol* 19. Nabokov's discussion of *poshlost'* (or *poshlust* as he writes) is found in *Gogol* 63–74.

26. Iurii Lotman emphasizes the importance of the boundedness of the old-world landowners' space in "Problema khudozhestvennogo prostranstva v proze Gogolia," *Trudy po russkoi i slavianskoi filologii,* Vol. 11: *Literaturovedenie. Uchenye zapiski Tartuskogo gosudarstvennogo universiteta* 209 (Tartu, 1968), 22–23.

27. In this case "The Carriage" ("Koliaska") also comes to mind, for it too describes a town in terms of its surrounding enclosures, as well as a vehicle in terms of its enclosing trunk. And the spaces within are as spiritually vacant as the Polish town and the landowners' yard.

28. Andrei Belyi [Bugaev], *Masterstvo Gogolia: issledovanie* (Moscow-Leningrad: Gosudarstvennoe izdatel'stvo khudozhestvennoi literatury, 1934); G. A. Gukovskii, *Realizm Gogolia* (Moscow-Leningrad: Gosudarstvennoe izdatel'stvo khudozhestvennoi literatury, 1959).

29. Simon Karlinsky, *The Sexual Labyrinth of Nikolai Gogol* (Cambridge, Mass., and London: Harvard University Press, 1976), 67–77. According to Kar-

linsky, it is also a "female," the house cat of Pul'kheriia Ivanovna, that destroys the world of the old-world landowners.

Chapter Four. Death Transcended and the Female Threat

1. The term *tur* (aurochs) refers to a now almost extinct breed of wild bison that is much beloved in Russian folk literature. It may also signify a type of Caucasian goat, but a reference earlier to *buitur* (Mordovtsev, *Sagaidachnyi, PS* 1:67), reminiscent of the "valiant aurochs" of *The Lay of Igor's Campaign,* clearly suggests the former definition.

2. Mordovtsev, *Sagaidachnyi, PS* 1:80.

3. See the boast of one chief that his unit has known no deserters to marriage in Nestor Kukol'nik, *Zaporozhtsy, Istoricheskie povesti* (St. Petersburg: Izdanie A. S. Suvorina, 1902), 5:1.

4. Mordovstev, *Sagaidachnyi, PS* 1:12.

5. G. P. Danilevskii, "Pesnia bandurista," *Sochineniia G. P. Danilevskogo v 24-kh tomakh* (St. Petersburg: Izdanie A. F. Marksa, 1901), 3:162.

6. Mordovtsev, *Sagaidachnyi, PS* 1:197. The Eastern captive whose relations with a Cossack provoke consternation among the men is an echo of the story of Razin and his Persian princess. See explanation of the Razin legend in Chapter 7.

7. Vasilii Narezhnyi, *Zaporozhets, Romany i povesti Vasiliia Narezhnago,* 2d ed. (St. Petersburg: Tipografiia Aleksandra Smirdina, 1836), 8:184–85.

8. Cf. Ezekiel 23:31–34; Matthew 20:22 and 30:39; John 18:11.

9. See Dmitrii Merezhkovskii, *Gogol'. Tvorchestvo, zhizn', religiia* (St. Petersburg: Panteon, 1909), for a more in-depth study of Gogol's depiction of the devil. James B. Woodward also discusses the association of women and the devil in *The Symbolic Art of Gogol: Essays on His Short Fiction* (Columbus, Ohio: Slavica, 1981), 39.

10. See Fanger, *Creation of Nikolai Gogol* 100; Gary Cox, "Geographic, Sociological, and Sexual Tensions in Gogol''s Dikan'ka Stories," *Slavic and East European Journal* 24 (1980): 219–32; George Grabowicz, "The Myth of the Ukraine in Gogol'," unpublished lecture, Columbia University, 1980, and his already cited dissertation; Woodward, *Symbolic Art of Gogol* 12; and Karlinsky, *Sexual Labyrinth of Nikolai Gogol* 36, 59.

11. In an effort to place *Taras Bul'ba* in the context of the pathos of most of Gogol's other stories, many critics have incorrectly interpreted the death of Taras Bul'ba at the end of the story as an indication of the disappearance of Cossackdom. As Alex de Jonge states: "When [Taras Bul'ba] is finally hunted down his world dies with him. . . . Thus negative values triumph on every level. Bul'ba pursues a downward path till he has outlived his sons and practically outlived *kazachestvo.* One feels that with the end of the book one witnesses the end of the Cossacks' golden age." "Gogol'" 81. The Cossack tradition endures, however, as Bul'ba's disciples disappear "into the sunset." They may exit any semblance of historical time, but they consequently enter fully into the reality of myth. See next chapter for a more detailed explanation.

12. An interesting comparison of cowboy and Cossack texts can be made on this score. See John G. Cawelti, *The Six-Gun Mystique* (Bowling Green, Ohio: Bowling Green University Popular Press, n.d.), pp. 62, 82.

13. Babinsky, *Mazeppa Legend* 46, 137.

14. Juliusz Słowacki, *Mazeppa, Polish and American: A Translation of Słowacki's 'Mazeppa,' Together with a Brief Survey of Mazeppa in the United States*. Translated by Marion Moore Coleman (Cheshire, Conn.: Cherry Hill Books, 1966), 41.

15. Ryleev, *Voinarovskii* 201–3, ll. 372–437.

16. See, for example, Joseph Campbell, *Hero of a Thousand Faces,* rpt. of 2d ed. (Princeton: Princeton University Press, 1973), 93, 140–43, for a discussion of the mythic connection between violence and life or regeneration.

17. Gogol borrows this convention from an article of the same title by D. V. Venevitinov in *Severnaia lira* of 1827. Venevitinov in turn borrowed it from Wilhelm Wackenroder. Gogol's explicit aesthetic statements are by no means original and have usually been dismissed by scholars, but the hidden assumptions revealed in his choice of vocabulary deserve a second look. For more on sculpture, painting, and music in this article and in *Mirgorod,* see my article "Gogol' and the Muses of *Mirgorod,*" *Slavic Review* 50, no. 2(Summer 1991):309–16.

Chapter Five. Space and Time Unbounded

1. D. I. Tschiżewskij, "Gogol: Artist and Thinker," *Forum Slavicum,* Vol. 12: *Gogol'-Turgenev-Dostoevskij-Tolstoj zur Russischen Literatur des 19 Jahrhunderts,* ed. Tschiżewskij (Munich: Wilhelm Fink Verlag, 1966), 91–92.

2. Kukol'nik, *Zaporozhtsy, Istoricheskie povesti* 5:13.

3. See Victor Turner, *The Ritual Process* 107, for discussion of Christian monks who have achieved a permanent state of liminality.

4. Kukol'nik, *Zaporozhtsy,* v:14.

5. Mordovtsev, *Sagaidachnyi* 10.

6. Ibid. 53.

7. Ibid. 89.

8. Danilevskii, *Beglye v Novorossii, Sochineniia* 1:99.

9. Danilevskii, "Pensil'vantsy i Karolintsy," *Sochineniia* 17:26.

10. See Frederick Jackson Turner, *The Frontier in American History* (1920; New York: Holt, Rinehart and Winston, 1962), 4.

11. Ibid. 3.

12. "In cossack history there is a dialectic between a people and their land: the qualities and quantities of their space shaped their personal lives and social structures, as the people shaped the social and political order and use of that space." Gordon, *Cossack Rebellions* 11. Gordon also states: "The Ukraine, like other frontiers, attracted certain kinds of personalities. Despite the heaviest oppression, only exceptional people, and usually not the poorest, leave their homelands for the unknown. In sixteenth-century eastern Europe such breaks were even more disorienting than in the modern world: they often meant leaving the security of communities

where families had lived for generations longer than memory, and setting out for a borderland known in the folk tales for its bloodthirsty infidels, the cruelty of its winters, the loneliness of its vast plains. On the other hand the Ukraine was also legendary for its fertility; the attraction of potential prosperity explains why the archetypal cossack personality had two sides: fearless and hopeful, free-spirited and ambitious, independent and self-serving, anti-authoritarian and aggressive" (75).

13. For further discussion of the distinction between European borders and the American frontier, see Richard Slotkin, *Regeneration through Violence: The Mythology of the American Frontier, 1600–1860* (Middletown, Conn.: Wesleyan University Press, 1973), 369–76.

14. Slotkin (ibid. 373) presents the example of Chateaubriand, to whom "America offered an exotic setting for the symbolic drama of a Romantic novel pitting reason against passion, savagery against civilization, rebellious anarchism against respect for order and precedence."

15. Ronald LeBlanc briefly discusses the "frontier consciousness" of American literature in relation to Russian "imitations" of European literature in *The Russianization of Gil Blas* 15. For more on American literature's rebellion see Albert von Frank, *The Sacred Game: Provincialism and Frontier Consciousness in American Literature* (Cambridge: Cambridge University Press, 1985).

16. Slotkin, *Regeneration through Violence* 23, 100.

17. Countries besides Russia and America also have frontiers, of course, or at least areas far from their cultural/political centers, and we do find in their literature characters that to some extent resemble the Cossacks. Walter Scott's Highlanders, for instance, live far from civilized London and are at once English and decidedly not English. The differences, however, could provide material for another study altogether.

18. Again, it is useful to compare the many times Gogol playfully inverts or parodies the frontier which he so ardently establishes in *Taras Bul'ba.* Boasting, Nozdrev indicates the boundaries of his estate in *Dead Souls,* and then willfully pushes "his" frontier into a false liminality by claiming that everything on this side *and* on that side belongs to him. And Khlestakov's departure at the end of act 4 of *The Inspector General* is essentially "into the sunset" over the Russian expanse, as his voice emerges from beyond the boundary of the stage, and the bell of his carriage rings from afar as the curtain falls.

19. See also "About Little Russian Songs," where Gogol evokes the "wonderous, immeasurable steppe [chudesnaia, neizmerimaia step']" with its "unbounded blue sky" (*PSS* 8:91).

20. We are here discussing spatial manifestations of boundlessness, but from this example we can see the temporal ramifications as well. More will be discussed about the timelessness of the Cossacks in the following pages.

21. In his dissertation "N. V. Gogol's Unfinished Historical Novel 'The Hetman,'" Paul Karpuk convincingly demonstrates that historical inaccuracies in Gogol's fiction may indeed be traced to misinformation in his sources. Like Karpuk, I assume that we must take Gogol's historical aspirations seriously, and then attempt to determine the consequences of those aspirations.

22. Faddei Bulgarin, *Mazepa, Sochineniia* (St. Petersburg, 1834), 2:12.

23. A classic example can be found in *Vladimir* (1705) in which the author, Feofan Prokopovich, praised Mazepa in the prologue and epilogue as a great leader, a godly man, and a patriot, but changed the text itself after Mazepa joined Charles XII against Peter I. Discussed in Babinsky, *Mazeppa Legend* 80, 85.

24. Babinsky points out that Russian (and Polish) writers reshaped the West European Mazepa legend by placing history at the center of their works. While Byron used historical material for background, the Russians molded the entire story in order to make a political/historical point. *Mazeppa Legend* 94.

25. On Nov. 9, 1833, Gogol wrote to M. A. Maksimovich: "I have now set to work on a history of our one and only poor Ukraine. Nothing soothes me like history. My thoughts are beginning to flow more calmly and regularly. It seems to me that I will indeed write it and that I will say much that has previously gone unsaid" (10:284). On Jan. 11, 1834, he wrote to M. P. Pogodin: "I am now totally immersed in my Little Russian History and my General History, and both are beginning to move along" (10:294). Neither historical work ever materialized.

26. V. V. Gippius reminds us that Gogol "is not an archeologist but a poet. He is capable of confusing chronology by entire centuries, simply not realizing in which historical period the action is taking place, any more than the oral epic does." *Gogol*, ed. and trans. Robert A. Maguire (Ann Arbor: Ardis, 1981), 65. For a contrasting opinion, see Karpuk.

27. Gippius points out that "as far as Gogol was concerned, the dividing line between a scholarly and an artistic approach toward history was virtually imperceptible, and he crossed it time and again in his writings." Gogol moves in his article on Schloezer, Mueller, and Herder from a discussion of those three historians to a discussion of three artists: Schiller, Walter Scott, and Shakespeare. See *Gogol* 60. In the introduction to *PSS*, Gippius also reminds us that in Gogol's time the boundaries between "science" (*nauka*) and "letters" (*slovesnost'*) and between history and historical romance were extremely unstable (1:28).

28. *Taras Bul'ba* is in this way curiously modern. Joseph Frank discusses the transmutation of "the time-world of history into the timeless world of myth" in epic works such as Joyce's *Ulysses* by means of a "continual juxtaposition between aspects of the past and present, in such a way that both are fused in one comprehensive view. . . . By this juxtaposition . . . history becomes unhistorical." "Spatial Form in Modern Literature," in *Criticism: The Foundations of Modern Literary Judgment*, ed. Mark Schorer, Josephine Miles, Gordon McKenzie (New York: Harcourt Brace, 1948), 392.

29. Cf. *The Iliad of Homer*, translated and with an introduction by Richmond Lattimore (Chicago and London: University of Chicago Press, 1951), 5:560, 13:178, 13:389, 16:482.

30. Ryleev, *Polnoe sobranie stikhotvorenii* 201, ll. 388–90.

31. Bulgarin, *Mazepa, Sochineniia* 2:34.

32. If anything, *Taras Bul'ba* is closer to Gogol's definition of a "minor type of epic" that deals with a single hero through whom the author can present "a true picture of all that is significant in the traits and manners of the time he has chosen, an earthly, almost statistically comprehensible picture [for all who] look in the past to find living lessons for the present" (8:479). In this definition we see Gogol's emphasis

on "statistics" which would bring this genre much closer to history than to the epic, which "embraces not several traits, but a whole epoch in time" (8:478). We can also see how Gogol relates the past to the present by means of this genre. He gives the examples of Ariosto and Cervantes (thus expanding the epic genre to include prose works), though his own *Taras Bul'ba* would also conform. See "Epopeia" and "Men'shie rody epopei" in "Uchebnaia kniga slovesnosti dlia russkogo iunoshestva," *Vybrannye mesta iz perepiski s druz'iami* (8:478–79).

33. Gogol thus participates in a "consummatory" stage of mythmaking in order to "recapture the lost innocence of the primitive mythopoeic attitude by transcending narrative, logical, and linguistic forms which romantic mythologizing [like Homer] accepts and utilizes." Philip Wheelwright, "Semantic Approach to Myth," in *Myth: A Symposium,* ed. Thomas Sebeok (Bloomington: Indiana University Press, 1965), 96. In this type of mythmaking the artist turns himself into a prophet: "shaking minds and hearts with new visions rather than providing customary balm for normal social and personal anxieties" (Slotkin, *Regeneration through Violence* 13). The modern or consummatory myth of the Cossack thus resembles but is not identical to ancient myth with its closed and self-sufficient world. Boundaries in ancient myth are sealed, in myths of national identity, transcended.

34. Iurii Lotman argues that the image of mirrors and reflection almost always points to Gogol's model of unbounded space and to a shift of perspective above and beyond the ordinary world. See "Problema khudozhestvennogo prostranstva v proze Gogolia" 31.

35. Gogol conveniently places himself, Hitchcock-style, into this mythic landscape in the form of the goldeneye duck, a *gogol'* in Russian.

36. My thanks to Professor Paul Valliere of Butler University for his suggestion of this biblical association. A comparison of the Cossacks with the early Americans in the "New Israel" is called for at this point, but must wait for another time.

37. Only "St. John's Eve" was ever printed independently and then in a much different form—in *Otechestvennye Zapiski,* Feb. and March 1830, under the title, "Bisavriuk, ili vecher nakanune Ivana Kupala. Malorossiiskaia povest' (iz narodnogo predaniia, rasskazannaia d'iachkom Pokrovskoi tserkvi)." Many scholars insist on the structural integrity of *Evenings.* See Zeldin, *Nikolai Gogol's Quest for Beauty* 202 (n. 9).

38. Viktor Vinogradov speaks of "a series [verenitsa] of narrators." "He [Gogol] freely creates an artistic work, like a scale of complex and abrupt interruptions of speech which suggests the illusion of a continual shift of narrators and of their unexpected metamorphosis into the writer-scribe." *Etiudy o stile Gogolia* (Leningrad: Akademia, 1926), 41–42.

39. See Wasyl Hrishko, "Gogol's Ukrainian-Russian Bilingualism and the Dualism of Gogolian Style," Diss., University of Washington, 1973, for lists of Ukrainianisms throughout Gogol's oeuvre.

40. Gary Cox has done an extensive analysis of the narrative style of *Evenings* and concludes that the stories reveal a contest between two different narrators, an oral narrator and a literary one. My analysis differs from his only in that I see the contest as taking place between many more than two, with none taking a totally dominant stand. See Gary Duane Cox, "A Study of Gogol's Narrators," Diss., Columbia University, 1978. See also Gippius, *Gogol* 36–37, who divides the types of

narration in *Evenings* into four categories: (1) epic monologue ("Vecher nakanune Ivana Kupola"); (2) lyric-dramatic ("Sorochinskaia iarmarka," "Maiskaia noch'"); (3) dramatic-epic ("Noch' pered Rozhdestvom," "Shpon'ka"); (4) lyrical monologue ("Strashnaia mest'"). This analysis is quite convincing, but the very need to distinguish so many voices supports my thesis: Gogol consciously combines many different stances into one cycle.

41.　Martin P. Rice, "On 'Skaz'," *Russian Literature Triquarterly* 12(Spring 1975):409–23.

42.　Lotman speaks of the loss of a fixed reference frame in passages when Gogol moves the point of view to a place above the action. "Problema khudozhestvennogo prostranstvo v proze Gogolia" 20.

43.　Tzvetan Todorov, *The Fantastic: A Structural Approach to a Literary Genre,* trans. Richard Howard, forward by Robert Scholes (Ithaca, N.Y.: Cornell University Press, 1975), 33.

44.　Ibid. 113.

45.　Ibid. 118.

46.　At this point the hero forms himself a bandura and begins to sing, connecting this fantastic passage with an element discussed earlier: epic song.

47.　Todorov identifies stories in which internal desires leave the inner world and become embodied (usually in witch or devil figures) in the external world. Given a tangible existence of their own, they drive the hero mad. *Fantastic* 127.

48.　Todorov reminds us about the fantastic that "the limit between matter and mind is not unknown here, as it is in mythical thought, for instance; it remains present, in order to furnish the pretext for incessant transgressions." *Fantastic* 116.

49.　For another discussion of the fantastic in the works of Gogol, see Iurii Mann, "Fantasticheskoe i real'noe u Gogolia," *Voprosy literatury* 13, no. 9 (1969): 106–25.

Chapter Six. Conclusion: The Ambivalent Tolstoi

1.　*The Cossacks* recalls Pushkin's narrative poems *The Gypsies* and *The Caucasian Prisoner* more than *The Captain's Daughter.* Tolstoi began his Cossack novel eleven years earlier than its final publication, at a time when he was still particularly involved in a study of romantic ideas. In this sense, it belongs with his highly romantic *Sevastopol Stories* of the 1850s and not with the later novels.

2.　For a brief investigation of the Caucasus in Russian literature, see Susan Layton, "The Creation of an Imaginative Caucasian Geography," *Slavic Review* 45, no. 3(Fall 1986):470–85.

3.　Lev Tolstoi, *Polnoe sobranie sochinenii* [henceforth *PSS*] (Moscow-Leningrad: Gosudarstvennoe izdatel'stvo, 1929), 6:11. Further references to Tolstoi will be from this edition and indicated in the text.

4.　Boris Eikhenbaum, *The Young Tolstoi,* translated by Gary Kern (Ann Arbor: Ardis, 1972), 89–94. Tolstoi must also have had in mind Pushkin's *The Caucasian Prisoner,* in which the hero has an experience with a mountain girl.

5. Gary Saul Morson discusses the importance for Tolstoi of the ordinary in relation to his theory of "prosaics" in *Hidden in Plain View: Narrative and Creative Potentials in 'War and Peace'* (Stanford: Stanford University Press, 1987), 126. For his use of the term "mess," see "Prosaics and *Anna Karenina*," *Tolstoy Studies Journal* 1 (1988):1–12.

6. C. J. G. Turner, "Tolstoy's 'The Cossacks': The Question of Genre," *Modern Language Review* 73 (1978):563–72, traces the development of the genre of the work.

7. Turner, "Tolstoy's 'The Cossacks': The Question of Genre" 567. Tolstoi's diary entry from 1857 is found in *PSS* 47:146.

8. For a provocative study of Tolstoi's fiction in terms of the categories of "securely loved" vs. "orphan," or, more broadly, "resident" vs. "stranger," see Richard F. Gustafson, *Leo Tolstoy, Resident and Stranger: A Study in Fiction and Theology* (Princeton: Princeton University Press, 1986).

9. Tolstoi borrows the technique of a supposedly objective ethnographic description from the physiological sketch. Contemporary readers considered this writing "realistic," although it is actually quite romantic. For suggestions of the relationship of Tolstoi's Caucasian fiction to the sketch, see Carol Carbone Eros, "Tolstoj's Tales of the Caucasus and Literary Tradition," Diss., University of Wisconsin, 1973, 7–8.

10. As John Hagan states, "Cossack and Moscow values are not as far apart as the reader and Olenin at first suppose." "Ambivalence in Tolstoy's 'The Cossacks'," *Novel: A Forum of Fiction* 3 (1969):33.

11. Cf. ibid. 28–47, and Laura Jepsen, "To Kill like a Cossack," *South Atlantic Bulletin* 43 (1978):86–94.

Chapter Seven. Introduction: From Myth to History

1. Seaton, *Horsemen of the Steppes* 194–95; and Longworth, *Cossacks* 267–68.

2. As Longworth succinctly states: "The old pattern of trade by which the Cossack imported food and exported revolution was reversed. The Don exported food now—and imported its ideas." *Cossacks* 250.

3. Robert H. McNeal argues that the Cossacks were a costly anachronism in the twentieth century. Nonetheless, "the horseman's tactical usefulness was not so obsolescent in one kind of war, the class conflict that had erupted in Russia's cities and villages in 1905." *Tsar and Cossack, 1855–1914* (London: Macmillan Press in association with St. Antony's College, Oxford, 1987), 220.

4. John Bushnell, *Mutiny amid Repression: Russian Soldiers in the Revolution of 1905–1906* (Bloomington: Indiana University Press, 1985), 109–10.

5. For a discussion of the distribution of land to the Cossack estate, see McNeal, *Tsar and Cossack* 166–89.

6. Seaton, *Horsemen of the Steppes* 216.

7. Ibid. 223.

8. Ibid. 216–17, 219.

9. It is possible that the Cossacks joined the Whites less out of antipathy to the

Revolution, and more in response to what they felt was "sacrilegious" behavior of the Reds in their villages. As one scholar explains: "The main causes of the Cossack counterrevolution were fear of losing their former privileges and a part of their land as a result of the levelling agrarian policy of the local Soviet regime and numerous acts of robbery and violence which were perpetrated by undisciplined Red bands." William Henry Chamberlin, *The Russian Revolution: 1917–1921* (New York: Macmillan, 1935), 2:135.

10. See Longworth, *Cossacks* 310.

11. Seaton, *Horsemen of the Steppes* 233.

12. Many of the Cossacks were recruited from Nazi POW camps and granted freedom if they agreed to fight against their homeland.

13. Longworth, *Cossacks* 329.

14. For a discussion of *lubok* literature, see Jeffrey Brooks, *When Russia Learned to Read: Literacy and Popular Literature, 1861–1917* (Princeton: Princeton University Press, 1985). Brooks discusses Cossack heroes mostly in his chapter on bandits (166–213). He sees Ermak as the most popular "non-military historical subject" (79 and 364 [Table 14]).

15. Vasilii Kamenskii, *Stikhotvoreniia i poemy*, ed. N. L. Stepanov, Biblioteka Poeta, Bol'shaia seriia, 2d ed. (Moscow-Leningrad: Sovetskii pisatel', 1966), 460.

16. Ibid. 179. *Saryn'* refers to the crew members of a boat captured by Razin's men, who were ordered to the front of the boat to remove them from the robbers' way. The call loses its original purpose in literature and becomes a fixed cry of the brigand Cossacks.

17. Ibid. 180.

18. See N. Chuzhak, *Pravda o Pugacheve. Opyt literaturno-istoricheskogo analiza* (Moscow: Vsesoiuznoe obshchestvo politicheskikh katorzhan i ssyl'no-poselentsev, 1926); *Pugachevshchina. Iz arkhiva*, edited by S. A. Golubtsov, 3 vols. (Moscow-Leningrad: Gosudarstvennoe izdatel'stvo, 1926, 1929, 1931); N. N. Firsov, *Pugachevshchina. Opyt sotsiologo-psikhologicheskoi kharakteristiki*, 2d ed. (1908; Moscow: Gosudarstvennoe izdatel'stvo, 1921).

19. S. G. Tomsinskii, introduction to Firsov, *Pugachevshchina* viii.

20. Scholars disagree sharply about the existence and role of these women, who do not seem to appear in contemporary folk songs, but emerge with any consistency only in nineteenth- and twentieth-century texts. (The Persian princess was mentioned, however erroneously, by Jan Struys in *The Voyages and Travels of John Struys* [London, 1684]. It is this foreign account with which later writers may have been familiar.) See Avrich, *Russian Rebels* 75, 280 n. 41.

21. See for example Kamenskii's play *Sten'ka Razin. P'esa v 9 kartinakh* (Kharkov: Gosudarstvennoe izdatel'stvo Ukrainy, 1923), 12–13.

22. Petr Struve, "Intelligentsia and Revolution," in *Landmarks*, edited by Boris Shragin and Albert Todd, translated by Marian Schwartz (New York, Karz Howard, 1977), 140.

Chapter Eight. Isaak Babel and His Red Cavalry Cossacks

1. D. S. Mirsky, *A History of Russian Literature,* ed. Francis J. Whitfield (New York: Alfred A. Knopf, 1949), 151. Babel's Red Army stories comprise the cycle *Konarmiia,* an abbreviation for Horse Army or Cavalry, but generally translated as *Red Cavalry.*

2. Maksim Gor'kii, "Rabselkoram i voenkoram o tom, kak uchilsia pisat'," *Pravda,* Sept. 30, 1928, 3. See also Patricia Carden, *The Art of Isaac Babel* (Ithaca: Cornell University Press, 1972), 59, 76, 127; James E. Falen, *Isaac Babel, Russian Master of the Short Story* (Knoxville: University of Tennessee Press, 1974), 52–54; Martin B. Klotz, "Poetry of the Present: Isaak Babel's *Red Cavalry,*" *Slavic and East European Journal* 18 (1974):160; Judith Stora-Sandor, *Isaac Babel', 1894–1941, l'homme et l'oeuvre* (Paris: Klincksieck, 1968), 77; I. A. Smirin, "Na puti k *Konarmii,*" *Literaturnoe nasledstvo* 74 (Moscow: Nauka, 1965):482.

3. Steven Marcus, "The Stories of Isaac Babel," *Partisan Review* 22, no. 3 (Summer 1955):403. See also Lionel Trilling, Introduction to *Isaac Babel: The Collected Stories,* trans. and ed. Walter Morrison (Cleveland and New York: New American Library, 1955), 18, published also in Trilling, *Beyond Culture: Essays on Literature and Learning* (New York: Viking Press, 1965); Ragna Grøngaard, *An Investigation of Composition and Theme in Isaak Babel's Literary Cycle Konarmija* (Aarhus: Arkona, 1979), 87; R. W. Hallett, *Isaac Babel* (Letchworth, Hertfordshire: Bradda Books, 1972), 51.

4. Although Khadzhi Murat is not a Cossack, he can be understood as an extension of the highly ambivalent heroes portrayed in *The Cossacks,* as discussed in Chapter 6. Renato Poggioli claims that *Red Cavalry* resembles *Khadzhi Murat* much more than it does *The Cossacks.* "Isaak Babel in Retrospect," *The Phoenix and the Spider* (Cambridge: Harvard University Press, 1957), 234.

5. Interview during a celebratory evening at the Writers' Union, Sept. 28, 1937, first published in *Nash Sovremennik* 4(1964). Reprinted as "O tvorcheskom puti pisatelia," in *Zabytyi Babel',* ed. Nikolai Stroud (Ann Arbor: Ardis, 1979), 267.

6. From "Moi Listki," an early story published in *Zhurnal zhurnalov,* no. 51 (1917):4–5, under the transparent pseudonym Bab-El'. Republished in *Zabytyi Babel'* 48–51.

7. *Zabytyi Babel'* 48–49, 50.

8. The best available biography of Babel is by Judith Stora-Sandor, *Isaac Babel',* cited above. Babel's own autobiography is fascinating, but not necessarily accurate.

9. Babel thus concealed his obviously Jewish name from the traditionally anti-Semitic Cossacks. But he could not adopt a pseudo-character as well. If his stories are any indication of his experience, the Cossacks were painfully aware of "Liutov's" intellectualism, symbolized by his glasses and associated with the educated Jewish population.

10. Patricia Carden feels Gor'kii's advice may be apocryphal, or at least exaggerated by Babel as he developed a "self-created legend," but that his search for material among the Cossacks was real (*Art of Isaac Babel* 11, 12–13).

11. Babel of course suffered a period of about twenty-five years when his works did not appear in the Soviet Union. He was "rehabilitated" after Stalin's death.

12. Gogol died at the age of forty-three, apparently from self-starvation. Babel, at the age of forty-seven, fell victim to the Stalinist purges.

13. Gogol', Letter of Feb. 1, 1833, *PSS* 10:257.

14. I. Babel', *Konarmiia. Odesskie rasskazy. P'esy* (Letchworth, Hertfordshire: Bradda Books, 1965), 262. Page numbers in the text will refer to this edition unless otherwise cited.

15. Konstantin Paustovskii, "Neskol'ko slov o Babele: Memuary," first published in *Nedelia,* nos. 11–17 (Sept. 1966). Translated in *Isaac Babel: You Must Know Everything,* trans. Max Hayward, ed. Nathalie Babel (New York: Farrar, Straus and Giroux, 1966):281.

16. See Gogol's December 24, 1844, letter to Smirnova quoted in Chapter 3, above.

17. Poggioli, *Phoenix and the Spider* 230. Cited in Carden, *Art of Isaac Babel* 8.

18. To this date, Soviet-Yiddish writers have been insufficiently studied. For some background, see *Ashes out of Hope: Fiction by Soviet-Yiddish Writers,* edited and introduction by Irving Howe and Eliezer Greenberg (New York: Schocken Books, 1977).

19. As Donald Fanger writes about Gogol: "Gogol capitalized on this appeal [the exoticism of Ukraine] as a mediator; by embracing his Ukrainian heritage, he became a Russian writer." *Creation of Nikolai Gogol* 87–88.

20. See Stora-Sandor's comment in *Isaac Babel'* 85, 92.

21. Nils Åke Nilsson suggests that the passage appears as a temporal chain on a metonymic plane, but that when experienced metaphorically it is detached from either temporal or causal progression. "Isaak Babel's 'Perechod čerez Zbruč," *Scando-Slavica* 23(1977):69–70.

22. Victor Terras, "Line and Color: The Structure of I. Babel's Short Stories in *Red Cavalry,*" *Studies in Short Fiction* 3, no. 2 (1966):153. See also Rochelle H. Ross, "The Unity of Babel's Konarmija," *South Central Bulletin* 41, no. 4 (Winter 1981): 116; Toby W. Clyman, "Babel' as Colorist," *Slavic and East European Journal* 21 (1977):333.

23. See "The Road to Brody," "My First Goose," "Gedali," "The Rebbe," "The Death of Dolgushov," "The Brigade Commander," "Konkin," and "Berestechko." For the suggestion that sunset also refers to the traditional symbol of demarcation of temporal power and the beginning of the sacred Sabbath, see Efraim Sicher, "The Road to a Red Calvary: Myth and Mythology in the Works of Isaak Babel' of the 1920's," *Slavonic and East European Review* 60, no. 4(Oct. 1982):540.

24. Nilsson, "Perekhod" 65, and Falen, *Isaac Babel* 137, also read the crossing, as Nilsson states, as "a transition from one world to another."

25. Sicher, "Road to a Red Calvary" 538.

26. From the traditional Passover Haggadah. Italics mine.

27. Passover falls in spring, not early summer, when the Polish campaign actually began. The dishes may be scattered because the invading soldiers removed them from storage, but Babel's choice to mention them specifically, and not other stored

items, gives credence to this interpretation. Babel was not interested in temporal fidelity here.

28. See Elizabeth A. Warner, *The Russian Folk Theater* (The Hague and Paris: Mouton, 1977), 95–98, for a discussion of the Cossack in Russian and Ukrainian folk theater. For an early-nineteenth-century play strongly influenced by the eighteenth-century folk plays, see *Kazak-stikhotvorets* by A. A. Shakhovskoi (1812).

29. Carden, *Art of Isaac Babel* 49, 112–13.

30. For a discussion of the specific Hasidic references in these stories, see Maurice Friedberg, "Yiddish Folklore Motifs in Isaak Babel's *Konarmija*," *American Contributions to the Eighth International Congress of Slavists,* Vol. 2 (Columbus, Ohio: Slavica, 1978), 192–203.

31. Herbert Marder, "The Revolutionary Art of Isaac Babel," *Novel: A Forum on Fiction* 7(1973):56.

32. Babel, *The Forgotten Prose,* ed. and trans. Nicholas Stroud (Ann Arbor: Ardis, 1978), 129–30.

33. Or: "Hyperbolic, surrealistic elements," according to Michael Falchikov, "Conflict and Contrast in Isaak Babel's *Konarmiya,*" *Modern Language Review* 72 (1977):128.

34. J. J. van Baak, "The Function of Nature and Space in *Konarmija* by I. E. Babel'," in *Dutch Contributions to the Eighth International Congress on Slavists: Zagreb, Ljubljana, 1978* (Amsterdam: Benjamins, 1979), 44. Many critics have noticed Babel's use of epic. Terras's article "Line and Color" sees a travesty of epic (142), and Sicher claims Babel's use of myth gives the illusion of epic while mocking it ("Road to a Red Calvary" 531). See also Carol Luplow, *Isaac Babel's "Red Cavalry"* (Ann Arbor: Ardis, 1982), 40; Carden, *Art of Isaac Babel* 118, 126; Falen, *Isaac Babel* 80, 83–84, 119, 191–25; J. Catteau, "L'épopée dans la *Cavalerie Rouge* de I. Babel," in *VII Międzynarodowy Kongres Slawistów w Warszawie. 1973: Streszczenia referatów i komunikatów* (Warsaw: PAN, 1973), 700–701; Milton Ehre, "Babel's *Red Cavalry*: Epic and Pathos, History and Culture," *Slavic Review* 40, no. 2(1981): 228–40; Martin B. Klotz, "Poetry of the Present: Isaak Babel's *Red Cavalry,*" *Slavic and East European Journal* 18(1974):160–69; A. B. Murphy, "The Style of Isaak Babel'," *Slavonic and East European Review* 44(1966):369.

35. John G. Gunnell, *Political Philosophy and Time* (Middletown, Conn.: Wesleyan University Press, 1968), 11.

36. Frank, "Spatial Form in Modern Literature" 393.

37. Terras, "Line and Color" 152; Carden, *Art of Isaac Babel* 48.

38. L. Livshits, "Materialy k tvorcheskoi biografii I. Babelia," *Voprosy literatury* 4(1964):122.

39. Frank, "Spatial Form in Modern Literature" 392.

40. Raymond Rosenthal, "The Fate of Isaak Babel," *Commentary* 3, no. 2(Feb. 1947); Trilling, Introduction to *Collected Stories,* and Falchikov, "Conflict and Contrast"; Gareth Williams, "Two Leitmotifs in Babel's *Konarmija,*" *Die Welt der Slaven* 17(1972):308–17; van Baak, "Function of Nature and Space" 37–55.

41. As Patricia Carden states, "the easy division between Cossack and Jew is inadequate" (*Art of Isaac Babel* 121). Louis Irabarne writes of the paradox of the

"beautiful-bad Cossack" vs. "ugly-good Jew," in "Babel's *Red Cavalry* as a Baroque Novel," *Contemporary Literature* 14(1973):68; see also Stanley Edgar Hyman, "The Problem of Jewish Identity: Identities of Isaac Babel," *The Promised End* (New York: World Publishing, 1963), 322; and Luplow, *Isaac Babel's "Red Cavalry"* 10.

42. See Falen, *Isaac Babel* 141, on the theme of rebirth, and Hyman, "Problem of Jewish Identity" 321, who sees changes of identity through rituals of rebirth as a major theme of *Red Cavalry*.

43. Livshits, "Materialy k tvorcheskoi biographii I. Babelia" 131.

44. Milk, a typically female symbol, is frequently associated with non-Cossack behavior in *Red Cavalry*. Matvei Pavlichenko describes himself in his young life as wasting away as a herdsman—not a warrior—surrounded by and infused with the smell of milk, for he has not yet entered true adult Cossackdom (73). The Polish enemy cries "white tears, real human milk" ("Konkin" 85) to express his fear of death. And the Cossack Akinfiev calls Liutov a *molokan* (a member of a pacifist sect named from the word *moloko* or milk) when he fails to act like a Cossack and cannot kill without regret ("After the Battle" 140).

45. My thanks to Robert A. Maguire for suggesting this allusion.

46. See Carden, *Art of Isaac Babel* 135–36.

47. Klotz, "Poetry of the Present" 161.

48. Terras, "Line and Color" 145.

49. In his autobiography, Babel describes his schoolboy world in just such chaotic and creative terms: "[At my school] studied the sons of foreign merchants, the children of Jewish brokers, imposing Poles, Old-Believers, and many overgrown billiard players. During breaks I would go out to the pier at the port or to the Greek coffee houses to play billiards, or to the Moldavanka to drink cheap Bessarabian wine in the cellars" (*Konarmiia* 19).

50. Cf. Gogol, *Taras Bul'ba, PSS* 2:43.

51. *Oktiabr'*, no. 4(1924):224. See also Budennyi's outraged remarks in "Babizm Babelia," *Oktiabr'*, no. 3(1924):196–97 and "Otkrytoe pis'mo M. Gor'komu," in *Pravda*, Oct. 26, 1928.

Chapter Nine. Modern Poets and Their Cossack Rebels

1. Vasilii Kamenskii, *Put' entuziasta* (Moscow: Federatsiia, 1931), 208–9. Cited in "Vasilii Kamenskii," Introduction to *Stikhotvoreniia i poemy*, ed. N. L. Stepanov, Biblioteka Poeta series, 2d ed. (Moscow-Leningrad: Sovetskii pisatel', 1966), 24.

2. Khlebnikov draws attention to the unique position of Astrakhan: "I belong to the Meeting Place of the Volga and the Caspian Sea [Sigai]. More than once over the centuries it held in its hand and shook the scales of all Russian deeds." In V. Khlebnikov, *Neizdannye proizvedeniia*, ed. N. Khadzhieva and T. Gritsa (Moscow: Khudozhestvennaia literatura, 1940), 352 [henceforth *NP*]. Also cited in Nikolai Stepanov, *Velimir Khlebnikov. Zhizn' i tvorchestvo* (Moscow: Sovetskii pisatel', 1975), 7–8.

3. See Vladimir Markov, *The Longer Poems of Velimir Khlebnikov* (Berkeley

and Los Angeles: University of California Press, 1962), 14; and Ronald Vroon, "Velimir Chlebnikov's 'Chadži-Tarchan' and the Lomonosovian Tradition," *Russian Literature* 9 (1981), 107–31.

4. Quoted in Stepanov, *Velimir Khlebnikov* 106.

5. See A. E. Parnis, "Iuzhnoslavianskaia tema Velimira Khlebnikova," in *Zarubezhnye slaviane i russkaia kul'tura*, ed. M. P. Alekseev (Leningrad: Nauka, 1978), 223–51.

6. *Sobranie proizvedenii Velimira Khlebnikova*, ed. Iu. Tynianov and N. L. Stepanov (Leningrad: Izdatel'stvo pisatelei v Leningrade, 1928–33), 3:201 [henceforth *SP*].

7. These include "The Death of Palivoda" ("Smert' Palivody"), which is the fourth section of "Children of the Otter" ("Deti vydry," *SP* 2:153–57); "The Great Day" ("Velik-Den'," 1911, *SP* 5:121–23); and "The Inhabitants of the Mountains" ("Zhiteli gor," 1912, *NP* 305–9).

8. See commentary to "The Inhabitants of the Mountains" in *NP* 457. Mentioned also in Robert A. McLean, "The Prose of Velimir Xlebnikov," Diss., Princeton University, 1973, 75.

9. E.g., Palivoda "died for holy Rus'" (pogib za sviatuiu Rus') (*SP* 2:155). See the comments of McLean, "Prose of Velimir Xlebnikov" 77–78.

10. "Pesn' mne," *NP* 205–8.

11. The reference to Huns perhaps recalls Valerii Briusov's poem "The Coming Huns" ("Idushchie gunny," 1904–5), which forecasts the destruction of Russia by invading Eastern elemental forces, greeted joyfully by the poet.

12. "Obed," *SP* 3:302–3.

13. In *Velimir Khlebnikov's Shorter Poems: A Key to the Coinages* (Ann Arbor: University of Michigan Press, 1983), 45, Ronald Vroon explains the neologism *vol'ba* as meaning the act of willing, desiring, or preferring, related to *volia*, or will. The line could then read: " . . . of the willful act of doves, of the firing of wills. . . ."

14. *SP* 1:115–21.

15. The term *kumach* is also found in the opening of "Inhabitants of the Mountains," not referring specifically to Razin. Chances are the word simply meant rebellion to Khlebnikov, with all the usual connotations of the color red: anger, emotion, strength, violence. It is ironic that *kumach* also became the color of the Soviet flag.

16. Khlebnikov defines the cry in an idiosyncratic way: "Saryn' est' sarych'—khishchik. Saryn' na kichku—znachit korshun na golovu; tak razboiniki obrashivalis' na suda." *NP* 331. Quoted in Jean-Claude Lanne, *Velimir Khlebnikov. Poète futurien* (Paris: Institut d'études slaves, 1983), 84.

17. It is also the name of the Egyptian sun-god, again bringing in mythic associations and Eastern motifs. See Markov, *Longer Poems of Velimir Khlebnikov* 111. Ronald Vroon analyzes the relationship between *Ra* (the sun) and -*zin* (an old Slavic root for vision) in Khlebnikov's poem "*Ra*—vidiashchii ochi svoi . . ." and concludes that Razin is a double and mirror image of the sun. "Metabiosis, Mirror Images and Negative Integers: Velimir Chlebnikov and His Doubles," in *Velimir Chlebnikov (1885–1922): Myth and Reality*, ed. Willem G. Weststeijn (Amsterdam: Rodopi, 1986), 252.

18.   Vroon, "Velimir Chlebnikov's 'Chadži-Tarchan' and the Lomonosovian Tradition" 124–25.

19.   "Zakliatie smekhom," *SP* 2:35. See Vroon, "Velimir Chlebnikov's 'Chadži-Tarchan' and the Lomonosovian Tradition" 125.

20.   *SP* 3:365.

21.   Vroon discusses Razin as a "metabiotic" double for Khlebnikov in "Metabiosis, Mirror Images and Negative Integers" 268–73.

22.   *SP* 1:233–45.

23.   See Lanne, *Velimir Khlebnikov* 81.

24.   *SP* 1:202–14.

25.   See Salomon Mirsky, *Der Orient im Werk Velimir Chlebnikovs, Slavistische Beitrage* 85 (Munich: Verlag Otto Sagner, 1975), 92.

26.   A loose translation of this passage, disregarding sound play, palindromes, and agrammatical omissions might read:

> He struck the milk with a stake,
> Grown fiercely independent.
>   A boor's broad gesture
>   Or
> He waved at the executioner's blocks.
>   Or
> A falcon near the scythes!
>   Search!
>   Go!
> Beckon, bondsman, the gentlemen!
>   There, the braziers of a thief,
>   And the rubies burned brightly
>   Once to the dawn.

27.   See Markov, *Longer Poems of Velimir Khlebnikov* 158, for an explanation of this translation.

28.   The poem "Ladomir" (*SP* 1:183–201) also unites the poet, Lobachevskii, and Razin. See Vroon, "Velimir Chlebnikov's 'Chadži-Tarkhan'" 121.

29.   "Ustrug Razina," *SP* 1:246–51.

30.   "Razin. Dve troitsy," 1922, *SP* 4:146–50.

31.   Vroon calls it Khlebnikov's *apologia pro vita sua.* "Velimir Khlebnikov's 'Razin: Two Trinities': A Reconstruction," *Slavic Review* 39, no. 1 (March 1980): 69.

32.   Ronald Vroon analyzes this work in detail in "Velimir Khlebnikov's 'Razin: Two Trinities': A Reconstruction." He shows the poet's close association with the Cossack, "denying Razin's death by virtue of his own reincarnation as the rebel" (78). I disagree only with the author's contrast of Razin and Khlebnikov in the statement: "Razin is a prophet of violence. The poet is a prophet of love" (84). Khlebnikov, I believe, did not divide the traits of love (or creation) and violence between himself and the rebel, but rather juxtaposed and combined the opposites within both personalities. Vroon retracts somewhat in his essay on doubles ("Metabiosis") and suggests the opposition occurs only over the issue of the drowned princess (272–3 and again in the discussion on 289).

33. *SP* 5:303. My thanks to Ronald Vroon for directing me to this quotation. Cited also in Lanne, *Velimir Khlebnikov* 84.

34. "Kto on, Voronikhin stoletii," 1921–22, *SP* 5:103–6.

35. For other important poems with Cossack themes, see Razin in "Rech' v Rostove na Donu," "Ra—vidiashchii ochi svoi . . . ," "Ia videl iunoshu proroka," and "Ladomir"; and Ermak in "Uravnenie dushi Gogolia" and "Zametki."

36. Vladimir Orlov, "Marina Tsvetaeva. Sud'ba. Kharakter. Poeziia," Introductory essay to Tsvetaeva, *Izbrannye proizvedeniia* (Moscow-Leningrad: Sovetskii pisatel', 1965), 15.

37. For a detailed biography, see Simon Karlinsky, *Marina Tsvetaeva: The Woman, Her World, and Her Poetry* (Cambridge and New York: Cambridge University Press, 1985).

38. Marina Tsvetaeva, *Izbrannaia proza v dvukh tomakh. 1917–1937* (New York: Russica Publishers, 1979), 2:249–79. Whenever possible, reference to Tsvetaeva's prose will be to this edition [henceforth *IP*], and referred to in the text by volume and page. In the case of her poetry, references are to *Stikhotvoreniia i poemy v piati tomakh* (New York: Russica, 1982–1983) [henceforth *S&P*].

39. *IP* 2:280–302. Both "My Pushkin" and "Pushkin and Pugachev" have been translated in Marina Tsvetaeva, *A Captive Spirit: Selected Prose*, ed. and trans. J. Marin King (Ann Arbor: Ardis, 1980).

40. *S&P* 2:198.

41. The first of Pushkin's Razin poems tells the story of the princess's death, but without remorse on the Cossack's part. The drowning of the girl is a sacrifice to the Mother Volga.

42. *S&P* 2:198.

43. "Tsar' i Bog! Prostite malym—" (1918) *S&P* 2:78–79.

44. *S&P* 4:296.

45. "Tsar'-devitsa," *S&P* 4:9–90. See also Razin in "Za devkami dogliadyvat'. . ."; the adjective "of Razin" (*Razinskie*) in "Maslianitsa shiroka"; a mention of "Black Sea forelocks" (*chuby*) in "Naiada."

46. My sincere thanks for help received from Marilyn Smith, who has done extensive research and analysis of Tsvetaeva's work.

47. See his dedication in *Vechernie Izvestiia Moskovskogo Sovieta*, no. 230, May 2, 1919.

48. Khlebnikov's first mention of the Cossack rebel was in 1911, four years before the first publication of Kamenskii's so-called "free novel" (*privol'nyi roman*) *Sten'ka Razin*, and a full year before Kamenskii confesses to have conceived the idea.

49. Kamenskii, *Put' entuziasta* 22. Cited in the introduction to Vasilii Kamenskii, *Stikhotvoreniia i poemy* [*Stikh*], ed. N. L. Stepanov (Moscow-Leningrad: Sovetskii pisatel', 1966), 6. References to this volume will henceforth appear in the text.

50. The archive with Kamenskii's manuscripts apparently contains an incomplete narrative poem on Ermak Timofeevich as well. See commentary to *Stikh* 477.

51. Kamenskii, *Ego-moia biografiia velikogo futurista* (Moscow, 1918), 152–53. Quoted in *Stikh* 486.

52. Kamenskii, *Sten'ka Razin* 10–11.

53. Ibid. 11.

54.   Kornei Chukovskii, *Futuristy* (Petrograd: Poliarnaia Zvezda, 1922), 38–39.

55.   Chuzhak, *Pravda o Pugacheve 5*, 23.

56.   Introduction to *Stikh* 40.

57.   Rough draft of a letter to N. F. Chudak, in TsGALI, cited in introduction to *Stikh* 34.

Chapter Ten. Mikhail Sholokhov and Transfer of the Staff of Power

1.   Sholokhov wrote a famous letter attacking the now emigré writer Andrei Siniavskii for having published abroad, and was subsequently condemned as a hack by Iurii Galanskov, a dissident of the mid-sixties. Sholokhov's adherence to the Party line in all official speeches did not earn many friends among the young, post-Stalin writers.

2.   Questions about the accuracy of Sholokhov's observations of Don Cossack life have added fuel to the plagiarism controversy that has surrounded Sholokhov since shortly after the publication of *The Quiet Don*. An excellent survey of the accusations and rebuttals is found in Herman Ermolaev, *Mikhail Sholokhov and His Art* (Princeton: Princeton University Press, 1982), 264–300. The present study assumes Sholokhov to be the legitimate author. Ultimately, the text stands on its own in the history of the myth, regardless of author.

3.   Mikhail Sholokhov, *Sobranie sochinenii v deviati tomakh* (Moscow: Khudozhestvennaia literatura, 1965–69), 4:62. All references will be to this edition, and indicated in the text. Translations are my own, although I have consulted the available English editions. None of the latter have been published unabridged.

4.   References to *War and Peace* can be found as well, as in the ironic statement on "heroism" found in 2:284. Yet Helen Muchnic finds a basic difference between Sholokhov and Tolstoi, both aesthetic and philosophical. See "Sholokhov and Tolstoy," *Russian Review* 16(April 1957), pp. 25–34.

5.   See Tolstoi, *Kazaki, PSS* 6:56.

6.   Chubatyi is usually called by the name Uriupin in the most widely read English translation, *And Quiet Flows the Don*, trans. Stephen Garry (New York: Vintage Books, 1966). The original repeats the given name Chubatyi much more often, however, to stress the Cossackness of the character—he wears a *chub,* a traditional Cossack forelock.

7.   In the article "Tragic Features in the Character of Grigorii Melexov," *Slavic and East European Journal* 23(1979): 65, Robert F. Price claims that the family history singles Grigorii out as an unusual individual and that Prokofii's choice of a Turkish bride is his first "violation of Cossack mores." He states: "The message of the family introduction is that Grigorij has inherited from his grandfather and grandmother an exotic individuality, high self-esteem, and impetuous courage." I agree with this last statement, but would claim that while this indeed makes him less like his peasantized Cossack neighbors, it nonetheless makes him more like the Cossacks of myth.

8.   For a discussion of similarities between *The Quiet Don* and *The Lay of Igor's*

Campaign and *Zadonshchina*, see P. V. Bekedin, "Drevnerusskie motivy v *Tikhom Done* M. A. Sholokhova (k postanovke voprosa)," *Russkaia literatura* 2(1980): 92–108.

9.   "Suddenly we are struck by the painful realisation of the awful connection between the time honoured Cossack way of life and traditions, and Uryupin's [Chubatyi's] degenerate, inhuman philosophy. The reader suddenly finds himself associating the Melekhov family and their way of life with Uryupin and his heinous ideas." Lev Yakimenko, *Sholokhov: A Critical Appreciation*, trans. Bryan Bean (Moscow: Progress Publishers, 1973), 57.

10.   Sholokhov claims the upper, northern Cossacks on the front joined the Reds, while the lower Cossacks entrenched themselves in Cossack nationalist fervor and drove out the Reds to free their land. To a large extent this is true, although there were major exceptions on both sides.

11.   Sholokhov also pays considerable attention to the Korshunovs and the eventual burning of their farmstead. Critics who cite *The Quiet Don* as a model of socialist realism must ignore the ironic link Shokholov draws between the death of the Cossacks and that of the bourgeoisie.

12.   Gogol', *Taras Bul'ba*, PSS 2:164.

13.   Michael Klimenko argues that Bunchuk belonged to an earlier project called *Donshchina* that Sholokhov dropped when he decided to write the much more all-encompassing *The Quiet Don*. According to Klimenko, characters and whole passages from the fragment were then incorporated into the final novel. He implies that the Bunchuk story is not fully integrated into the main narrative of *The Quiet Don*. *The World of Young Sholokhov: Vision of Violence* (North Quincy, Mass.: Christopher Publishing House, 1972).

14.   Ermolaev points to an uncorrected blunder in early editions of *The Quiet Don* that refers to Bunchuk's "hairy wide *palms*." German Ermolaev, "Politicheskaia Pravka *Tikhogo Dona*," *Mosty* 15(1970): 266.

15.   Associations with the female savior in the Mazepa story (cf. *Voinarovskii*) may be quite apt.

16.   Katerina Clark, *The Soviet Novel: History as Ritual* (Chicago and London: University of Chicago Press, 1981), 139.

17.   Ibid. 138.

Chapter Eleven. Socialist Realism and Death to the Cossack Myth

1.   Abram Terts, *Sud idet*, in *Fantasticheskii mir Abrama Tertsa* (Paris: Inter-Language Literary Associates, 1967), 274. This story has been translated by Max Hayward in Abram Tertz, *The Trial Begins* (Berkeley and Los Angeles: University of California Press, 1960). Terts (or Tertz) is the pseudonym of Andrei Siniavskii.

2.   Terts, *Sud idet* 210.

3.   Abram Terts, "Chto takoe sotsialisticheskii realizm," in *Fantasticheskii mir* 416–17.

4.   See the essay discussing the relationship of the characters in Rufus W. Mathew-

son, Jr., *The Positive Hero in Russian Literature,* 2d ed. (Stanford: Stanford University Press, 1978), 182–90.

5. Dmitrii Furmanov, *Chapaev* (Leningrad: Khudozhestvennaia literatura, 1974), 30. All references to this book will be to this edition and indicated in the text.

6. Gogol', *Taras Bul'ba, PSS* 2:68.

7. As Clark points out: "Furmanov does not so much *de*mythologize, however, as *counter*mythologize: he sets himself/Klychkov up (impersonally) as a counterexample to that of the then popular hero type, the 'spontaneous' folk leader." *Soviet Novel* 88.

8. A. P. Chapygin, *Sobranie sochinenii v piati tomakh* (Leningrad: Khudozhestvennaia literatura, 1968), 3:676.

9. Sergei Petrov, *Russkii sovetskii istoricheskii roman* (Moscow: Sovremennik, 1980), 78.

10. Ibid. 389–90.

11. Brooks, *When Russia Learned to Read* 167, 169, 171, 174. Cossacks were so popular in this fiction that many traditional and folk heroes, including Il'ia Muromets, were sometimes made into Cossacks. See 176.

12. S. P. Zlobin, *Stepan Razin* (Moscow-Leningrad: Izdatel'stvo detskoi literatury, 1939), 16. Henceforth page references will be found in the text. The full version is found in Zlobin, *Sobranie sochinenii* (Moscow: Khudozhestvennaia literatura, 1981), Vols. 3 and 4.

13. Dmitrii Petrov-Biriuk, *Syny stepei donskikh* (Moscow: Voennoe izdatel'stvo Ministerstva oborony SSSR, 1970), p. 107.

14. Petrov-Biriuk, *Syny stepei donskikh* 250–52.

15. Semen Petrovich Babaevskii, *Stanitsa. Sobranie sochinenii* (Moscow: Khudozhestvennaia literatura, 1981), 5:114.

16. Evgenii Evtushenko, *Bratskaia GES,* in *Stikhi i poemy* (Moscow: Sovetskii pisatel', 1967), 69–239. Available in English in *Bratsk Station and Other New Poems by Yevgeny Yevtushenko,* trans. Tina Tupskina-Glaessner, Geoffrey Dutton, Igor Mezhakoff-Koriakin (New York: F. A. Praeger, 1967).

17. Evtushenko, *Bratskaia GES* 100.

18. Ibid. 101.

19. Ibid. 102.

Chapter Twelve. Conclusion: Nabokov's Postmortem

1. Vladimir Nabokov, *Pnin* (New York: Avon Books, 1957), 118.

2. In fact, Gogol's Akakii Akakievich in "The Overcoat" might make a better parallel. Akakii, too, preserves lifeless texts through endless and mindless copying.

3. Gogol', *Taras Bul'ba, PSS* 2:43.

Selected Bibliography

Allen, W. E. D. *The Ukraine: A History*. Cambridge: The University Press, 1940.

Anderson, Roger B. "A Study of Petr Grinev as the Hero of Pushkin's *Kapitanskaia dochka.*" *Canadian-American Slavic Studies* 5 (1971): 477–86.

Antonovich, V., and M. Dragomanov, eds. *Istoricheskie pesni malorusskago naroda.* Kiev, 1877.

Arianova-Perets, V. P., ed. *Voinskie povesti drevnoi Rusi.* Moscow: Izdatel'stvo Akademii Nauk SSSR, 1949.

Avrich, Paul. *Russian Rebels: 1600–1800.* New York: Schocken Books, 1972.

Baak, J. J. van. "The Function of Nature and Space in *Konarmija* by I. E. Babel'." *Dutch Contributions to the Eighth International Congress on Slavists:* Zagreb, Ljubljana, 1978. Amsterdam: Benjamins, 1979.

Babaevskii, Semen Petrovich. *Sobranie sochinenii.* Moscow: Khudozhestvennaia literatura, 1981.

Babel, Isaac. *You Must Know Everything.* Trans. Max Hayward and ed. Nathalie Babel. New York: Farrar, Straus and Giroux, 1966.

Babel, Isaac. *The Forgotten Prose.* Ed. and trans. Nicholas Stroud. Ann Arbor: Ardis, 1978.

Babel', Isaak. *Konarmiia. Odesskie rasskazy. P'esy.* Letchworth, Hertfordshire: Bradda Books, 1965.

Babel', Isaak. "Moi Listki." *Zhurnal zhurnalov* 51 (1917): 4–5.

Babel', Isaak. "O tvorcheskom puti pisatelia." *Zabytyi Babel',* ed. Nikolai Stroud. Ann Arbor: Ardis, 1979.

Babel', Isaak. *Sochineniia v dvukh tomakh,* ed. A. N. Pirozhkova. Moscow: Khudozhestvennaia literatura, 1990.

Babinsky, Hubert. *The Mazeppa Legend in European Romanticism.* New York and London: Columbia University Press, 1974.

Bahrij-Pikulyk, Romana Myroslawa. "*Taras Bul'ba* and *The Black Council:* The Adherence to and Divergence from Walter Scott's Historical Novel Pattern." Diss., University of Toronto, 1978.

Bakhtin, Mikhail. *Rabelais and His World.* Trans. Helene Iswolsky. Cambridge, Mass.: M.I.T. Press, 1968.

Barthes, Roland. *Mythologies.* Trans. Annette Lavers. London: Jonathan Cape, 1972.

Barzun, Jacques, ed. *European Writers: The Romantic Century.* New York: Charles Scribner's Sons, 1985.

Bekedin, P. V. "Drevnerusskie motivy v *Tikhom Done* M. A. Sholokhova (k postanovke voprosa)." *Russkaia literatura* 2 (1980): 92–108.

Belinskii, V. G. *Polnoe sobranie sochinenii V. G. Belinskogo.* 13 vols. Moscow: Akademiia nauk SSSR, 1953–59.

Belyi [Bugaev], Andrei. *Masterstvo Gogolia: issledovanie.* Moscow-Leningrad: Gosudarstvennoe izdatel'stvo khudozhestvennoi literatury, 1934.

Borschak, Elie. *La légende historique de l'Ukraine 'Istorija Rusov'.* Paris: Institut d'Etudes Slaves, 1949.

Brokgauz, F. A., and I. A. Efron, eds. *Entsiklopedicheskii slovar'.* St. Petersburg, 1897.

Brooks, Jeffrey. *When Russia Learned to Read: Literacy and Popular Literature, 1861–1917.* Princeton: Princeton University Press, 1985.

Bulgarin, Faddei. *Sochineniia.* St. Petersburg, 1827–34.

Bushnell, John. *Mutiny amid Repression: Russian Soldiers in the Revolution of 1905–1906.* Bloomington: Indiana University Press, 1985.

Byron, George Gordon, Lord. *The Complete Poetical Works.* Oxford: Clarendon Press, 1986.

Campbell, Joseph. *Hero of a Thousand Faces,* rpt. 2d ed. Princeton: Princeton University Press, 1973.

Carden, Patricia. *The Art of Isaac Babel.* Ithaca: Cornell University Press, 1972.

Catteau, J. "L'épopée dans la *Cavalerie Rouge* de I. Babel." *VII Międzynarodowy Kongres Slawistów w Warszawie.* 1973: Streszczenia referatów i komunikatów. Warsaw: PAN, 1973.

Cawelti, John G. *The Six-Gun Mystique.* Bowling Green, Ohio: Bowling Green University Popular Press, n.d.

Chamberlin, William Henry. *The Russian Revolution: 1917–1921.* New York: Macmillan, 1935.

Chapygin, A. P. *Sobranie sochinenii v piati tomakh.* Leningrad: Khudozhestvennaia literatura, 1968.

Cherniavsky, Michael. "'Holy Russia': A Study in the History of an Idea." *American Historical Review* 63, no. 3 (1958): 617–37.

Cherniavsky, Michael. *Tsar and People: Studies in Russian Myths.* New Haven and London: Yale University Press, 1961.

Chteniia v imperatorskom obshchestve istorii i drevnostei rossiiskikh pri Moskovskom Universitete. Nos. 1–3, 1846.

Chukovskii, Kornei. *Futuristy.* Petrograd: Poliarnaia zvezda, 1922.

Chulkov, M. D. *Sobranie raznykh pesen. Sochineniia Mikhaila Dmitrievicha Chulkova 1770–1773.* Rpt. St. Petersburg: Otdelenie russkogo iazyka i slovesnosti Imperatorskoi Akademii Nauk, 1913.

Chuzhak, N. [N. F. Nasimovich]. *Pravda o Pugacheve. Opyt literaturno-istoricheskogo analiza.* Moscow: Vsesoiuznoe obshchestvo politicheskikh katorzhan i ssyl'noposelentsev, 1926.

Clark, Katerina. *The Soviet Novel: History as Ritual.* Chicago and London: University of Chicago Press, 1981.

Clyman, Toby W. "Babel' as Colorist." *Slavic and East European Journal* 21 (1977): 332–43.

Cox, Gary. "Geographic, Sociological, and Sexual Tensions in Gogol''s Dikan'ka Stories." *Slavic and East European Journal* 24 (1980): 219–32.

Cox, Gary Duane. "A Study of Gogol's Narrators." Diss., Columbia University, 1978.

Danilevskii, G. P. *Sochineniia G. P. Danilevskogo v 24-kh tomakh.* St. Petersburg: Izdanie A. F. Marksa, 1901.

Dashkevich, N. P., ed. *Pamiati Gogolia. Nauchno-literaturnyi sbornik.* Kiev, 1902.

Davies, Norman. "Izaak Babel's *Konarmiya* Stories and the Polish-Soviet War," *Modern Language Review* 67 (1972): 845–57.

Debreczeny, Paul. "Narrative Voices in *Poltava.*" *Russian Literature* 24 (1988): 319–48.

Debreczeny, Paul. "Nikolay Gogol and His Contemporary Critics." *Transactions of the American Philosophical Society,* n.s. 56, Part 3, April 1966.

Debreczeny, Paul. *The Other Pushkin: A Study of Alexander Pushkin's Prose Fiction.* Stanford: Stanford University Press, 1983.

Edie, James M., James P. Scanlan, and Mary-Barbara Zeldin, eds. *Russian Philosophy,* Vol. 1: *The Beginnings of Russian Philosophy. The Slavophiles. The Westerners.* Knoxville University of Tennessee Press, 1965, 1976.

Ehre, Milton. "Babel's *Red Cavalry:* Epic and Pathos, History and Culture." *Slavic Review* 40 (1981): 228–40.

Ehrman, Jacques, ed. *Structuralism.* New York: Anchor Books, 1966.

Eikhenbaum, Boris. *The Young Tolstoi.* Trans. Gary Kern. Ann Arbor: Ardis, 1972.

Ekimov, B. P., ed. *Pesni donskikh kazakov.* Volgograd: Nizhne-Volzhskoe knizhnoe izdatel'stvo, 1982.

Emel'ianov, L. I., ed. *Russkaia istoricheskaia pesnia,* Biblioteka Poeta series. Leningrad: Sovetskii pisatel', 1987.

Emerson, Caryl. *Boris Godunov: Transpositions of a Russian Theme.* Bloomington: Indiana University Press, 1986.

Erlich, Victor. *Gogol.* New Haven: Yale University Press, 1969.

Ermolaev, German. "Politicheskaia Pravka *Tikhogo Dona.*" *Mosty* 15 (1970): 265–89.

Ermolaev, Herman. *Mikhail Sholokhov and His Art.* Princeton: Princeton University Press, 1982.

Eros, Carol Carbone. "Tolstoj's Tales of the Caucasus and Literary Tradition." Diss., University of Wisconsin, 1973.

Evtushenko, Evgenii. *Bratsk Station and Other New Poems by Yevgeny Yevtushenko.* Trans. Tina Tupskina-Glaessner, Geoffrey Dutton, and Igor Mezhakoff-Koriakin. New York: F. A. Praeger, 1967.

Evtushenko, Evgenii. *Stikhi i poemy.* Moscow: Sovetskii pisatel', 1967.

Fairchild, Hoxie Neale. *The Noble Savage: A Study in Romantic Naturalism.* New York: Columbia University Press, 1928.

Falchikov, Michael. "Conflict and Contrast in Isaak Babel's *Konarmiya.*" *Modern Language Review* 72 (1977): 125–33.

Falen, James E. *Isaac Babel, Russian Master of the Short Story.* Knoxville: University of Tennessee Press, 1974.

Fanger, Donald. *The Creation of Nikolai Gogol.* Cambridge, Mass. and London: Belknap Press of Harvard University Press, 1979.

Fennel, John, ed. *Nineteenth-Century Russian Literature: Studies of Ten Russian Writers.* Berkeley and Los Angeles: University of California Press, 1973.

Finke, Michael, "Puškin, Pugačev, and Aesop." *Slavic and East European Journal* 35, no. 2 (1991): 179–92.

Firsov, N. N. *Pugachevshchina. Opyt sotsiologo-psikhologicheskoi kharakteristiki.* 2d ed. Moscow: Gosudarstvennoe izdatel'stvo, 1921.

Frank, Albert von. *The Sacred Game: Provincialism and Frontier Consciousness in American Literature.* Cambridge: Cambridge University Press, 1985.

Frank, Joseph. "Spatial Form in Modern Literature." In *Criticism: The Foundations of Modern Literary Judgement,* ed. Mark Schorer, Josephine Miles, and Gorden McKenzie. New York: Harcourt Brace, 1948. 379–92.

Friedberg, Maurice. "Yiddish Folklore Motifs in Isaak Babel's *Konarmija.*" *American Contributions to the Eighth International Congress of Slavists,* Vol. 2. Columbus, Ohio: Slavica, 1978. 192–203.

Furmanov, Dmitrii. *Chapaev.* Leningrad: Khudozhestvennaia literatura, 1974.

Gippius, V. V. *Gogol.* Ed. and trans. Robert A. Maguire. Ann Arbor: Ardis, 1981.

Glazkov, V. G. *History of the Cossacks.* New York: R. Speller, 1972.

Gogol', N. V. *Polnoe sobranie sochinenii.* Moscow: Izdatel'stvo Akademii Nauk SSSR, 1937–52.

Gogol', N. V. *Sochineniia N. V. Gogolia.* 10th ed. Ed. Nikolai Tikhonravov. Moscow, 1889.

Golubtsov, S. A., ed. *Pugachevshchina. Iz arkhiva.* 3 vols. Moscow-Leningrad: Gosudarstvennoe izdatel'stvo, 1926, 1929, 1931.

Gordon, Linda. *Cossack Rebellions: Social Turmoil in the Sixteenth-Century Ukraine.* Albany: State University of New York Press, 1983.

Gordon, Linda. "Revolutionary Banditry: An Interpretation of the Social Roles of the Ukrainian Cossacks in Their First Rebellions, 1590–96." Diss., Yale University, 1970.

Gor'kii, Maksim. "Rabselkoram i voenkoram o tom, kak uchilsia pisat'." *Pravda,* September 30, 1928, 3.

Grabowicz, George G. "The History and Myth of the Cossack Ukraine." Diss., Harvard University, 1975.

Green, Militsa. "Pushkin and Sir Walter Scott." *Forum for Modern Language Studies* I (1965): 207–15.

Grøngaard, Ragna. *An Investigation of Composition and Theme in Isaak Babel's Literary Cycle Konarmija.* Aarhus: Arkona, 1979.

Gubaroff, George V. *Cossacks and Their Land: In Light of New Data.* Trans. John Nelson Washburn. Providence, R.I.: Cossack American National Alliance, 1985.

Gudzy, N. K. *History of Early Russian Literature.* Trans. Susan Wilbur Jones from 2d Russian ed. New York: Macmillan, 1949.

Gukovskii, G. A. *Realizm Gogolia.* Moscow-Leningrad: Gosudarstvennoe izdatel'stvo khudozhestvennoi literatury, 1959.

Gunnell, G. John. *Political Philosophy and Time.* Middletown, Conn.: Wesleyan University Press, 1968.

Gustafson, Richard F. *Leo Tolstoy, Resident and Stranger: A Study in Fiction and Theology.* Princeton: Princeton University Press, 1986.

Gutsche, George J., and Lauren G. Leighton, eds. *New Perspectives on Nineteenth-Century Prose.* Columbus, Ohio: Slavica, 1981.

Hagan, John. "Ambivalence in Tolstoy's 'The Cossacks.'" *Novel: A Forum on Fiction* 3 (1969): 28–47.

Hallett, R. W. *Isaac Babel.* Letchworth, Hertfordshire: Bradda Books, 1972.

Howe, Irving, and Eliezer Greenberg, eds. *Ashes out of Hope: Fiction by Soviet-Yiddish Writers.* New York: Schocken Books, 1977.

Hrishko, Wasyl. "Gogol's Ukrainian-Russian Bilingualism and the Dualism of Gogolian Style." Diss., University of Washington, 1973.

Hugo, Victor. *Oeuvres complètes.* 18 vols. Paris: Club Français du livre, 1967–69.

Hyman, Stanley Edgar. "The Problem of Jewish Identity: Identities of Isaac Babel." In *The Promised End.* New York: World Publishing, 1963. 319–29.

Iakovliv, Andriy. "Istoriya Rusov and Its Author." *Ukrainian Academy of Arts and Sciences in the U.S.,* Annals 3 (1953): 620–69.

Iakubovich, D. P. "*Kapitanskaia dochka* i roman V. Skotta." *Vremennik pushkinskoi komissii* 4–5 (1939): 165–97.

Irabarne, Louis. "Babel's *Red Cavalry* as a Baroque Novel." *Contemporary Literature* 14 (1973): 58–77.

Jepson, Laura. "To Kill like a Cossack." *South Atlantic Bulletin* 43 (1978): 86–94.

Jonge, Alex de. "Gogol'." In *Nineteenth-Century Russian Literature: Studies of Ten Russian Writers,* ed. John Fennell. Berkeley and Los Angeles: University of California Press, 1973. 69–129.

Kamanin, I. M. "Nauchnye i literaturnye proizvedeniia N. V. Gogolia po istorii Malorossii." *Pamiati Gogolia. Nauchno-literaturnyi sbornik,* ed. N. P. Dashkevich. Kiev, 1902.

Kamenskii, Vasilii. *Ego-moia biographiia velikogo futurista.* Moscow, 1918.

Kamenskii, Vasilii. *Put' entuziasta.* Moscow: Federatsiia, 1931.

Kamenskii, Vasilii. *Sten'ka Razin. P'esa v 9 kartinakh.* Kharkov: Gosudarstvennoe izdatel'stvo Ukrainy, 1923.

Kamenskii, Vasilii. *Stikhotvoreniia i poemy.* Ed. N. L. Stepanov. Biblioteka Poeta series, 2d ed. Moscow-Leningrad: Sovetskii pisatel', 1966.

Karlinsky, Simon. *Marina Tsvetaeva: The Woman, Her World, and Her Poetry.* Cambridge and New York: Cambridge University Press, 1985.

Karlinsky, Simon. *The Sexual Labyrinth of Nikolai Gogol.* Cambridge, Mass., and London: Harvard University Press, 1976.

Karpuk, Paul A. "Gogol's Unfinished Historical Novel 'The Hetman,'" *Soviet and East European Journal* 35, no. 1 (1991): 36–55.

Karpuk, Paul A. "N. V. Gogol's Unfinished Historical Novel 'The Hetman.'" Diss., University of California, Berkeley, 1987.

Kazaki: narod ili russkoe soslovie. Izdanie organizatsii kazach'ikh natsionalistov, n.d.

Khlebnikov, Velimir. *Neizdannye proizvedeniia.* Ed. N. Khadzhieva and T. Gritsa. Moscow: Khudozhestvennaia literatura, 1940.

Khlebnikov, Velimir. *Sobranie proizvedenii Velimira Khebnikova.* Ed. Iu. Tynianov and N. Stepanov. Leningrad: Izdatel'stvo pisatelei v Leningrade, 1928–33. Rpt. *Sobranie Sochinenii.* Munich: Wilhelm Fink Verlag, 1968.

Khomiakov, Aleksei Stepanovich. *Polnoe sobranie sochinenii.* 8 vols. Moscow: Universitetskaia tipografiia, 1900–1904.

Kirdan, B. P. *Ukrainskie narodnye dumy.* Moscow: Nauka, 1972.

Klimenko, Michael. *The World of Young Sholokhov: Vision of Violence.* North Quincy, Mass.: Christopher Publishing House, 1972.

Klotz, Martin B. "Poetry of the Present: Isaak Babel's *Red Cavalry.*" *Slavic and East European Journal* 18 (1974): 160–69.

Kornblatt, Judith Deutsch. "Gogol' and the Muses of *Mirgorod.*" *Slavic Review* 50, no. 2 (Summer 1991): 309–16.

Krafcik, Patricia Ann. "Sten'ka Razin in Russian Historical Folksongs: A Robin Hood of the Volga." Diss., Columbia University, 1980.

Kukol'nik, Nestor. *Istoricheskie povesti.* St. Petersburg: Izdanie A. S. Suvorina, 1902.

Lanne, Jean-Claude. *Velimir Khlebnikov. Poète futurien.* Paris: Institut d'Etudes Slaves, 1983.

Layton, Susan. "The Creation of an Imaginative Caucasian Geography." *Slavic Review* 45 no. 3 (1986): 470–85.

Lazanova, A. N., ed. *Pesni i skazaniia o Razine i Pugacheve.* Moscow-Leningrad: Akademiia, 1935.

LeBlanc, Ronald D. *The Russification of Gil Blas: A Study in Literary Appropriation.* Columbus, Ohio: Slavica, 1986.

Lednicki, Wacław. "Pouchkine et Mickiewicz." *Revue de littérature comparée* 17 (1937): 129–44.

Lednicki, Wacław, ed. *Adam Mickiewicz in World Literature: A Symposium.* Berkeley and Los Angeles: University of California Press, 1956.

Lewis, Bernard. *History Remembered, Recovered, Invented.* Princeton: Princeton University Press, 1975.

Livshits, L. "Materialy k tvorcheskoi biografii I. Babelia." *Voprosy literatury* 4 (1964): 110–35.

Longworth, Philip. *The Cossacks.* New York: Holt, Rinehart and Winston, 1969.

Longworth, Philip. Letter. *Slavic Review* 33 (1974): 411–14.

Lotman, Iurii M. "Problema khudozhestvennogo prostranstva v proze Gogolia." *Trudy po russkoi i slavianskoi filologii,* Vol. 11: *Literaturovedenie. Uchenye zapiski Tartuskogo gosudarstvennogo universiteta* 209 (1968): 5–50.

Luckyj, George S. N. *Between Gogol' and Ševčenko: Polarity in the Literary Ukraine, 1798–1847.* Munich: Wilhelm Fink Verlag, 1971.

Luckyj, George. *Panteleimon Kulish: A Sketch of His Life and Times.* Boulder, Colo.: East European Monographs, 1983.

Lukashevich, Platon. *Malorossiiskie i Chervonorusskie narodnye dumy i pesni.* St. Petersburg, 1836.

Luplow, Carol. *Isaac Babel's "Red Cavalry."* Ann Arbor: Ardis, 1982.

Magarshack, David. *Gogol: A Life.* New York: Grove Press, 1957.

Maksimovich, Mikhail. *Malorossiiskiia pesni.* Moscow, 1827.

Maksimovich, Mikhail. *Sbornik ukrainskikh pesen, izdavaemykh M. Maksimovichem.* Moscow, 1849.

Maksimovich, Mikhail. *Ukrainskie narodnye pesni.* Moscow, 1834.

Mann, Iurii. "Fantasticheskoe i real'noe u Gogolia." *Voprosy literatury* 13, no. 9(1969): 106–25.

Marcus, Steven. "The Stories of Isaac Babel." *Partisan Review* 22, no. 3(1955): 400–411.

Marder, Herbert. "The Revolutionary Art of Isaac Babel." *Novel: A Forum on Fiction* 7 (1973): 54–61.

Markevych, N. A. *Ukrainskie melodii.* Moscow, 1831.

Markov, Vladimir. *The Longer Poems of Velimir Khlebnikov.* Berkeley and Los Angeles: University of California Press, 1962.

Mathewson, Rufus W., Jr. *The Positive Hero in Russian Literature,* 2d ed. Stanford: Stanford University Press, 1978.

McLean, Hugh. "Gogol's Retreat from Love: Towards an Interpretation of *Mirgorod.*" *American Contributions to the Fourth International Congress of Slavists.* The Hague: Mouton, 1958.

McLean, Robert A. "The Prose of Velimir Xlebnikov." Diss., Princeton University, 1973.

McNeal, Robert H. *Tsar and Cossack, 1855–1914.* London: Macmillan Press in association with St. Antony's College, Oxford, 1987.

Merezhkovskii, Dmitrii. *Gogol'. Tvorchestvo, zhizn', religiia.* St. Petersburg: Panteon, 1909.

Mikkelson, Gerald E. "The Mythopoetic Element in Pushkin's Historical Novel *The Captains Daughter,*" *Canadian-American Slavic Studies* 7(1973): 296–313.

Mikkelson, Gerald E. "Pushkin's *History of Pugachev:* The Litterateur as Historian." In *New Perspectives on Nineteenth-Century Prose,* ed. George J. Gutsche and Lauren G. Leighton. Columbus, Ohio: Slavica, 1981.

Mintz, Samuel I., Alice Chandler, and Christopher Mulvey, eds. *From Smollett to James: Studies in the Novel and Other Essays Presented to Edgar Johnson.* Charlottesville: University Press of Virginia, 1981.

Mirsky, D. S. *A History of Russian Literature.* Ed. Francis J. Whitfield. New York: Alfred A. Knopf, 1949.

Mirsky, Salomon. *Der Orient im Werk Velimir Chlebnikovs. Slavistische Beitrage* 85. Munich: Verlag Otto Sagner, 1975.

Mocha, Frank. "Pushkin's 'Poltava' as a Reaction to the Revolutionary Politics and History of Mickiewicz's 'Konrad Wallenrod' and Ryleev's 'Vojnarovskij.'" *Antemurale* 19 (1975): 91–147.

Mordovtsev, Daniel. *Polnoe sobranie istoricheskikh romanov, povestei i razskazov.* St. Petersburg: Izdatel'stvo P. P. Soikina, n.d.

Morson, Gary Saul. *Hidden in Plain View: Narrative and Creative Potentials in "War and Peace."* Stanford: Stanford University Press, 1987.

Morson, Gary Saul. "Prosaics and *Anna Karenina.*" *Tolstoy Studies Journal* 1 (1988): 1–12.

Muchnic, Helen. "Sholokhov and Tolstoi." *Russian Review* 16 (1957): 25–34.

Murphy, A. B. "The Style of Isaak Babel'." *Slavonic and East European Review* 44 (1966): 361–80.

Nabokov, Vladimir. *Nikolai Gogol.* New York: New Directions, 1961.

Nabokov, Vladimir. *Pnin.* New York: Avon Books, 1957.

Nakhimovsky, Alexander D., and Alice Stone Nakhimovsky, eds. *The Semiotics of Russian Cultural History*. Ithaca: Cornell University Press, 1985.

Narezhnyi, Vasilii. *Romany i povesti Vasiliia Narezhnago,* 2nd ed. St. Petersburg: Tipografia Aleksandra Smirdina, 1836.

Neiman, B. V. "*Kapitanskaia dochka* Pushkina i romany V. Skotta." *Sbornik otdeleniia russkogo iazyka i slovesnosti AN SSSR* 101 (1928): 440–443.

Nilsson, Nils Åke. "Isaak Babel's 'Perechod čerez Zbruč." *Scando-Slavica* 23 (1977): 63–71.

Novikov, N. I., ed. *Novoe i polnoe sobranie rossiiskikh pesen.* Moscow: Universitetskaia tipografiia 1780–81.

Nud'ga, G. A., ed. *Dumi.* Biblioteka Poeta series. Kiev: Radians'kii pis'mennik, 1969.

Ohloblyn, Oleksandr. "Where Was Istoriya Rusov Written?" *Ukrainian Academy of Arts and Sciences in the U.S., Annals* 3 (1953): 670–95.

Oksman, Iurii. "Neosushchestvlennyi zamysel istorii Ukrainy." *Literaturnoe nasledstvo* 58 (1952): 211–21.

Oksman, Iurii. "Pushkin v rabote nad *Kapitanskoi dochkoi.*" *Literaturnoe nasledstvo* 58 (1952): 222–42.

Orlov, Vladimir. "Marina Tsvetaeva. Sud'ba. Kharakter. Poeziia." Introduction to *Izbrannye proizvedeniia* by Marina Tsvetaeva. Moscow-Leningrad: Sovetskii pisatel', 1965. 5–54.

Parker, W. M. "Scott and Russian Literature." *Quarterly Review* 305 (April 1967): 172–78.

Parnis, A. E. "Iuzhnoslavianskaia tema Velimira Khlebnikova." In *Zarubezhnye slaviane i russkaia kul'tura,* ed. M. P. Alekseev. Leningrad: Nauka, 1978.

Pauls, John J. "Two Treatments of Mazeppa: Ryleyev's and Pushkin's." *Etudes slaves et est-européennes* 8 (1963): 97–109.

Paustovskii, Konstantin. "Neskol'ko slov o Babele: Memuary." *Nedelia,* nos. 11–17, Sept. 1966.

Peace, Richard. *The Enigma of Gogol: An Examination of the Writings of N. V. Gogol and Their Place in the Russian Literary Tradition.* Cambridge: Cambridge University Press, 1981.

Pereverzev, V. F. *Tvorchestvo Gogolia.* 3d ed. Ivanovo-Voznesensk: Osnova, 1928.

Petrov, Sergei. *Russkii sovetskii istoricheskii roman.* Moscow: Sovremennik, 1980.

Petrov-Biriuk, Dmitrii. *Syny stepei donskikh.* Moscow: Voennoe izdatel'stvo Ministerstva oborony SSSR, 1970.

Petrunina, N. N. *Proza Pushkina (Puti evoliutsii).* Leningrad: Nauka, 1987.

Poggioli, Renato. "Isaac Babel in Retrospect." *The Phoenix and the Spider.* Cambridge: Harvard University Press, 1957.

Price, Robert F. "Tragic Features in the Character of Grigorii Melexov." *Slavic and East European Journal* 23 (1979): 63–71.

Pushkin, Alexander. *The History of Pugachev.* Trans. Earl Sampson. Ann Arbor: Ardis, 1983.

Pushkin, A. S. *Polnoe sobranie sochinenii.* 16 vols. Moscow-Leningrad: Izdatel'stvo Akademii Nauk SSSR, 1937–49.

Putilov, B. N., ed. *Istoricheskie pesni XVII veka.* Moscow-Leningrad: Nauka, 1966.

Putilov, B. N., ed. *Narodnye istoricheskie pesni.* Biblioteka Poeta series. Moscow-Leningrad: Sovetskii pisatel', 1962.

Raeff, Marc. *The Decembrist Movement.* Englewood Cliffs, N.J.: Prentice-Hall, 1966.

Raleigh, John Henry. "Scott and Pushkin." In *From Smollett to James: Studies in the Novel and Other Essays Presented to Edgar Johnson,* ed. Samuel I. Mintz et. al. Charlottesville: University Press of Virginia, 1981.

Rice, Martin P. "On 'Skaz'." *Russian Literature Triquarterly* 12 (Spring 1975): 409–23.

Rogger, Hans. *National Consciousness in Eighteenth-Century Russia.* Cambridge, Mass.: Harvard University Press, 1960.

Rosenthal, Raymond. "The Fate of Isaak Babel." *Commentary* 3, no. 2 (1947): 126–31.

Ross, Rochelle H. "The Unity of Babel's Konarmija." *South Central Bulletin* 41, no. 4 (1981): 114–19.

Rubinshtein, N. L. *Russkaia istoriografiia.* Moscow: Gospolitizdat, 1941.

Rudnytsky, Ivan L. Reply to letter of Philip Longworth. *Slavic Review* 33 (1974): 414–16.

Rudnytsky, Ivan L. "A Study of Cossack History." Review of *The Cossacks,* by Philip Longworth. *Slavic Review* 31 (1972): 870–75.

Ryleev, Kondratii. *Polnoe sobranie stikhotvorenii,* Biblioteka Poeta series. 2d ed. Leningrad: Sovetskii pisatel', 1971.

Sakharov, I. P., ed. *Pesni russkogo naroda.* St. Petersburg, 1838–39.

Schorer, Mark. "The Necessity of Myth." *Daedalus* 88, no. 2 (1959): 359–62.

Seaton, Albert. *The Horsemen of the Steppes: The Story of the Cossacks.* London: Bodley Head, 1985.

Setchkarev, Vsevolod M. *Gogol: His Life and Works.* New York: New York University Press, 1965.

Shaw, J. Thomas. "The Problem of the *Persona* in Journalism: Puškin's Feofilakt Košičkin." *American Contributions to the Fifth International Congress of Slavists, Sofia, 1963.* The Hague: Mouton, 1963.

Shaw, J. Thomas, ed. *The Letters of Alexander Pushkin.* Bloomington: Indiana University Press, 1963.

Sholokhov, Mikhail. *And Quiet Flows the Don.* Trans. Stephen Garry. New York: Vintage Books, 1966.

Sholokhov, Mikhail. *Sobranie sochinenii v deviati tomakh.* Moscow: Khudozhestvennaia literatura, 1965–69.

Shragin, Boris, and Albert Todd, eds. *Landmarks.* Trans. Marian Schwartz. New York: Karz Howard, 1977.

Sicher, Efraim. "The Road to a Red Calvary: Myth and Mythology in the Works of Isaak Babel' of the 1920's." *Slavonic and East European Review* 60, no. 4 (1982): 528–46.

Simmons, Ernest J. *English Literature and Culture in Russia, 1553–1840.* Cambridge: Harvard University Press, 1935.

Simpson, George W. "The Names 'Rus,' 'Russia,' 'Ukraine,' and Their Historical Background." *Slavistica* 10 (1951): 5–18.

219

Sirskyj, Wasyl. "Ideological Overtones in Gogol's *Taras Bulba.*" *Ukrainian Quarterly* 35 (1979): 279–87.

Slonimskii, A. *Masterstvo Pushkina.* Moscow: Gosudarstvennoe izdatel'stvo khudozhestvennoi literatury, 1959.

Slotkin, Richard. *Regeneration through Violence: The Mythology of the American Frontier, 1600–1860.* Middletown, Conn.: Wesleyan University Press, 1973.

Słowacki, Juliusz. *Mazeppa, Polish and American: A Translation of Słowacki's "Mazeppa," Together with a Brief Survey of Mazeppa in the United States.* Trans. Marion Moore Coleman. Cheshire, Conn.: Cherry Hill Books, 1966.

Smirin, I. A. "Na puti k *Konarmii.*" *Liternaturnoe nasledstvo* 74 (1965): 462–82.

Soimonov, A. D., ed. *Istoricheskie pesni XVIII veka.* Leningrad: Nauka, 1971.

Sreznevskii, I. I. *Zaporozhskaia starina.* Kharkov, 1833–38.

Stepanov, Nikolai. *Velimir Khlebnikov. Zhizn' i tvorchestvo.* Moscow: Sovetskii pisatel', 1975.

Stilman, Leon. "Nikolaj Gogol' and Ostap Hohol." *Orbis Scriptus. Dmitrij Tschiźewskij zum 70. Geburtstag.* Munich: Wilhelm Fink Verlag, 1966.

Stora-Sandor, Judith. *Isaac Babel', 1894–1941, l'homme et l'oeuvre.* Paris: Klincksieck, 1968.

Terras, Victor. "Line and Color: The Structure of I. Babel's Short Stories in *Red Cavalry.*" *Studies in Short Fiction* 3, no. 2 (1966): 141–56.

Terras, Victor, ed. *Handbook of Russian Literature.* New Haven and London: Yale University Press, 1985.

Terts, Abram. *Sud idet. Fantasticheskii mir Abrama Tertsa.* Paris: Inter-Language Literary Associates, 1967.

Tertz, Abram. *The Trial Begins.* Trans. Max Hayward. Berkeley and Los Angeles: University of California Press, 1960.

Thorslev, Peter L. *The Byronic Hero: Types and Prototypes.* Minneapolis: University of Minnesota Press, 1962.

Todorov, Tzvetan. *The Fantastic: A Structural Approach to a Literary Genre.* Trans. Richard Howard. Forword by Robert Scholes. Ithaca: Cornell University Press, 1975.

Tolstoi, Lev. *Polnoe sobranie sochinenii.* 90 vols. Moscow-Leningrad: Gosudarstvennoe izdatel'stvo, 1928–58.

Tretiak, Jozef. *Mickiewicz i Puszkin: Studya i szkice.* Warsaw: Nakładem Księgarni E. Wende I Sp., 1906.

Trilling, Lionel. *Beyond Culture: Essays on Literature and Learning.* New York: Viking Press, 1965.

Trilling, Lionel. Introduction. *Isaac Babel. The Collected Stories.* Trans. and ed. Walter Morrison. Cleveland and New York: New American Library, 1955.

Troyat, Henri. *Divided Soul: The Life of Gogol'.* Trans. Nancy Amphoux. Garden City, N.Y.: Doubleday, 1973.

Tschiźewskij, D. I. "Gogol: Artist and Thinker." *Forum Slavicum,* Vol. 12: *Gogol'-Turgenev-Dostoevskij-Tolstoj zur Russischen Literature des 19 Jahrhunderts.* Ed. Tschiźewskij. Munich: Wilhelm Fink Verlag, 1966.

Tsertelev, N. A. *Opyt sobraniia starinnykh malorossiiskikh pesen.* Moscow, 1819.

Tsvetaeva, Marina. *A Captive Spirit: Selected Prose.* Ed. and trans. J. Marin King. Ann Arbor: Ardis, 1980.

Tsvetaeva, Marina. *Izbrannaia proza v dvukh tomakh, 1917–1937.* New York: Russica Publishers, 1979.

Tsvetacva, Marina. *Izbrannye proizvedeniia.* Moscow-Leningrad: Sovetskii pisatel', 1965.

Tsvetaeva, Marina. *Stikhotvoreniia i poemy v piati tomakh.* New York: Russica, 1982–83.

Turner, C. J. G. "Tolstoy's 'The Cossacks': The Question of Genre." *Modern Language Review* 73 (1978): 563–72.

Turner, Frederick Jackson. *The Frontier in American History.* New York: Holt, Rinehart and Winston, 1920, 1947, 1962.

Turner, Victor. *The Ritual Process: Structure and Anti-Structure.* Ithaca: Cornell University Press, 1969.

Vinogradov, Viktor. *Etiudy o stile Gogolia.* Leningrad: Akademia, 1926.

Vinogradov, V. V., et al., eds. *Slovar' iazyka Pushkina.* Moscow: Gosudarstvennoe izdatel'stvo inostrannykh i natsional'nykh slovarei, 1957.

Vroon, Ronald. "Metabiosis, Mirror Images and Negative Integers: Velimir Chlebnikov and His Doubles." In *Velimir Chlebnikov (1885–1922): Myth and Reality,* ed. Willem G. Weststeijn. Amsterdam: Rodopi, 1986.

Vroon, Ronald. "Velimir Chlebnikov's 'Chadži-Tarchan' and the Lomonosovian Tradition." *Russian Literature* 9 (1981): 107–31.

Vroon, Ronald. "Velimir Khlebnikov's 'Razin: Two Trinities': A Reconstruction." *Slavic Review* 39, no. 1 (1980): 70–84.

Vroon, Ronald. *Velimir Khlebnikov's Shorter Poems: A Key to the Coinages.* Ann Arbor: University of Michigan Press, 1983.

Walicki, Andrzej. *The Slavophile Controversy: History of a Conservative Utopia in Nineteenth-Century Thought.* Oxford: Clarendon Press, 1975.

Warner, Elizabeth A. *The Russian Folk Theater.* The Hague and Paris: Mouton, 1977.

Wheelwright, Philip. "Semantic Approach to Myth." In *Myth: A Symposium,* ed. Thomas Sebeok. Bloomington: Indiana University Press, 1965.

White, Hayden. *Metahistory: The Historical Imagination in Nineteenth-Century Europe.* Baltimore and London: Johns Hopkins University Press, 1973.

White, Hayden. *Tropics of Discourse: Essays in Cultural Criticism.* Baltimore and London: Johns Hopkins University Press, 1978.

Williams, Gareth. "Two Leitmotifs in Babel's *Konarmija.*" *Die Welt der Slaven* 17 (1972): 308–17.

Woodward, James B. *The Symbolic Art of Gogol: Essays on His Short Fiction.* Columbus, Ohio: Slavica, 1981.

Yakimenko, Lev. *Sholokhov: A Critical Appreciation.* Trans. Bryan Bean. Moscow: Progress Publishers, 1973.

Zeldin, Jesse. *Nikolai Gogol's Quest for Beauty: An Exploration into His Works.* Lawrence: Regents Press of Kansas, 1978.

Zhirmunskii, V. M. *Bairon i Pushkin.* Leningrad: Academia, 1924.

Zhirmunskii, V. M. "Pushkin i zapadnye literatury." *Vremennik pushkinskoi komissii* 3 (1937): 66–103.

Ziolkowski, Margaret. *Hagiography and Modern Russian Literature*. Princeton: Princeton University Press, 1988.

Zlobin, S. P. *Sobranie sochinenii*. Moscow: Khudozhestvennaia literatura, 1981.

Index

America: myths of, 3–4, 13, 17; frontier of 3–4, 20, 72–75, 195*nn13,17;* cowboys in, 3, 19, 39, 194*n12;* literature of, 73–74
Ataman, definition of, 8, 166
Averbakh, L. L., 110
Azov, Sea of, 158
Azov, Tale of Taking of, The, 22, 39

Babaevskii, Semen: *The Cossack Village,* 172
Babel, I. E., 107–25; sexuality in, 19, 119–20; Gogol and, 107, 108–11, 113, 117, 119, 122, 123–25; Tolstoi and, 107, 122; diary of Budennyi campaign, 108, 115–16, 119; Sholokhov and, 108, 151; biographical information on, 108–11, 202*nn11,12;* Jews in, 109–11, 114–16, 118–19; timelessness in, 112, 116–17; Chagall and, 112, 117; liminality in, 112–13, 114, 202*nn23, 24;* epic in, 113, 116, 203*n34;* rebirth in, 114, 115, 118–19, 204*n42;* women in, 115, 119–20, 204*nn44;* reconciliation of opposites in, 118, 120–22; violent creativity in, 120–22; mentioned, 141, 149
—works: *Red Cavalry,* 102, 108, 110, 111–25, 201*n1;* "Odessa," 108, 118; "Guy de Maupassant," 109, 120; "Crossing the Zbruch," 111, 116, 118, 119, 202*n21;* "The King," 114; "How It Was Done in Odessa," 114; "The Rebbe's Son," 114, 115, 117; "Gedali," 114, 115, 117, 202*n23;* "The Rebbe," 114, 117, 202*n23;* "The Catholic Church at Novograd," 114, 119; "Berestechko," 116, 202*n23;* "Argamak," 117; "Continuation of Story of a Horse," 117, 119, 122, 124–25; "Story of a Horse," 117, 122–24; "The Life

Story of Pavlichenko, Matvei Rodionych," 118, 119; "My First Goose," 119, 120, 122, 202*n23;* "Sashka the Christ," 119; "Evening," 119; "The Death of Dolgushov," 120, 151, 202*n23;* "Pan Apolek," 120–21; "Timashenko and Mel'nikov," 125; autobiography, 201*n8,* 204*n49;* "The Road to Brody," 202*n23;* "The Brigade Commander," 202*n23;* "Konkin," 202*n23*
Bakhtin, M. M., 15
Bandura, 185*n17. See also* Bandurist
Bandurist (Ukrainian epic bard), 24, 80–81, 83, 86, 116, 198*n46. See also* Epic: bards
Belinskii, V. G., 34, 44, 190*n13*
Bible, references to, 25, 63, 67, 69, 72, 81, 82, 113, 121, 152, 158, 197*n36*
Blok, A. A., 130
Bogatyr' (Russian folk hero), 27, 162–63
Bolotnikov, Ivan (Cossack leader), 145–48, 173, 181*n16*
Briusov, V. Ia.: "The Coming Huns," 205*n11*
Budennyi, S. M., 100, 108
Bulavin, Kondrat (Cossack leader), 172
Bulgarin, F. V.: *Mazepa,* 30, 67, 76; Pushkin and, 187*nn40,41;* mentioned, 26
Burliuk, D. D., 142
Byron, George Gordon, Lord (author of *Mazeppa*): Cossack hero in, 15, 29, 30, 34, 196*n24;* depiction of women in, 63; rebirth in, 66; frontier in, 73; mentioned, 171, 174

Catherine the Great, Tsaritsa, 9, 11, 37–38, 105, 129, 189*n62*
Catholicism: Gogol and, 192*n22. See also* Poland

223

Caucasus: myth of, 92, 198*n*2. *See also*
   Cossack: Terek (Caucasian)
Chaadaev, P. Ia., 17–18
Chapygin, A. P.: *Razin Stepan,* 168
Charles XII of Sweden. *See* Poltava,
   Battle of
Coincidenatia oppositorum, 71
Cooper, James Fenimore, 73, 93
Cossack hosts: Ukrainian (Hetmanate),
   6–8, 10, 19, 28; Zaporozhian, 6–8, 9,
   10, 17, 23, 27, 28, 39, 40, 45, 61, 62,
   63, 74, 78, 127, 153, 170; Black Sea, 8;
   Don, 8, 9, 17, 19, 149, 150, 152, 153,
   160, 170, 190*n*13; Kuban, 8, 9, 39;
   Iaik (Ural), 8, 11, 19, 104, 160; Grebensk, 8, 160; Terek (Caucasian), 9, 39
Cossacks: freedom and, 3, 4, 16–19, 26,
   96, 102, 143, 148, 160; boundlessness
   of, 3, 15, 71–75, 82, 113, 121, 143,
   148, 159–60, 163, 164, 168, 175; reconciliation of opposites of, 4, 5, 15,
   16, 36, 45–46, 55–56, 65–66, 70, 71,
   110, 135, 141, 148, 153; definition of
   term, 5–6; Slavic "purity" of, 5, 6, 48,
   96; historical account, 5–13; Service,
   6; *domovitye* (house-owning), 9, 10;
   golutvennye (destitute), 9, 10; in Imperial Army, 12, 99, 101, 199*n*3; in
   Revolution and Civil War, 12, 99–101,
   200*n*9; nationalism of, 12, 100–101,
   151; exoticism of, 13, 15, 27, 29, 41,
   44, 96; violence of, 13, 15, 36, 49, 66,
   68, 104, 106, 107, 120, 126, 129, 130,
   136, 142, 148, 153, 157; as essential
   Russians, 13, 16, 25–26, 39–41, 44–
   49, 103, 106, 120, 127, 143–44; liminality of, 14–15, 41, 71, 96, 106, 148,
   153, 194*n*12; forelock (*chub, oseledets*), 15, 39, 208*n*6; sexuality and,
   19, 63–66, 119–20; *dzhigitovka* (trick
   horsemanship), 39; *ustrug* (boat on
   Volga), 39; "holy," 39, 41, 49, 62, 127;
   kuren' (military unit) 39, 153; *pestrota*
   (multicolored diversity), 47; passion
   of, 47, 114, 157, 175; wholeness of,
   49–54, 192*n*24; *khladnokrov'e* (cold-
   bloodedness), 50, 51, 53; women and,
   50, 61–66, 105–6, 155, 157, 193*n*3;
   vitality of, 54–58, 68, 143, 175; masculinity of, 60, 61–63, 66, 106, 115,
   119–20, 122, 123, 139, 175, 182*n*27;
as monks, 62–63, 96; rebirth and,
   66–68, 118–20, 154–55, 161–62;
   timelessness of, 75–82, 90, 116–17; in
   Red Army, 100–101, 108, 120, 141; folk
   theater and, 113–14, 165, 203*n*28;
   bunchuk, 161. *See also* Bolotnikov,
   Ivan; Bulavin, Kondrat; Ermak, Timofeevich; Khmel'nitskii, Bogdan;
   Mazepa, Ivan; Ostranitsa, Stepan;
   Pugachev, Emel'ian; Razin, Stepan;
   Sech (Zaporozh'e); Babel, I. E.; Gogol,
   N. V.; Kamenskii, V. V.; Khlebnikov,
   V. V.; Pushkin, A. S.; Sholokhov,
   M. A.; Tolstoi, L. N.; Tsvetaeva, M. I.
Cossackia, 12
Cowboys. *See* America, cowboys in

Daniel Boone, 13. *See also* America:
   myths of
Danilevskii, G. P., 93, 193*n*5, 194*nn*8,9
Decembrists: Cossacks and, 18, 26;
   political program of, 23, 26–27, 186*n*27;
   mentioned, 173. *See also* Glinka,
   F. N.; Ryleev, K. F.
Denikin, A. I., 100, 134
Dnepr River, 6, 10, 150
Dnestr River, 81, 82, 113
Don River, 5, 9, 10, 12, 21, 22, 149, 150,
   152, 153, 156, 160
Dostoevskii, F. M., 73
Dumy: definition of, 24, 188*n*46; by Ma-
   zepa, 31, 33; Gogol's interest in, 42.
   See also Folk literature; Ryleev, K. F.

Efron, Sergei (husband of Tsvetaeva),
   134, 141
Epic: *The Lay of Igor's Campaign,* 13,
   80, 116, 181*n*21, 193*n*1, 208*n*8; *bylina,*
   definition of, 21; Homer, *Iliad,* 24,
   26, 80–81, 113, 116, 167; bards (often
   blind), 24, 33, 80–81, 154, 167; search
   for, Russian, 26; birds and, 44, 80,
   166; battle as wedding in, 62; "modern," 196*n*28; "minor," 197*n*32. *See
   also* Babel, I. E.: epic in; Bandurist;
   Gogol, N. V.: epic in; Sholokhov,
   M. A.: epic in
Ermak Timofeevich (Cossack leader): in
   lubki, 103, 200*n*14; biographical
   information on, 180*n*10; mentioned,
   10, 22, 128, 166, 167, 207*nn*35,50

Esenin, S. A., 142, 144
Europe, Western: attitude toward Russians, 13, 46; Russians attitude toward, 15, 16, 17–18, 126; literature of, 29–30, 34, 73, 195nn14,15; attitude toward frontier, 73. *See also* Westernizers
Evtushenko, E. A.: *The Bratsk Hydro-Electric Station* ("The Execution of Sten'ka Razin"), 172–73

Fantastic in literature, the, 87–88, 163, 198nn47,48,49
Folk literature: Cossacks in, 21–24, 34; romantic imitations of, 22; Pushkin and, 36–37, 91; Gogol's interest in, 42, 45; women in, 62; neoromantic interest in, 105; puppet plays, 113–14, 165, 203n28; Tsvetaeva's interest, 134; Russian vs. Ukrainian, 184n16. *See also Bogatyr'; Dumy*
Frontier: Cossacks on, 5–11 *passim,* 46, 194n12; liminal associations of, 14, 17, 72–75; resemblance of Russian to American, 20. *See also* America: frontier of
Furmanov, D. A.: *Chapaev,* 102, 165–68, 169, 210n7
Futurism, 102, 105, 126, 129, 130, 133, 134, 142, 149. *See also* Kamenskii, V. V.; Khlebnikov, V. V.

Glazunov, A., 142
Glinka, F. N.: "The Foray of the Zaporozhian Cossacks from the Sech to the Volyn," 27
Gnedich, N. I. (translator of *Iliad*), 26
Gogol, N. V.: 39–90; on geography, 5, 48–49, 68, 77; sexuality in, 19, 63–66; Cossack heritage, alleged, 41, 190n9; biographical information on, 41–42, 108–111, 202n12; Ukraine and, 41, 43–44, 77, 87, 109–110, 202nn16,19; on history, 42–43, 68, 76, 77, 191n14, 196nn21,25,26,27; reconciliation of opposites in, 43–44, 46, 48, 55, 65–66, 82; russification of Cossacks in, 43–46, 191n19; epic in, 44, 45, 68, 80–81, 197n32, 198n46; wholeness in, 49–54; women in, 50, 63, 64–66, 193nn29,9; music and dance in, 54–58, 68–69, 107–8; painting and sculpture in, 57–58, 68–69; devil in, 63–65, 193n9; rebirth in, 67–68; aesthetic as feminine in, 69; boundlessness in, 72, 74–75, 82, 85–90, 197n34; timelessness in, 77–82; narrative strategies in, 82–90, 197n38, 198n40; *skaz* in, 86; fantastic in, 87–88, 198nn46,49; Babel and, 107, 108–111, 117, 122, 123–25; Khlebnikov and, 127; Sholokhov and, 150–57 *passim,* 160; Sir Walter Scott and, 191n15; contemporary reaction to, 191n17; mentioned, 20, 34, 37, 93, 105, 107, 123, 126, 175, 179n5
—works: *Taras Bul'ba,* 14, 38, 41, 44, 45, 46, 48, 49–60, 64–79 *passim,* 80–82, 86, 88–90, 92, 105, 107, 108, 111, 113, 116, 119, 127, 141, 145, 147, 150–57 *passim,* 160, 166, 167, 170, 175, 190n70, 193–94n11, 195n18, 196n28, 197n32; *The Inspector General,* 38, 41, 58, 195n18; *Dead Souls,* 38, 41, 58, 195n18; "About Little Russian Songs," 41, 42, 57, 107, 195n19; *Evenings on a Farm near Dikan'ka,* 41, 43, 44, 45, 64, 76, 78, 83, 85, 88, 117, 190n7; "A Glance at the Composition of Little Russia," 41, 44, 45–46, 47–48, 57, 69; *Arabesques,* 41, 57, 107; *Mirgorod,* 41, 58, 59, 64, 87, 124, 125, 190n7; "Vii," 41, 64, 67, 87–88, 190n7; "The Hetman," 41, 78, 79; "The Tale of How Ivan Ivanovich Quarreled with Ivan Nikiforovich," 43, 58–59, 123–24, 156; "The Fair at Sorochintsyi," 43, 78, 83, 84, 87; "Christmas Eve," 45, 64, 67, 83, 84; "The Lost Letter," 45, 64, 78, 83, 87; "Old-World Landowners," 58–60, 190n7, 192n26; "A May Night or The Drowned Girl," 64, 83, 84, 87; "A Terrible Vengeance," 67, 78, 79, 83, 84, 86; "St. John's Eve," 67, 78, 83, 87, 197n37; "Sculpture, Painting, and Music," 68–69, 107; "The Bloody Bandura Player," 78; "An Enchanted Spot," 83; "Ivan Shpon'ka and his Auntie," 83, 84; "The Nose," 108; "The Portrait," 108; "Notes of a Madman," 108; "The Carriage," 192n27; "The Overcoat," 210n2

Golden Horde (Mongol Yoke). *See* Tatars

Gor'kii, Maksim (Peshkov), 107, 108, 142, 168, 202*n10*

Great Russia: Little Russia vs., 23–24, 25

Guro, E. G., 142

Hetman: definition of, 8

History of the Russes or Little Russia, The: Koniskii as author, 25; Pushkin and, 25, 191*n14;* Cossacks and, 25–26; Gogol and, 43, 191*n14;* as unreliable history, 186*nn23,24*

Homer. *See* Epic: Homer

Hugo, Victor (author of "Mazeppa"): Cossacks in, 15, 29–30; frontier in, 73; mentioned, 174

Iaik (Ural) River, 9

I'lf, Il'ia (Fainzilberg) and Petrov, Evgenii (Kataev), 110

Jews: Cossacks and, 6, 14, 39, 79; pogroms, Cossack participation in, 12, 99; Exodus of, 82, 113, 202*nn26, 27;* Yiddish literature, 109–110, 202*n18;* and Soviet intelligentsia, 110; Hasidism, 114–15; Wandering Jew, 159; Khmel'nitskii and, 180*n11;* mentioned, 67, 80. *See also* Babel, I. E.

Kamenev, L. B., 110

Kamenskii, V. V.: 142–48; Cossack as rebel in, 102, 103–4, 126–27; Razin and, 103–4, 126–27, 142–44, 147, 207*n48;* biographical information on, 142–43; Pugachev and, 144–45; Bolotnikov and, 146–48; Ermak and, 207*n50;* mentioned, 132, 133

—works: *Native Heart—Sten'ka Razin,* 103, 142; *Sten'ka Razin (poema),* 103–4; *The Way of the Enthusiast,* 142; *Sten'ka Razin* (novel), 142; *Stepan Razin* (novel), 142; *Sten'ka Razin* (play), 142, 143–44; *Stepan Razin (poema),* 142–43, 144, 145, 146; *His-My Biography of a Great Futurist,* 143; *Emel'ian Pugachev (poema),* 143, 144, 145–46; *Ivan Bolotnikov (poema),* 143, 145–48; *Emel'ian Pugachev* (play), 144

Karamzin, N. M., 21, 183*n2*

Kataev, V. P., 110

Kerenskii, A. F., 100

Khlebnikov, V. V.: 127–33; Cossacks as rebel in, 102, 126, 132–33; biographical information on, 127, 132; East vs. West and, 127, 128, 204*n2;* Gogol and, 127; attitude toward Rus' of, 127–28, 129–30; Razin and, 127–33, 205*n17,* 206*nn21,28,* 207*n48;* Pugachev and, 128–29; Ermak and, 128, 207*n35;* mentioned, 138, 142

—works: "An Imitation of Gogol," 127; "Khadzhi-Tarkhan," 127, 128–29; "The Trumpet of Gul'-mulla," 127, 130, 132; "The Great Day," 127, 205*n7;* "The Death of Palivoda," 127, 205*n7;* "A Song to Me," 128; "A Dinner," 128; "Incantation to Laughter," 129; "Zangezi," 129; "Razin," 130–32, 206*n26;* "Razin's Boat," 132; "Razin: Two Trinities," 132, 206*nn31, 32;* "Who is he, Voronikhin of the centuries," 133; "Slap in the Face of Public Taste," 133; "Children of the Otter," 205*n7;* "Inhabitants of the Mountains," 205*nn7,8,15;* "Ladomir," 206*n28,* 207*n35;* "Speech in Rostov-on-the-Don," 207*n35;* "Ra—Its Seeing Eye," 207*n35;* "I Saw the Youth of the Prophet," 207*n35;* "The Equation of Gogol's Soul," 207*n35;* "Notes," 207*n35*

Khmel'nitskii, Bogdan (Cossack leader): Ukrainian history and, 26, 28; and Gogol, 77, 83; and Babel, 116; biographical information on, 180*n11;* mentioned, 10, 27

Khomiakov, A. S., 192*n24*

Kievan Academy, 49–50

Koniskii, Bishop Georgii, *See History of the Russes, The*

Kotliarevskii, Ivan, 43, 84

Krasnov, P. N., 100

Kukol'nik, N. V.: *The Zaporozhians,* 71, 193*n3*

Kulish, P. A., 184*n12*

Lay of Igor's Campaign. See Epic

Lenin, V. I., 142

Lermontov, M. Iu.: Mountain charac-

ters, 15, 92; Cossack folk imitations,
183*n*7
Liminality, definition of, 14–15, 182*n*23,
194*n*3. *See also* Babel, I. E.: liminality
and; Cossacks: liminality of; Gogol:
liminality and
Little Russia, *See* Ukraine; Great Russia
Liutov, K. V. (assumed name of Babel in
Red Army), 108, 201*n*9
Lubki (chapbooks), 103, 142, 170,
200*n*14, 210*n*11

Maiakovskii, V. V., 126
Maksimovich, M. A., 42, 56, 185*n*16,
196*n*25
Marlinskii, A. A. (Bestuzhev), 15, 92
Mazepa, Ivan (Cossack leader): Euro-
pean depiction of, 15, 28–30, 196*n*24;
biographical information on, 28;
spelling of name, 186*n*31. *See also*
Bulgarin, F. V.; Byron, George Gor-
don, Lord; Hugo, Victor; Prokopo-
vich, Feofan; Pushkin, A. S.; Ryleev,
K. F.; Voltaire
Melville, Herman, 73
Mickiewicz, Adam: *Konrad Wallenrod,*
30, 186*n*35
Mirsky, D. S., Prince, 107, 108
Mongol Yoke (Golden Horde). *See*
Tatars
Montaigne, Michel Eyquem de, 15
Mordovtsev, Daniel: *Sagaidachnyi,* 14,
40, 61, 62, 72; mentioned, 93
Myth: definition of, 4–5, 179*nn*2,3,
197*n*33

Nabokov, Vladimir: and Gogol, 41,
190*n*7; *Pnin,* 174–75
Napolean: War of 1812, 12, 27, 171
Narezhnyi, V. T.: *The Zaporozhian,* 27,
62, 76; *The Seminarian: A Little Russian Tale,* 27, 43; "Two Ivans or a
Passion for Litigation," 43; and development of Russian novel, 186*n*30
Narod, the: Cossacks as representatives
of, 23, 36, 103–4, 143; romantic historiography and, 25; neoromantic
interest in, 105; in socialist realism,
169, 172; intellectuals and, 184*n*10
Nationalism. *See* Cossacks: nationalism
of; Ukraine: Ukrainian nationalism

Nicholas I, Tsar, 23, 35, 112
Nikon, Patriarch, 10
Noble savage, the, 15–16, 107

Old Believers, 10, 93, 181*n*13
Olesha, Iu. K., 110
Orthodoxy, Russian: upheld by Cossacks, 3, 16, 40, 49, 50; and *Raskol,*
10; attitude toward women of, 63. *See
also* Rus', "holy"; Uniate Church
Ostranitsa, Stepan (Cossack leader), 78,
79, 181*n*16

Paustovskii, K. G., 109, 110
Peter the Great, Tsar: Mazepa and, 28,
30, 32, 188*n*45; mentioned, 9, 11, 16,
18, 29, 112, 123, 157, 165
Petrov-Biriuk, Dmitrii: *Sons of the Don
Steppes,* 171–72; mentioned, 102
Petrovskii, Dmitrii, 142
Pil'niak, Boris (Vogau), 130
Pogodin, M. P., 42, 109, 196*n*25
Poland: attempts to register Cossacks of,
8–9; enemy of Cossacks, 3, 17, 30, 39,
49, 50, 52–54, 57, 67, 75, 76, 78, 79,
80, 114, 123; Jews of, 114–15, 118;
mentioned, 4–10 *passim,* 28, 46, 64,
66, 112, 120, 121
Polish-Lithuanian empire. *See* Poland
Poltava, Battle of, 28–33
Poshlost' (zemnost'), 18, 58, 59, 192*n*25
Prokopovich, Feofan, 196*n*23
Pugachev, Emel'ian (Cossack leader):
rebellion (Pugachevshchina), 9, 11,
34–38, 128; biographical information
on, 11; in folk poetry, 22; Pushkin
and, 34–38, 134–37; as proto-Bolshevik, 104–5, 173; Khlebnikov and,
128–29; Tsvetaeva and, 134–37, 138–
39, 141; Terts and, 164; in socialist
realism, 164, 167–70 *passim;* mentioned, 5, 10, 102, 106, 163, 166, 167,
168
Pugachevshchina. *See* Pugachev: rebellion
Pushkin, A. S.: 30–38; superfluous man
in, 18; folk imitations by, 22–23; Sir
Walter Scott and, 34, 37; on history,
34–35, 188*n*52; Tolstoi and, 95; use of
term *kazak* in, 183*n*8; Bulgarin and,
187*nn*40,41; mentioned, 20, 21, 105,
108, 145, 151

Pushkin, A. S.: (*continued*)
—works: *The Gypsies,* 15, 16, 198*n1*;
The Captain's Daughter, 19, 35–38,
40, 42, 43, 44, 91, 92, 94, 134–37,
188*n53*, 189*n59*, 198*n1*; *The Brigand
Brothers,* 22; *Songs of Sten'ka Razin,*
22, 31, 33, 103, 139–40, 207*n41*; *Poltava,* 30–34, 38, 42, 94, 187–88*n43*,
188*nn45, 47*; *The Tales of Belkin,* 31,
38; *The History of Pugachev,* 35, 40,
42, 61, 136, 188*n53*, 189*n57*; *Boris
Godunov,* 182–83*n1*; *The Caucasian
Prisoner,* 198*n1*, 199*n4*

Rape and pillage. *See* Cossacks: violence
of
Raskol (Great Schism). *See* Old Believers
Razin, Stepan (Cossack leader): biographical information on, 10–11; in
folk poetry, 22–23; Pushkin and, 22–
23, 33, 34, 103, 188*n53*; in *lubki,*
103; Kamenskii and, 103–4, 126–
27, 142–44, 146; as proto-Bolshevik, 103–5; neoromantic interest in,
105; and women, 105–6, 193*n6*,
200*n20*; Khlebnikov and, 127, 128,
129–33; *kumach* (red calico), 129, 141,
205*n15*; "Rabble to the Bow" (*saryn' na
kichku*), 129, 200*n16*, 205*n16*; Tsvetaeva and, 137–38, 139–41; Terts and,
164–65; Furmanov and, 166; in socialist realism, 167–71; Evtushenko and,
172–73; mentioned, 5, 39, 102, 106,
142, 163
Repression vs. Freedom: dichotomy of
Russian culture, 15; Cossacks as reconcilers, 16–17, 18. *See also* Cossacks:
freedom and
Robin Hood, 11
Romanticism: attitude toward history
of, 25–28, 43, 185*nn18, 19,* 199*n9*;
mentioned, 13, 16, 21–28 *passim,* 34,
38, 92, 96
Rus', "holy": Cossacks and, 12, 39, 45,
46, 47–48, 96, 103, 127, 141, 144,
145, 148; as "soul" of Russia, 16, 23,
25, 33, 127, 170, 181*n21*, 189*n2*; on
name, 191*n20*. *See also* Russian "soul"
Russian "soul" (*russkaia dusha*): Cossacks and, 40, 44–49, 60, 103, 120,
143; Pushkin and, 40–41; as synthesis

of East and West, 46. *See also* Rus',
"holy"
Ryleev, K. F.: *dumy* and, 24, 27, 184*n15*;
Nalivaiko, 27; *Oleg the Wise,* 27;
Sviatoslav, 27; *Sviatopolk,* 27; *Dmitrii
Donskoi,* 27; *Bogdan Khmel'nitskii,*
27; *Voinarovskii,* 27, 30, 66, 187*n39*,
209*n15*

Sagaidachnyi, Petr (Cossack leader), 83,
181*n16*
Schelling, Friedrich Wilhelm Joseph von,
25
Scott, Sir Walter: publications of in Russia, 34; Pushkin and, 34, 37; Mordovtsev and, 39; Gogol and, 191*n15*;
mentioned, 91, 169, 171, 195*n17*,
196*n27*
Sech (Zaporozh'e): as female, 49, 61–65
passim; as boundless, 54, 71, 74–75,
89; as music and dance, 57; mentioned, 6–11 *passim,* 40, 42, 44, 50,
56, 76, 90, 100, 105, 127, 170, 180*n9*.
See also Cossack, Zaporozhian
Self vs. Other: dichotomy of Russian
culture, 15; Cossacks as reconcilers,
16, 36, 37, 44, 85, 148. *See also* Cossacks, reconciliation of opposites of;
Cossacks, exoticism of
Senkovskii, O. I. (editor of *Library for
Reading*), 34
Serfdom, 6, 8, 17
Shakhovskoi, A. A.: *The Cossack-Poet,*
203*n28*
Shishkov, V. Ia., 102
Sholokhov, M. A.: 149–63; Babel and,
108, 149, 151; biographical information on, 149; socialist realism and,
149, 208*n1*; Tolstoi and, 149, 150–51,
208*n4*; Gogol and, 150–57 *passim,*
160; socialists in, 151, 152, 161–62,
167; liminality in, 153–54; women in,
153, 155, 157; reconciliation of opposites in, 153, 208*n7*; epic in, 154,
208*n8*; rebirth in, 154–55, 161–62,
209*n15*; sexuality in, 155, 157; boredom in, 156, 159, 160; Cossack dissension in, 157–61, 209*n10*; Jews in,
159; plagiarism and, 208*n2*; bourgeoisie in, 209*n11*; mentioned, 102,
148, 167

—works: *The Quiet Don,* 102, 149–62, 172; *Don Stories,* 149
Siniavskii, A. D. *See* Terts
Slavophiles, 17–18, 46, 182*n29*
Slowacki, Juliusz. *Mazeppa,* 66, 187*n42*
Smirnova, A. O. (friend of Gogol), 43
Sobornost', 192*n24. See also* Cossacks: wholeness of
Socialist realism: historical fiction and, 102, 165, 168–70; Cossack hero in, 106, 148, 163, 167–68; Sholokhov and, 149, 108*n1;* Terts and, 164–65. *See also* Chapygin; Furmanov; Petrov-Biriuk; Shishkov; Zlobin
Stalin: collectivization of, 12. *See also* Socialist realism
Steppe: as female, 22, 54, 61–66 *passim,* 105–06, 115, 123, 145, 153, 167; as boundless, 48, 54, 72–75, 153, 159, 175, 195*n19;* as music, 57; mentioned, 6, 8, 17, 20, 28, 33, 89, 100, 127, 132, 137, 149, 150, 156, 160, 161, 165, 166, 168
Struve, P. B., 106
Superfluous man, 3, 18, 96
Suvorov, A. V., 164

Tatars: influence on Cossacks, 6, 8; Mongol Yoke (Golden Horde), 16–17; Cossack enemies, 17, 39; mentioned, 46, 47, 48, 51, 127
Terek River, 9, 94
Terts, Abram (Siniavskii): *The Trial Begins,* 164; "On Socialist Realism," 164–65; mentioned, 169, 173, 208*n1*
Tolstoi, L. N., 91–96; Russian self-definition as Cossack, 13; sexuality in, 19; Pushkin and, 95; Babel and, 107, 122; Sholokhov and, 150–51, 208*n4;* mentioned, 3, 20, 105, 120, 149, 179*n5*
—works: *War and Peace,* 3, 208*n4; The Cossacks,* 91, 92–96, 122, 150, 198*n1,* 201*n4;* "Khadzhi-Murat," 95, 107, 201*n4; Sevastopol Stories,* 198*n1*
Trenev, Konstantin, 142, 144
Trotskii, Lev (Bronshtein), 110
Tsvetaeva, M. I., 133–42; sexuality in, 19; Pushkin and, 19, 134–37, 139–40; Cossack as rebel in, 102, 136, 141; Rus' and, 133, 141; biographical information on, 133–34; Khlebnikov

and, 133–34; Pugachev and, 134–37, 138–39, 140; Razin and, 137–38, 139–41, 207*n45;* Gogol and, 141
—works: "My Pushkin," 134; "Pushkin and Pugachev," 134–37; "Free Passage," 137–38; "Razin's Dream," 138; "October in the Train," 138–39; *Swan's Encampment,* 140; "Tsar and God! Forgive the small —," 140–41; *Perekop,* 141; *The Tsar-maiden,* 141; "To keep an eye out for the girls," 207*n45;* "Broad Shrovetide," 207*n45;* "The Naiad," 207*n45*
Turgenev, I. S., 18
Turks: Cossack enemies, 3, 17, 39, 50; influence on Cossacks, 6; mentioned, 9, 22, 153

Ukraine ("Little Russia"): Poland and, 4, 6, 180*n11;* Ukrainian nationalism, 12, 24, 180*n9;* names for, 23, 45, 184*nn11, 13;* Russian fascination with, 23–24, 27, 109–110; folk poetry of, 24, 184*n16;* in *History of the Russes, The,* 25, 186*n24;* Decembrists and, 26–27; literature of, 28, 43, 179*n1,* 180*n9;* Gogol and, 41–48 *passim,* 77, 87, 109–10; mentioned, 72, 87, 88, 127. *See also* Cossacks; *Dumy*
Uniate Church, 27, 79, 80, 180*n10,* 186*n24. See also* Orthodoxy, Russian
Ural River. *See* Iaik (Ural) River

Venevitinov, D. V., 194*n17*
Vladimir, Saint, 40
Vlasov, A. A., 101
Volga River, 9, 21, 22, 39, 105, 127, 129, 132, 143, 160
Voloshin, M. A., 142
Voltaire: Mazepa and, 29; mentioned, 174

Westernizers, 17–18, 46, 182*n29*

Yiddish literature. *See* Jews

Zamiatin, E. I., 130
Zaporozhian Sech. *See* Sech (Zaporozh'e)
Zinov'ev, G. Ia., 110
Zlobin, Stepan: *Stepan Razin,* 170–71; mentioned, 102